A NEW LINK TO INTARSIA
AnneTarsia KNITS

Anne Berk

Foreword by Lucy Neatby

DOUBLE VISION PRESS

Copyright © 2014 by Anne Berk

All rights reserved. No part of this publication may be reproduced, distributed, or transmitted in any form or by any means, including photocopying, recording, or other electronic or mechanical methods, without the prior written permission of the publisher, except in the case of brief quotations embodied in critical reviews and certain other noncommercial uses permitted by copyright law.

All business names, product names, and trademarks used within are the property of their respective owners.

First published in 2014 by Double Vision Press

12020 SE Sunnyside Rd, Clackamas OR

ISBN: 978-0-9894638-0-5

LCN number available from the Library of Congress.

Printed and bound in China through Asia Pacific Offset.

10 9 8 7 6 5 4 3 2 1

Technical Photographs copyright © 2014 Anne Berk

Photographs on pages 17, 82 (top right), 85 (bottom left), 97, 105 (right), 137–140, 190, 193, 194 (top left), 195–197, 200 (bottom right) by Jessica Keaveny

Photographs on the first page of the Table of Contents (left and right) and pages 4 (left and right), 6, 82 (top left), 84, 92, 95, 116, 118, 119, 120, 158, 166, 170–172, 178, 194 (top right), 220 by Raina Stinson

Photographs on pages 8 (top center), 18 (top right, bottom left) by Anne Berk

Photograph on page 124 by Nancy Nord King

Photos of The Village Yarn & Fiber Shop and Dizzy T. Sheep and the Gang copyright © The Village Yarn & Fiber Shop, LLC.

All other photographs copyright © 2014 Bill Berk

Editor: Ann Budd

Technical Editor: Tracey Davidson

Copy Editors: William Thomas Berk and Marcia Weinert

Director of Photography and Photo Editor: Bill Berk

Book and Cover Design: Sarah Jaworowicz

Title Design: Joya Menashe

Stylist: Cindy Taylor

Make-up and Hair Artist: Natalie Olson

Cover: Bill Berk (photographer), Sara Olson (model), Chelsea Kay Bowman (make-up artist)

Acknowledgments

Cat Bordhi—Thanks for being Gandalf to my Frodo. I wouldn't have taken this journey without you.

The Core Group

Every single one of these people was essential to getting this done. I have immense respect, love, and gratitude for each of them.

Bill Berk—My partner in all things. You always know what to say or do to keep me going. And, in the process of becoming a knitting photographer to help me, you have revealed immense talent. As usual, this project reflects both of us working together.

Tracey Davidson—You were the first person I asked to help me because I knew that I needed new charting methods to make this happen. Your creativity, imagination, and expertise are exceeded only by your work ethic. You made bringing Annetarsia to the knitting community possible.

Sarah Jaworowicz—We work so well together that it is hard to believe we are 3,000 miles apart most of the time. Hiring you is one of the best decisions I ever made. I had the ideas, and Tracey charted them, but you turned them into a book.

Ann Budd—You are an editing genius, and watching you rearrange and refine the text was a beautiful thing. You made everyone on the team better.

Donna Druchunas—Thanks for putting it all together and occasionally putting me back on track, as well. You've worn all sorts of hats at one time or another, and having your guidance made us all better.

The Team Who Gave Their Time and Talent to Make the Book Come Alive:

Production Support: Susan Santos, Dominic Cotignola, and William Thomas Berk.

Photography: Raina Stinson and Jessica Keaveny.

Additional Photography: Nancy Nord King.

Designers: Valerie McPherson, Marcia Weinert, Bobbie Hodges, and Nancy Powell Thompson.

Test-knitters: Deb Jaworowicz, Beth Popp, Shan Davis, and Tammie Stafford.

Wynona Knitters: Jennifer "JJ" Foster, Gwen Fuller, Ruth Chadd Beck, Eve, Suzie Failmezger, Danielle Aust, Charlene Fugel, Shelly Wert, Roxanne Baker Cummings-Basey, Taciana Simmons, Tammie Stafford, Arminda Barnes, Nancy Mackenroth, Nona Litch, Holly Chidsey-Gardner, MaryLou Wacek, Shan Davis, Chris Drefs, Linda Bell, and Willson (the shop dog).

Dizzy Knitters: Erin Brown, Lynn Charles, Megan Heberlein, Bobbie Hodges, Jodi Houlihan, Deb Jaworowicz, Paula Lane, Barbara Mauger, Valerie McPherson, Evelyn Mondo, Laura Mondo, Karen Petito, Beth Popp, Sarah Reilly, Caralyn Miller Ross, Marcie Shapiro, Andi Simmonsen, Esther Waldman, Marcia Weinert, and Susan Zuris.

The Village Yarn & Fiber Shop: Thanks for yarn support, moral support, and creating Dizzy T. Sheep.

Visionaries: I learned a lot from you. Special thanks to Hunter Hammersen and Nancy Powell Thompson.

Location Shoot Angels

CampFire Columbia: René Leger, Kim Summers, Mary-Kate Narcisi, Namanu CIT Class of 2014.

Oaks Park: Mary Beth Coffey.

Special thanks to Kelly Jarozek, Suzanne Pederson, Tina Newton, Sam and Randy, for their personal support during the creation of this book.

Table of Contents

06 **FOREWORD**

08 **INTRODUCTION:** THE BIRTH OF A TECHNIQUE
  10 *Annetarsia*

18 **CHAPTER 1:** YARN, TOOLS, AND TECHNOLOGY
  20 *Yarn Choice*
  25 *Yarn Management*
  27 *Yarn Supply Choices*
  31 *Linking Yarn at Color Changes*
  32 *Adding New Yarn*
  35 *All Those Loose Ends*
  38 *Tools*

38 *Terminology*
39 *Reading Charts*

46 **CHAPTER 2:** FOUNDATION WORKSHOPS
  48 *In the Kitchen*
    50 Project 1: Stockinette-Stitch Potholder Worked Flat
    54 Project 2: Garter-Stitch Potholder Worked Flat
    59 Project 3: Oven Mitt Worked "In the Round"
  64 *In the Loo*
    65 Project 1: Stockinette-Stitch Washcloth Worked Flat
    69 Project 2: Garter-Stitch Washcloth Worked Flat
    73 Project 3: Soap Bag Worked "In the Round"
  76 *Detours and How to Fix Them*

82 **CHAPTER 3:** PROJECTS
    86 *Dizzy Scarf*
    92 *Rose City Hat*
    98 *Astoria Socks*
    106 *Cannon Beach and Seaside Pillows*
    116 *Timberline Hat and Mitts*
    122 *Multnomah Coat*
    132 *Namanu Shawl and Variations*
        138 Blue Moon Variation
        142 Sandy Hook Variation
        146 Seneca Maples Variation
        150 Tawanka Variation
    158 *Columbia Suit*
    166 *Sunriver Scarf*
    172 *Willamette Valley Socks*
    180 *Oaks Park Socks*
    190 *Kelly Sweater*

200 **CHAPTER 4:** MOTIF LIBRARY

222 **ABBREVIATIONS**

223 **BIBLIOGRAPHY**

223 **YARN SUPPLIERS**

224 **INDEX**

Foreword

Have you ever wanted to knit something with a picture in it, perhaps to celebrate someone's special interest? Needed an intarsia-in-the-round technique that truly works in socks? We have all been there! After sober second thought, most knitters decide to avoid doing it, deterred by intarsia's reputation for billions of ends, rat's nest tangles, and lumpy appearance.

Avoid intarsia knitting no more! Here at last is a delightful little book celebrating the delights and joys of intarsia-style knitting. Intarsia knitting offers unmatched freedom in color use and infinite design possibilities. Anne Berk magically resolves the feared ends and tangles with simple common-sense solutions. She provides a revolutionary intarsia-in-the-round technique that truly works in socks!

In addition to offering a comprehensive, step-by-step course in traditional intarsia techniques and methods, she also elegantly solves the intarsia issue of having to work flat pieces of knitting—that then require seaming. Anne has come up with a new, true intarsia-in-the-round method, neatly explained, which is free of the compromises and unpleasant side issues that so many other lesser methods entail.

In this bright, fresh presentation Anne offers a project management approach that will make your work easier. The entire project is carefully divided into manageable stages: yarn management, needle and yarn choices, and analyzing a design to see what it entails. You will be able to foresee the areas that might cause difficulty and plan ahead how to deal with them. In addition, there is a reassuringly comprehensive section on detours and how to correct them. Armed with this knowledge, you will learn a great deal about your stitches and knit with ever greater confidence and pleasure.

In addition to the small practice projects (all photographed with a backdrop of magnificent Oregon scenery), there is something here for everyone. There are colorful scarves, exotic hats, mittens, shawls, socks, cushion covers, a child's sweater, a coat and a stylish skirt-and-top ensemble. All are presented in a format that encourages you to develop and add your own motifs and incorporate stitch patterns and texture within intarsia. In addition, there is a very useful chapter containing alphabet charts and other charted motifs to speed you on your way to creating something beautiful.

I have always loved intarsia knitting for its limitless expressive possibilities. I hope this book will help you to become an intarsia fan, as well. Discover for yourself that "intarsia" is not synonymous with "impossible"!

Make yourself and your stitches smile!

Happy Stitches,

Lucy Neatby

Author of *Cool Socks Warm Feet*,
Cool Knitters Finish in Style,
and the *Learn with Lucy* DVD series.

Valerie McPherson, designer of the Seneca Maples Shawl (page 146).

The amazing team from the photoshoot: **Back row:** Nevaeh Calhoun, Sarah Jaworowicz, Jessica Keaveny, Cindy Taylor, Raina Stinson, Scott Stinson, Anne Berk, Natalie Olson, Ann Budd, Julie Alexander. **Front row:** Bo Harris, Aspen Speas, Bill Berk, Sara Olson, Jade Himmelsbach.

Introduction:
The Birth of a Technique

Intarsia, the method of knitting that allows an unlimited number of colors in a single-layer fabric, is well known for the argyle patterns it produces. For this "color block" technique, a separate strand of yarn is used for each block or area of color, and the strands are twisted or "linked" together at color changes to prevent small holes from forming at those boundaries to result in a smooth fabric.

Mary Thomas's Knitting Book (originally published in 1938, but republished by Dover Publications in 1973) describes geometric knitting—which we now know as intarsia—as a technique in which "the colours are changed as the pattern demands by merely looping the two yarns, to avoid gaps." Thomas chose tartan (what we recognize today as argyle) socks as an example; knitted flat and seamed down the back of the leg. She also included a seamless option. "They can be done in Round Knitting providing after each round the knitting is turned, i.e., after completing a round, knit to the seam stitch, knit this stitch, turn, slip it and purl back in pattern."

Although the idea of working intarsia in the round has been largely ignored, the various methods that were developed in succeeding decades stemmed from this principle. In just a few short paragraphs in 1938, Mary Thomas summed up almost everything we've known about intarsia for the past 100 years. Although incomplete, her work has stood the test of time.

Intarsia remained popular in Britain, generally in geometric knitting motifs such as argyle, vertical stripes, or squares. In America, there was an enormous interest in argyle patterns after World War II, and a generation learned to knit by creating argyle socks. My mother learned to knit in her college dormitory. With her hair in curlers and yarn wound around matchbook covers for bobbins, she and her roommate made argyle socks for their boyfriends. Grace Ennis published patterns for socks and Christmas stockings with novelty motifs related to hobbies and interests in the 1950s, expanding intarsia beyond argyle motifs.

Kaffe Fassett's bold geometric designs created a renaissance for intarsia in the 1980s, which lasted through the decade. Sweater kits for Fassett designs, with more than a dozen colors of Rowan yarns, were assembled for bold, boxy sweaters in the style of the period. Missoni, Adrienne Vittadini, Betty Jackson, Michele Rose, Nicky Epstein, and Pam Allen designed lovely intarsia garments for *Vogue Knitting* in the very early 1990s. In her 1996 book, *Knitting in America*, Melanie Falick featured many talented American designers inspired by intarsia. Around this time, Lucy Neatby designed beautiful intarsia patterns that spurred me to explore the technique, and I was fortunate to learn from her expert instruction.

Intarsia knitting patterns have been continuously available, but precious little has been published about learning and practicing the technique. In the last century, knitters who were motivated to knit intarsia had great success. When intarsia came easily to someone, not much instruction was necessary. Many knitters, however, found the process non-intuitive and awkward. They naturally gravitated to other techniques.

Intarsia has not evolved significantly from Mary Thomas's simple definition—"colours are changed as the pattern demands by merely looping the two yarns, to avoid gaps."

ANNETARSIA

Although I'd been happily knitting intarsia for a long time, pleased with my easy, flat knitting and invisible mattress-stitch seams, I kept working out ways to make it easier and more fun, all while teaching other knitters to enjoy it as well. But in classes, I was always asked, "Can we do this in the round?"

None of the established methods for doing intarsia in the round (or "ITR," as I began to call it) appealed to me. The joins showed, the knitting was slow and fussy, and the fabric was lumpy. I typically told my students "No," or "Yes, but it isn't worth it." After those glib responses, I decided that if, indeed, it wasn't possible to make intarsia in the round as much fun as flat intarsia, I should prove it to myself before discouraging anybody else.

It also occurred to me that if I could find a way to easily do intarsia in the round, a whole world of design possibilities would suddenly open up for hats, mitts, gloves, socks, and other seamless projects. As my imagination took off, my motivation soared.

I started researching the topic at the same time as Suzanne Pederson was preparing for the Madrona Fiber Arts Retreat and brainstorming ideas for 90-minute "mini-classes." I blithely offered to teach intarsia in the round, which gave me a goal and a deadline: I had six months to solve the riddle.

Most knitters learn that intarsia paints pictures in knitting by using as many colors as necessary in each row according to a charted pattern, with a separate yarn source for each section of color. This means that there can be many yarns attached to any row of knitting. To prevent holes from forming at transitions from one color to the next, the old strand is linked over the new. The old strand is left behind as the new strand is knitted for the designated number of stitches, and so on across each row of knitting.

Everything goes smoothly when you're working back and forth in rows, but if you're working in rounds, you'll find that the yarn for a particular color section isn't where you need it. It is up ahead, at the end of the section worked on the previous round. It's like driving your car from your home to a parking garage, then taking a bus from there to work, and then getting a ride home from a friend. In the morning, you won't have a car to drive, because you left it at the garage. The yarn keeps moving out of reach when working intarsia in a circle— therein lies the problem.

I began by exploring all the in-the-round methods that I could find in my library. They weren't any more fun than I remembered, and I began to worry about my deadline. After a few months passed and my deadline approached, I began to admit that I couldn't find a way to make any of these methods as easy and efficient as I wanted.

I found this discouraging but I continued to ponder options. The physics would not allow me to actually work in the round, but perhaps I could make it look as if I did. Some intarsia patterns involve relatively long spaces between two sections of the same color and, in these cases, a length of yarn is carried to the new spot and woven in along the back as for stranded colorwork. I experimented with that concept, but it didn't work. It succeeded in getting me to the next color, but every strand was in the wrong place and I had to repeat the process along the entire row.

Then came my first "a-ha!" moment—I realized that I only needed to move one strand back to link one round to the next, and then work in the opposite direction. All of the other strands would be where I needed them to be and the piece should look as though it was knitted seamlessly in rounds.

After finishing a right-side row, I turned the work to the wrong side to test my theory. The yarn I needed was to my right! I picked up that strand and placed it over the yarn that I had been knitting with. As I started purling with the working yarn, I noticed that the working yarn "linked" the old strand against the wrong side, forming a loop of yarn to my right. I purled the entire row, picking up new colors and linking as I went. When I reached the loop, I simply pulled out enough yarn to purl the necessary number of stitches, then tucked the old yarn into the loop to link the yarns.

I purled the new section with the loop, then tugged the strand a bit to eliminate the loop and form an unbroken circle of perfect intarsia knitting. I couldn't believe it! And when I turned the piece to work a right-side row, the old yarn was to my right, exactly where it was needed. I simply created a new loop, worked around, and voilà! Success.

Months of experimentation followed and I made multiple attempts to write it down coherently. Although the method is quite simple to do, it's much more difficult to describe. My class handout was nearly two pages long and admittedly complicated. I was very nervous about whether I could explain the technique effectively and how it would be received.

As it turns out, Madrona was the perfect place to debut this technique and I'll be forever grateful to the dozen women who took my class. Within 30 minutes, every one of them was knitting perfect intarsia "in the round." We spent the remaining hour adding colors and discussing variations and possibilities.

A few months later, Valerie McPherson, a student from the class, e-mailed me to say she had re-written my instructions in her own language and had added hand-drawn illustrations. Her generous permission to use this material in subsequent classes, along with her support and encouragement, spurred me on.

I began designing with my in-the-round technique right away, but because I had only taught the method to twelve people, my audience was limited. But it wasn't long before Interweave Press invited me to tape an instructional DVD on Intarsia techniques (called *Inside Intarsia*) and, suddenly, my audience was much,

much larger. My first published in-the-round (or ITR, as I've come to call it) patterns are included with that DVD package.

At the Madrona conference the following year, I took Cat Bordhi's Personal Footprints sock class, thinking that socks were ideal for ITR applications—a spiral-in-the round pattern could flow uninterrupted from toe to heel and up the leg. Cat saw me knitting what would become the Oaks Park Socks (page 180) and asked, "What do you call that technique?"

I replied, "I call it Intarsia ITR, for 'in the round.'"

"That's not good enough," she said, looking at me expectantly.

I thought fast. "Umm, my husband calls it Annetarsia."

"THAT'S IT!" Cat exclaimed, hands in the air.

And so it began.

Annetarsia is intarsia, but worked according to my simple guidelines. It's designed to be fun and easy, with representational rather than complex motifs. All elements of Annetarsia are optional and all can be used to replace or supplement traditional intarsia as the knitter desires.

Basic Annetarsia "In the Round" (ITR)

To begin working Annetarsia ITR, work the first (right-side) round just as you would for normal intarsia. When you get to the end of the round, you will discover that the color you need to begin the next round is at the opposite edge of the motif (color block) for which it's needed.

The solution is to turn the work at the end of every row, just as you would when working flat. The difference is that you will link the last stitch of each row with the first section of color to fasten the edges of your work together into a seamless tube.

Purl "Round" (Wrong-Side Row)

Step 1. Turn your work so you are looking at the wrong (purl) side. Notice that the yarn you need to link to the stitches on your left needle is hanging from the far right-hand edge of the first color block on the right needle. Pick up this strand of yarn and bring it to the left, across the front (wrong side) of your knitting to place it over the yarn you just used to complete the previous row. Don't worry about the length of the loop that is formed; you'll find that the loop can magically be used to work the stitches of the last color section of this "round," and then you'll snug it up to make it disappear.

Step 1: (A) *Wrong side viewed after turning. The first stitch of this row will be yellow; the blue yarn is at the right edge of the section to the right (not visible in photo).*

Step 1: (B) *Bring the yarn from the right and drop it over the working yarn to form a strand across the last motif on the right needle.*

Step 2. Because the work has been turned, this row will begin with the same yarn used to complete the last row. Pick up this "old" yarn from under the strand you just brought from the right edge of the first color block on your right needle, and use it to purl the first stitch on your left needle. The stranded yarn will be locked in place by the first stitch worked on this row. (From now on, we'll call this "loop 'n' lock"!)

Step 2: Pick up the working yarn (in this case, yellow) from under the loop of stranded yarn.

Step 3. Purl around, linking the yarns at each color change by placing the old color over the new one, then picking up the new color from under the old. Remember to keep the links loose for a nice, relaxed look.

Step 3: At each color change, pick up the new color (in this case, yellow) yarn from under the old color (in this case, blue) to form a link.

Remember to keep stitches loose for nice, relaxed links.

Step 4. When you arrive at the loop of yarn formed in Step 1, you'll have reached the last color section of the row. Drop the yarn you just used through the loop, and pull gently on the loop to release enough yardage so that you can use the loop itself to purl across the remaining stitches in the row.

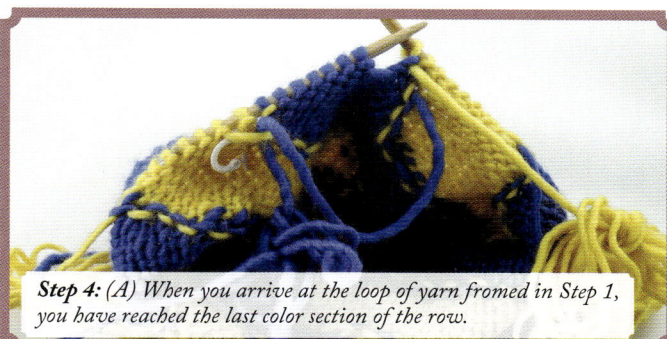

Step 4: (A) When you arrive at the loop of yarn fromed in Step 1, you have reached the last color section of the row.

Step 4: (B) Drop the yarn you just used (in this case, yellow) through the loop.

Step 4: (C) Use yarn from the loop itself (in this case, blue) to purl the next section.

Step 5: When you finish working this row, there will still be a loose loop of the yarn just used hanging from the wrong side of the fabric. Find where this yarn emerges from the fabric to the left of the link you formed when you started the row, and gently tug on the yarn until it smoothes itself in place and looks just like all the other links.

Step 5: Gently pull on the left-most end of the last strand of the row (in this case, blue) until the loop disappears.

Knit "Round" (Right-Side Row)

Step 1. Turn the work so the right side is facing you. The yarn you just used to complete the wrong-side row is in position to knit with, but the yarn you need to link to it is hanging from the far right edge of the wrong side of the color block on your right needle. Pick up the yarn from in back (wrong side) of the color block on your right needle, and bring it to the left, behind your work, to place it over the working yarn. Again, this forms a loose loop across the wrong side of the last color section of the row.

Step 1: Bring the yarn from the right (in this case, yellow) over the working yarn (blue) to form a loose strand across the wrong side of the last motif on the right needle.

Step 2. Pick up the working yarn from under the loop you just created, and use it to knit the first st of the row. This first stitch acts to "loop 'n' lock" the stranded yarn in place.

Step 2: (A) Work the first stitch of the row to lock the loop in place.

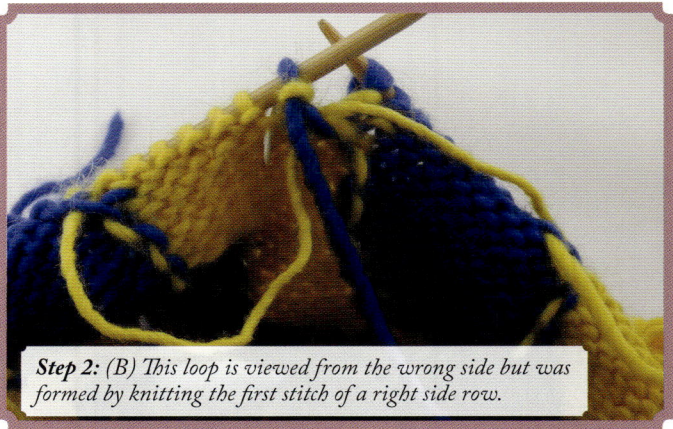

Step 2: (B) This loop is viewed from the wrong side but was formed by knitting the first stitch of a right side row.

Step 3. Knit around the row, always dropping the old color over the new color at the back of your work, and picking up the new color from under the old to loosely link each color section with its neighbor. Experiment with the tension needed to create the smoothest possible links.

Step 3: At each color change, pick up the new color (in this case, yellow) from under the old color (in this case, blue) to form a link.

Step 4. When you arrive at the loop formed in Step 1, you'll have reached the last color section of the row. Drop the yarn you just used through the loop and pull gently on the loop to release enough yardage so that you can use the loop itself to knit across the remaining stitches in the row.

Step 4: Drop the old (blue) yarn through the loop, then use the loop itself (yellow) to knit to the end of the row.

Step 5. When you finish working this row, there will be a loose loop of the yarn just used hanging from the wrong side of the fabric. Find where this yarn emerges from the fabric to the left of the link you formed when you started the row, and gently tug on the yarn until it smoothes itself in place and looks just like all the other links.

Repeat these two "rounds" as necessary for your design.

Shortcut Directions

Once you get the hang of Annetarsia ITR, you'll find that both "rounds" follow a simple repetition:

1. Turn the work.

2. Bring the yarn across the wrong side of the work from the far right edge of the right-hand motif and place it over the working yarn to form a loop.

3. Work the row as charted to the loop, drop the last strand through the loop and use the loop to complete the row.

Helpful Hints

The following tips should help if you get lost or confused.

» You are actually working back and forth, as in traditional intarsia. Rather than turning your work at the edge of the fabric, the turning point falls between two color sections, effectively producing a seamless tube. The edges of the two motifs that meet at the turning point are linked exactly like all the other motifs in the row.

» All links and loops for Annetarsia ITR are formed on the wrong side of the work, no matter whether you are working a right-side row or a wrong-side row.

» If you set down your work without turning and working a "loop 'n' lock," you may feel lost when you pick it up again. If the yarn you need in order to work the next color section is at the far end of its color block, then this is a signal that it's time to turn your work and loop 'n' lock. Better yet, learn to always turn your work and make a loop before setting aside your knitting.

» There should always be one, and only one, loop in each row. If you discover that you have two loops, you probably forgot to drop the working yarn into the loop for the last section of the previous "round." The first loop you come to is the false one. To remove it, simply pull on the loop to release the strand (you may need to unwind the yarn supply), and continue working.

The fun and functional projects included in this book will empower you to put pictures in your knitting whenever and wherever you wish. Many of the projects have been re-imagined by "real" knitters who share their experiences and invite you to learn from them as you venture into your own designs. Their enthusiasm and originality are truly inspiring.

With Annetarsia, you have the option of working intarsia as a flat piece or a seamless tube. Although not strictly worked in the round, Annetarsia ITR appears to be done so—there's no apparent beginning or end. Hats, socks, mitts, and sweaters all can be personalized with multi-colored motifs without adding the double thickness produced by color stranding.

One of the drawbacks of intarsia is estimating how much yarn is needed for each color. Using simple math, I'll teach you how to determine the length of yarn needed for each section. The process is fun and interesting, and it speeds up knitting and improves yarn management. You know all those ends that everyone moans about with intarsia? Stick with me, kids, because finishing is fast and efficient with an Annetarsia method to bury ends almost instantly.

To make it easy to keep track of the different sections of colors, I've put as much information on the charts as possible. The motifs I use are engineered to be easy to knit with new strands of yarn added at intuitive points.

The fundamentals of Annetarsia are easily mastered with practice. Every knitter can develop muscle memory so that the technique can be done quickly with increasingly little effort. As you hone your skills, you may be surprised to find yourself looking forward to the next project and eyeing your stash for possible combinations of color and texture. After you master Annetarsia, a whole new world of color will be at your fingertips.

My goal for *Annetarsia Knits* is to clarify and expand the reach of the intarsia technique. My hope is that it will become commonplace and no longer subject to the ebbs and flows of knitter fascination. Let's get started!

Chapter 1:
Yarn, Tools, and Terminology

Success with Annetarsia depends on proper yarn handling, so it's important to take some time to become familiar with the best ways to manage the yarn before you leap into a project. It's also a good idea to choose the best needles for your purpose, learn the terminology, and learn how to read the charts.

YARN CHOICE

Smooth solid-colored yarns are traditionally used for intarsia and are well suited for Annetarsia as well. Worsted-weight yarns in smooth and contrasting colors are good choices for practicing the technique. Once you're comfortable with Annetarsia, the sky's the limit! When it comes to selecting yarn for a project, you'll have choices in fiber content, yarn size or weight, texture, and of course, color. All of these factors will affect the overall appearance of your project in significant ways.

Fiber Content

Wool and other animal fibers are good choices for intarsia because they snuggle up easily beside adjacent stitches. Synthetic and machine-washable fibers may require more scrutiny when it comes to maintaining even tension, particularly at the links between color sections.

Texture

Traditionally, intarsia is worked with smooth yarns such as superwash or naturally processed wool, mercerized cotton, and smoothly spun acrylic. They create beautiful pictures because they make it easy to maintain even tension, particularly along the linked sections. In addition, smooth yarns tend to tangle less, or at least are easy to untangle.

A lightly processed wool yarn gives soft edges to the motif in this swatch.

Textured yarns, such as thick-and-thin, bouclé, and lightly processed yarns can create lovely depth and textural qualities and they can go a long way to obscure random spots of uneven tension. The largest projects in this book—the Columbia Suit (page 158) and Multnomah Coat (page 122)—are knitted with a thick-and-thin wool yarn that gives the fabric character, bounce, and durability. But it's important to respect that textured yarns can be sticky and create firmer tangles.

Knit swatches to see how the yarn works with the pattern and needles you've chosen. In general, "interesting" yarns are best reserved for the simple patterns, while smooth "plain" yarns work well with all types of patterns.

Size

Any size, or weight, of yarn will work well with intarsia, but you'll get the smoothest fabric and most consistent gauge if you use the same weight of yarn throughout a project. Keep in mind that the size of a yarn will affect the stitch and row gauges—the bigger the yarn (and needles), the fewer stitches and rows there will be per inch. You can use this to your advantage by choosing a lighter or heavier yarn (and adjusting needle size appropriately) to change the size of a motif or garment.

It's fine to mix yarn brands as long as you stick to standard weights, such as fingering, sport, Aran, or worsted. This is a great way to use up yarns leftover from other projects (imagine combining several leftover sock yarns). With caution, it's also possible to mix different weights and textures. As always, a good-size gauge swatch should be your first priority. You'll want to evaluate how the yarns fit together and whether the various weights and textures lead to an interesting design element or an unwanted distraction. This is often a fine line, as demonstrated by many Christmas sweaters.

Color

Color has a huge effect on a project. Impact is greatest when colors are clear and very different from the colors in adjacent areas. This is important to remember if you plan to use hand-dyed or variegated yarns. For example, placing a blue yarn next to another yarn that has bits of blue itself will muddy the motif.

Swatching is imperative! Simply holding skeins or strands of yarn next to each other will not tell you if a particular group of colors will play well together in a motif. Even if you knit just a small swatch with simple diagonal lines, you'll get valuable information that could save you a lot of time, yarn, and frustration in the long run. When color combinations are involved, results are often surprising and can be better or worse than you expect. Save yourself time and grief by swatching your color combination before you tackle a full-size project.

To provide a short-course in color interactions, I invited Nancy Powell Thompson to knit some of her signature felted intarsia bags and talk a bit about how she combines and plays with color in her knitting. See Nancy's Color Play on page 22.

You need to knit a swatch to see how colors will impact one another.

Color Play

by Nancy Powell Thompson

Although almost everyone claims to love color, combining colors becomes an almost insurmountable task for many who are afraid to make a mistake, fear judgment and criticism, or have forgotten what it's like to be a kid with no such concerns.

For the bags shown here, I used worsted-weight yarns (Donegal tweeds, Harrisville, Rowan, Jameison & Smith, and as well as oddballs of unknown origin). I knitted the bags at about 4 stitches/inch to allow for felting. To maintain my interest, I worked different patterns on the front and back of each bag. The beauty of these small bags is that you can experiment to your heart's content and learn something new with each one.

Softly Spring

I love to see the first yellow-green leaves emerge in the early spring. This bag incorporates multiple greens and yellow-greens with those pale lavender-pinks that often show themselves in the first flowers of the season. The orange and blue were added for a little "pop," but placed to maintain the dominant quiet mood. Generally, I place "pop" colors a little to the side, never in the center.

Softly Spring

Autumn Leaves

In early fall, I'm surrounded by cascading red, orange, gold, and green leaves that turn ordinary trees extraordinary. The pattern I used in this bag is a variation of the Sunshine and Shadows quilt motif. I'm pleased with the movement of the colors. Note that not all of the squares are a single color—I like to use short lengths of yarn and often move on to a slightly different color when I come to the end of a length.

Autumn Leaves

Winter Warm

I knitted this bag, composed of multiple squares, in midwinter. I was warmed by simply looking at the rich red and deep orange yarns and enjoyed playing with them. The alternation of dark and medium values in multiple hues avoids the static checkerboard pattern worked in just two colors.

Square One

For this bag, I turned to a color combination that I used in a pair of fingerless mitts for my sister. The result reminds me of old quilts.

Little Girls

The soft colors in this bag are reminiscent of my childhood favorites of pastel lavenders and blues, especially during the spring and summer months. I think these colors would also look nice as small squares instead of diagonals, if more variation were added to the colors.

Summer

For this bag, I wanted something bright and sunny that combined yellows and oranges with blues and blue-greens. I think it would be improved with small squares instead of diagonals and with more complementary colors in the main body in addition to the upper border. It's certainly worth a try.

Summer

Memories

I've always been attracted to deep violets, blues, and blue-greens. For this bag, I incorporated yarns leftover from my first diagonal intarsia sweater. As much as I like this arrangement, I'd like to try it again with more variation—perhaps with some red violets in the border.

Memories

Grounded

I like to play with colors of similar value and the dark colors combined in this bag provide a sense of the richness of the good Earth, which is necessary for good growth. The lighter beige and soft greens offer the necessary contrast. I think a quiet gold would add interest to the lighter diagonal, as it does to the border at the top of the bag.

Grounded

YARN MANAGEMENT

Although Annetarsia is quite simple once you get the hang of it, there are some keys to yarn management that will help you work most efficiently.

Calculating Yarn Supplies

Intarsia knitting involves a lot of different yarn supplies—one for each section of color. You can save yourself a lot of time and frustration if you figure out how much yarn you'll need for each section, then wind off just that amount of yarn instead of working with multiple balls or excessively long supplies. To do this, you'll need to work a swatch with each yarn you plan to use for your project. You'll cast on with waste yarn so that you can measure the length of yarn used for the stitches knitted.

Step 1. Knit a Swatch

With waste yarn, CO 20 sts.

Use a half-hitch knot to secure the working yarn to the waste yarn, as close to the last stitch cast on as possible, then continue to work 100 stitches with the working yarn as follows:

Rows 1, 3, and 5: Knit.

Rows 2 and 4: Purl.

Cut the working yarn close to the needle. Remove the needle and pull out the stitches to where the yarn is knotted to the waste yarn. Cut the yarn close to the knot, so that no tail is included in the measurement.

Remove the knot, then carefully measure the length of the working yarn, being careful not to stretch the yarn as you measure.

For this swatch of Cotton Fleece, the yarn measured 80" (203 cm) once I pulled out the stitches (I folded the length in quarters to make it easier to measure, then I multiplied that number by four).

Knit a swatch of 100 stitches to determine your yarn gauge.

Remove the stitches fron the needle.

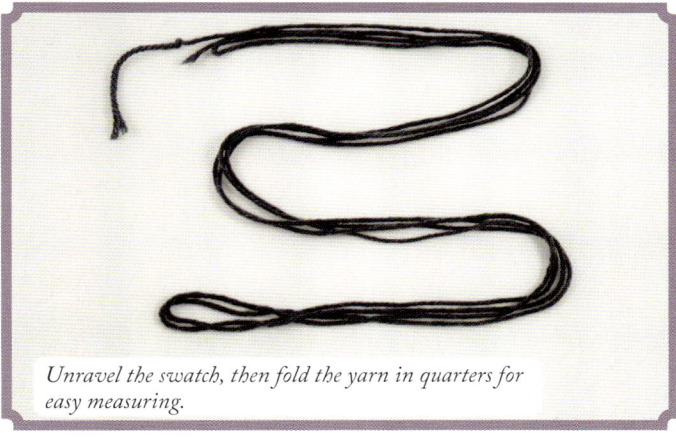

Unravel the swatch, then fold the yarn in quarters for easy measuring.

Step 2. Calculate the Yarn Gauge

To determine the yarn gauge, divide the length of yarn needed to knit 100 stitches (80" [203 cm], in the example) by the number of stitches knitted (100).

80 ÷ 100 = 0.80

Step 3. Determine the Number of Stitches Plus Rows in Each Section (S+R)

The next step is to count the number of stitches and rows in each section. For the number of stitches, simply count the number of cells on the chart in each color section. You can methodically count every cell or you can use some simple math to help you out. If the colors appear in stripes of constant widths that travel in a diagonal direction, you can count the number of stitches in a stripe and multiply that by the number of rows in that stripe.

For example, for the chart at right, the green stripe that begins at the lower right corner begins with 1 stitch and increases 1 stitch for 7 rows. The stripe remains 8 stitches wide for a total of 9 rows, and then narrows by 1 stitch per row for 7 more rows, to end again with a single stitch.

To determine the number of stitches in the area in which the stripe is its full width (outlined in purple), multiply the number of stitches by the number of rows.

8 stitches × 9 rows = 72 stitches

You'll also want to factor in the area where the stripe narrows (outlined in red). I find it easiest to simply count the number of stitches in these areas. For this stripe there are 28 stitches in the tapered areas on both the top and the bottom of the motif.

7 + 6 + 5 + 4 + 3 + 2 + 1 stitches = 28 stitches

Add the numbers together to determine the total number of stitches for this color.

72 stitches + 28 stitches (top) + 28 stitches (bottom) = 128 stitches total

Because a little extra yarn is needed to make the links and the number of links depends on the number of rows, add the number of rows in the total section to the number of stitches to get the number of stitches plus rows (S+R).

128 stitches total + 23 rows = 151 (S+R)

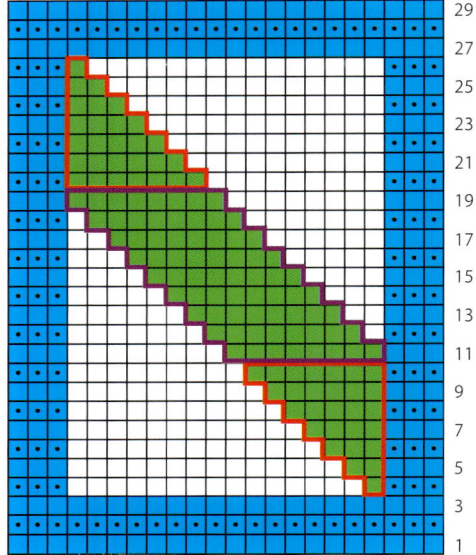

Step 4. Multiply Yarn Gauge by S+R

All that's left is to multiply the yarn gauge by the number of stitches plus rows (S+R) in the section to determine the total length of yarn you'll need.

0.80 × 151 = 120.8" (306.8 cm)

Step 5. Add Extra for Tails

To be sure that you'll have enough yarn to leave a 5" (12.5 cm) tail at each end of the color section, add an end allowance of 10" (25.5 cm) to this number.

121" + 10" = 131" (332 cm)

This tells you that you'll need 131" (332 cm) of yarn for that stripe. But, because it's easier to work in yards (or meters), you'll want to divide this by the appropriate number.

131" ÷ 36 inches/yard = 3.63 yards

332 cm ÷ 100 cm/meter = 3.32 meters

Round up to the next ½ yard (0.45 meters) for good measure:

4 yards

3.75 meters

The amount of yarn needed of each color section is provided at the beginning of each project in Chapter 3. This information is provided under the heading Yarn Preparation when multiple stands of various colors are required. The yarn supplies are listed in the order in which they are used.

YARN SUPPLY CHOICES

I find that new intarsia knitters generally prefer to work with short strands or bobbins. As their confidence increases and their knitting becomes faster, most find that bobbins get in the way and that short strands are used up quickly. When that happens, it's time to move to yarn butterflies.

Pull-Skeins and Balls

I rarely knit from full pull-skeins or balls for my Annetarsia projects. This is because they are too large and tangle too easily—instead, I opt for bobbins or butterflies when a lot of yarn is needed. If you feel that a pull-skein or ball would be appropriate for your project, contain the yarn in a bowl (there are lots of beautiful handmade bowls for this purpose), as this will minimize tangling. Also, frequently unwind it from the other strands, which will catch on the skein strand as you work.

Bobbins

Bobbins are preferable to pull-skeins or balls when a large amount of yarn is required (such as hat with a single, isolated motif). Bobbins are the "training wheels" of the intarsia world, and beginning intarsia knitters often find them comforting. They hold long lengths of yarn securely and are available in many shapes and sizes. As you progress across a row, you can unwind enough yarn to knit the necessary number of stitches, and then wind the extra back onto the bobbin before you move to the next color. As proficiency improves and speed increases, you may find that bobbins are "too slow," add weight, and get tangled with each other.

You can use a variety of bobbins and yarn butterflies.

Loose Strands

Loose strands of yarn are the best choice for beginning intarsia knitters. I suggest using strands that measure an arm's length to a wingspan (both arms spread apart). These loose strands will pull through tangles easily, but are often long enough for a few rows of a motif. If a wingspan isn't long enough for the number of stitches required, consider spit-splicing (page 34) new lengths as necessary. Simply stop when about 8" (20.5 cm) of yarn is left, then spit-splice a new length onto the old end.

The drawback to loose strands is that they tend to knit up quickly. There will likely be times when you won't notice that you're about to run out of yarn until there's not enough left to spit-splice. In these cases, it's best to un-knit stitches until you have the necessary 8" (20.5 cm) for splicing. If you're too near a link to un-knit, the best option is to join a new strand and bury both ends in the link at a later time.

Butterflies

I prefer yarn butterflies to bobbins because they provide a way to hold significant amounts of yarn without adding the weight of bobbins. Butterflies are, in effect, small center-pull "balls" of yarn that are made by winding yarn around your hand (see box on page 29). Butterflies are very useful if you're using yarns that can't be spit-spliced (such as machine-washable yarns). Beginning knitters often graduate to yarn butterflies from loose strands or bobbins fairly quickly.

The size of the butterfly is a matter of personal choice. Heftier butterflies mean fewer ends to bury; smaller butterflies mean more ends but less weight on your needles. Through experience, you'll learn what size works best for you. Begin with about ten to twenty wraps around your hand. As you become comfortable, you can increase the number of wraps (and, therefore, the length of the strand). For a sock, I typically wrap my hand thirty times, which makes a butterfly that goes a long way.

Before you cast on for a project, wind a good supply of butterflies so that you can keep knitting without interruption. Store the butterflies in a zip-top baggie in your project bag so they'll be ready when you need them. Leave the larger balls and skeins at home until you run out of butterflies.

It's important to note that the more yarn that has been pulled out of a butterfly, the looser and messier the butterfly will become and the more easily it will tangle with the other yarns. Only pull out the amount of yarn that is needed for a row—depending on your pattern, this could be as little as 2" (5 cm). Unlike a bobbin, you can't wind the yarn back onto a butterfly.

If it becomes too loose and sloppy, you'll have to unwind the butterfly completely and start over. When this becomes necessary, simply undo the half-hitch knot to release the yarn, then rewind the butterfly. When the yarn becomes less than a couple of arm lengths long, work with it as a loose strand.

For large projects, you'll probably end up undoing all of the butterflies and re-winding them at least once. Like burying ends, it's a good activity for when you're tired and need a break. The process is rhythmic, soothing, and productive.

A supply of yarn butterflies prepared for a project.

Keep butterflies close to needles for easy management and fewer tangles.

How to Wind a Yarn Butterfly

Step 1. Hold the tail of the yarn in your hand so that about 4" (10 cm) extends from the edge of your palm and the rest extends across your palm and over the back of your hand.

Step 2. Secure the yarn tail with your thumb, then wind yarn around your palm the desired number of times (start with 10 to 15 wraps), being careful not to pull so tightly that you won't be able to remove the loops from your hand. You can wind the yarn in a simple circle around your hand or in a figure eight around your thumb and little finger.

Step 3. Check to make sure that the strands are evenly spaced and not tangled on your palm.

Step 4. Cut the yarn source, leaving a tail about 6" (15 cm), pinch the fibers to keep the wraps secure, then gently slide them over your fingers and off your hand.

Step 5. Pinch the middle of the wraps to form the butterfly shape.

Step 6. Wind the outside tail fairly firmly around the middle of the butterfly three or four times, then twist the tail into a half-hitch knot.

Step 7. Pull the yarn from the center.

Alternatively, wind the yarn in a figure eight around your pinkie and thumb.

Wind the outside tail aroud the middle of the butterfly.

Wind the yarn around your hand.

Secure the tail with a half-hitch knot by making a simple backward loop, placing it over one end, and pulling firmly to secure.

Managing Tangles

Most of the time, your yarn supply will be a combination of sources—loose strands, yarn butterflies, and perhaps a bobbin or two to hold a large amount of yarn. How you manage them will depend on your mood and needs at a given time in a project.

Intarsia is messy, but that's one of the fun and crazy things about the technique. Don't despair—these messes are really quite easily fixed.

If tangled yarn supplies distract you, use bobbins and keep them close to the needles. When you need more yarn, unwind the necessary amount of yarn from the bobbin, knit the designated stitches, and then wind the yarn back up to the bobbin. This will keep your yarn under tight control and leave no long strands to tangle on one another. But the price you'll pay is that your progress will be reduced to a slow crawl.

When you're knitting, you'll want to focus on the stitches that are on the needles and those in the row below to make sure they match the charted pattern. You don't need to pay attention to the yarn supplies bouncing around on the wrong side. Instead, you can enjoy effortless knitting for a surprisingly long time before the yarns become so tangled that your knitting comes to a halt. See if you can train yourself to forget about the mess and just enjoy the knitting. Wait until something sticks, and then untangle everything.

When the yarns become so tangled that you can no longer release yarn from a butterfly, pull out the loose strands. If that doesn't do the trick, undo the half-hitch knot on one of the tangled butterflies, unwind it and pull the strand entirely free, then rewind the butterfly. If the yarn is less than a wingspan long, simply let it hang free as a loose strand. Do the same with as many other butterflies as necessary until the remaining strands untangle by themselves.

Once you're on a roll in your knitting and the yarn isn't getting caught and tangled, you'll find that intarsia knitting goes quite quickly. You may be surprised when you take a break and see how much progress you've made—the "spaghetti" hanging off the back of your work will attest to your speed, skill, and confidence. Be proud of the mess!

Tangled yarn supplies are inevitable.

Begin by pulling out loose strands, then unwind butterflies one at a time as needed to untangle the yarns.

Rewind the yarn supplies, and you're ready to knit!

LINKING YARN AT COLOR CHANGES

To prevent holes from forming at color changes, you'll need to link the two yarns. In general, you'll drop the old color over the new color, then bring the new color over the old in position to work the next stitch. Be careful not to pull the yarn too tightly at this point. You'll want to remove the slack, but if you pull too much, the neighboring stitches will be affected and may disappear from the motif.

Yarns are linked slightly differently on right- and wrong-side rows. But in either case, it doesn't matter which direction the colors are shifting (i.e., to the left or right).

Right-Side Rows

Step 1. Work to where you want the first stitch of the new color to appear, then insert the right needle tip into that stitch and drop the old color to the back of the work so that it crosses over the new color.

Right-Side Row Step 1. Place the old color (blue) over the new color (gray) in preparation to knit the next stitch.

Step 2. Knit with the new color to lock in the strand of old yarn.

Right-Side Row Step 2. After knitting the next stitch, the old color (blue) is linked securely with the new color (gray).

Wrong-Side Rows

Step 1. Work to where you want the first stitch of the new color to appear, then insert the right needle tip into that stitch and drop the old color to the front of the work so that it crosses over the new color.

Wrong-Side Row Step 1. Place the old color (gray) over the new color (blue).

Step 2. Pull the new color from under the old color, then purl the stitch with the new color.

Wrong-Side Row Step 2. Purl the next stitch with the new color (blue) to lock in the old color (gray).

Work one stitch with the new color (white).

ADDING NEW YARN

There will be times when you'll need to add yarn, both when new colors are specified by the motif and when you need to join more of the same color.

Adding a New Color

When you need to add a new color, as at the beginning of a motif or when additional colors are specified in the middle of a motif, drop the yarn that you've been working with (designated the "old" color), then insert the working needle into the next stitch and work it with the new yarn (designated the "new" color), leaving a 5" (12.5 cm) tail to be worked in later. Then lay the old color over the new and work a second stitch with the new color. This will lock the old color in place.

Place the old color (red) over the new color (white).

Work the rest of section with the new color (white), locking the link of the old color (red) between the first and second stitches.

You'll probably notice that the first stitch of the new color is loose. This is because the tail is hanging free without being attached to anything. If this bothers you, you can join the new color with a knot—you have three choices:

Option 1. Make a slipknot to form a loop in the new color. Put the right-hand needle through the first stitch on left-hand needle. Place a slip knot over the right-hand needle, and pull through to make the first stitch. Place the old color over the new to link between first and 2nd stitch. There will be a tiny knot at the base of the loop, which you can remove later.

Make a slipknot to form a loop in the new color (gray).

Option 2. Tie a loose overhand knot to join the new color to the strand of the old color, then begin knitting with the new color.

Option 3. Tie a small half-hitch knot around the old color with the new color, then begin knitting with the new color.

Joining a New Source of the Same Color

At some point in your knitting, you'll most likely come to the end of a yarn source and will have to join more yarn of the same color. You can add the new yarn with a simple join, in which case the tails will need to be woven in, or you can use the spit-splice or Russian join methods to eliminate the tails.

Simple Join

Plan to join a new source near a link, where the tails can be buried most easily. Ideally, you'll want to leave about 8" (20.5 cm) tails on both the old and new yarns.

Step 1. Work the first stitch of the section with the old strand to establish the link.

Step 2. Drop the old strand, then work the second stitch with the new strand.

Step 3. Lay the old strand over the new strand, then work the third stitch with the new strand, to lock in the old. Cut the old yarn, leaving a 5" (12.5 cm) tail for burying.

Because both strands are the same color, only the two tails will identify the join.

There are two methods that I use to splice the two ends together. Both eliminate the need to weave in extra ends and both are undetectable in the knitting. Both methods require tails about 8" (20.5 cm) long.

Spit-Splice

Spit-splicing is easy, requires no equipment, and is ideal for fibers that felt readily, such as wool and alpaca. It also works on blends in which wool or alpaca make up at least 50% of the fiber content. But this method doesn't work with superwash wools.

Spit-splicing takes advantage of a fiber's tendency to felt. Felting requires soap, water, and friction. Remarkably, knitters have all three elements at their disposal—in the form of their hands and their spit! The hands cause the friction, while human saliva, which contains enzymes that facilitate fusion, functions as both soap and water. This is a most convenient piece of luck for Annetarsia knitters. The only caveat is that the yarn has to be predominantly wool.

Step 1. Wash and dry your hands! This is for sanitary reasons, but also to avoid discoloring or damaging the yarn with anything that may be on your hands.

Step 2. To prepare the ends of the two strands, untwist the plies in each strand for about 4" (10 cm).

Step 3. Tear off one or two plies from each strand to reduce the thickness by half. This will ensure that the spliced strand will be the same thickness as the original yarn. It's best to tear the plies rather then cut them—a fuzzy, distressed end felts most efficiently.

Step 4. Moisten the unplied ends with saliva. You can lick your palms, spit into your palms or into a plate and press a palm onto the plate, or simply place the ends of yarn into your mouth.

Step 5. Place the strands in your palm so that the wet unplied ends overlap about 4" (10 cm).

Step 6. Rub your palms together vigorously, as if rubbing a stick to start a fire. The heat you feel is an indication that the fibers are felting. Checking the progress every 10 seconds or so, rub your palms until the two strands are firmly felted together.

Step 7. Wash your hands to remove the saliva. The yarn will be washed when being blocked.

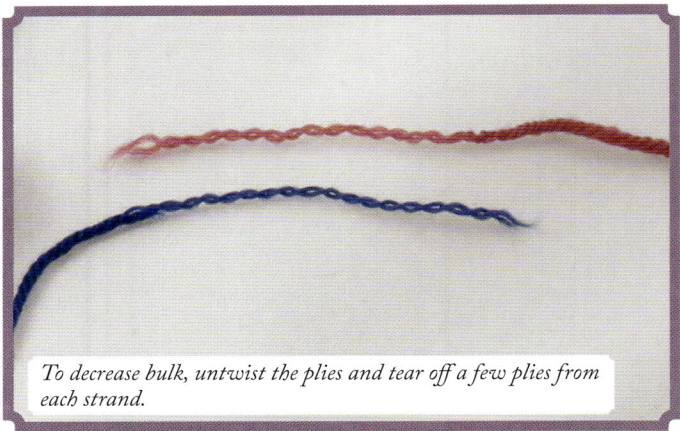

To decrease bulk, untwist the plies and tear off a few plies from each strand.

Overlap the wet ends on the palm of your hand.

The moisture and friction will felt the two ends together.

You can knit the spliced strand as soon as you'd like. After drying, the join will be strong and smooth.

Russian Join

For non-wool fibers or fibers that are loosely spun and soft, the Russian join is a good way to splice two ends together. You'll need a sharp chenille needle, as well as about 10" (25.5 cm) tails of the old and new yarn.

Step 1. Thread the working yarn onto a sharp needle. Weave the tip of the needle through the plies of the yarn for at least 1" (2.5 cm), starting from about 4" (10 cm) from the yarn end.

Step 2. Pull the needle through the plies of the yarn to create a 2" (5 cm) loop. Remove the needle.

Step 3. Bring the tail of the new piece of yarn through the loop of the working yarn and thread it through the needle. Reach around the loop of working yarn to weave the tip of the needle through the plies of the new yarn as in Steps 1 and 2. Remove the needle.

Step 4. Pull the ends to close the loops on both strands, leaving the ends to hang free (you'll deal with them later).

Step 5. After working a few rows, trim the ends by burying them in the wrong side of the fabric (preferably in a link) or simply trimming the ends, leaving 1" (2.5 cm) tails if they won't be visible in the finished piece.

ALL THOSE LOOSE ENDS

The first few rows of a project can be quite awkward. You'll be adding colors all at once and the working strands and their tails will all be very close to the needles and each other.

Unfortunately, you can't bury the tails (loose ends) until a few rows have been knitted—you'll just have to put up with them for a while.

Make a loop and draw the needle back through the plies.

Bring the other tail through loop and draw it through its own plies to create a second loop.

When the yarn is knitted, the join will not be detectable.

Weaving in Ends

Use this method to secure ends that you may want to undo in the future.

To weave in an end, thread the end onto a blunt tapestry or yarn needle, weave it around the links for about 1" (2.5 cm), then double back a little way to secure it. Cut the yarn, leaving enough end that you'll be able to find the end if you want to remove it later.

Note that superwash yarn will pull out most easily, especially if you avoid splitting plies when weaving in the ends. Wool yarn will be more secure, but may come loose when woven around the links.

*Weave ends **around** the links if you think you might want to remove them later.*

Burying Ends

Use this method when you want to quickly and easily secure the ends permanently.

The sharp tip of the chenille needle will allow you to draw the yarn through the plies of the link strands, rather than weaving around them. For sticky yarns, such as wool, a single pass of ½" to 1" (1.3 to 2.5 cm) will be sufficient.

For smooth yarns, such as superwash wool or synthetics, draw the end through the link, then double back and draw it through the plies again, catching it on itself as you do so.

Caution: Hold off on burying any ends until you're absolutely certain that you won't want to unknit, frog, or change anything about the knitting. Burying ends is a permanent move. If you want to tidy your knitting, but not permanently, trim the ends to about 5" (12.5 cm) lengths. Weave them in lightly or tie them in loose overhand knots to temporarily keep them out of the way. Removing a buried end is extremely difficult and will damage all of the links in which it was buried.

*To bury an end in the link, run the needle **through** the plies in one direction.*

Other Methods

Knots

Knots are quick, easy, relatively easy to undo, and they take care of two ends at once if you knot them together. However, they aren't as secure as buried ends and they tend to be visible and

Turn around and run the needle through the plies in the opposite direction to secure the end completely.

a bit messy. Knots are best used if you're working intarsia flat and the ends will be hidden in a seam. In this case, a knot won't affect the weight and structure of the surrounding stitches.

Fringe

In some cases, you might want to use the loose ends for fringe, tying them into overhand knots and letting them hang free. Doing so will take care of two or more ends with a single knot. But, in addition to creating unwanted bulk, these knots can distort the stitches in the knitting. While this type of treatment might provide a pleasing decorative element to a placemat or scarf, I recommend testing it along a short span to make sure you like the look. For a polished appearance, I recommend weaving in and burying the ends as usual to maintain the beautiful stitches all the way to the edge, and then adding fringe separately. This will ensure uniform and secure edges and fringe that wears better over time.

Managing the Ends

In many cases, the first rows have sections of just one or two stitches in a given color surrounded by a main color. Instead of joining separate sources of the main color, you can simply work the main color in the Fair Isle or color-stranding technique in which the main color is stranded across the back of the work behind these small sections of pattern colors. When the main-color sections are separated by more than five stitches, join new yarn sources so that each section is worked with a separate source. This spreads the loose ends over multiple rows and will help keep the first few rows snug and tidy.

Leave about 5" (12.5 cm) tails when joining new sources. This length should be heavy enough not to pull loose from the knitting, but not so long that you will knit with it by mistake. It's also a good length for weaving in or burying later.

To help separate the working ends from the tails, leave the tails on the wrong side of the work (where they will be woven in or buried) and flip the yarn butterflies, bobbins, or working strands to the right side of the work until you need them.

Resist working from full balls of yarn, even for the main color, at the beginning of a piece. Full balls simply will not stay out of the way. Wind the yarn into a butterfly for the first few rows. If desired, move to a full ball after the butterfly has been used—by then, you'll have worked a few rows and the other sources will be more secure.

After knitting for 2" to 3" (5.0 to 7.5 cm), take a break to assess your work. Pull gently on the loose ends to make sure you've used the correct colors and that you like the results. If all is well, consider burying in the loose ends along the links. But keep in mind that this is a permanent move. If there is any doubt that you might want to rip out, simply tighten the ends for now. Don't bury in the ends until you're sure that you won't want to start over.

Tie groups of ends in knots for a simple fringe.

For a more polished look, bury the ends, then add fringe.

Sometimes, I leave all of the ends hanging until I finish a project, then I have a marathon session of taking care of them. I enjoy getting it all done at once and watching the pile of snipped ends grow. At other times, I'm too tired to knit and pay attention to the chart, so I switch to taking care of the ends, which makes me feel that I'm accomplishing something without much effort. When the ends disappear, the sections become better defined. Whenever you choose to deal with the ends, you have a few choices—weaving them in, burying them, or taking care of them in other ways.

TOOLS

Every craft is improved with superior tools. Fortunately, a wide variety of quality tools is available to today's knitters. Let's look at the ones that you'll need for Annetarsia.

Knitting Needles

All types of knitting needles are appropriate for Annetarsia, and you'll likely develop your own preferences. Straight needles are fine for working back and forth in rows. Circular needles are ideal for working "in the round." Long circular needles used in the magic-loop technique work beautifully for narrow circumferences, such as socks. If you prefer double-pointed needles, be aware that the yarn supplies (loose strands, butterflies, bobbins, etc.) can tangle on the needle tips in annoying ways. Until you're comfortable with Annetarsia in the round, I suggest reserving double-pointed needles for swatching and small projects that are worked back and forth in rows.

Stitch Markers

Stitch markers are useful in many ways. I prefer the locking kind (the ones that look like tiny safety pins but without coils at the closed end). Use these markers to designate the right side of the work when working in garter stitch, to mark the turning point when working in the round, and to identify problems that need to be dealt with later, such as missed links and mistaken color shifts.

Chenille Sewing Needles

This type of color knitting results in a lot of ends of yarn that will need to be secured when you're done knitting. To facilitate this, you'll want a needle with a very sharp tip that will slide through individual plies, as well as an eye large enough to accommodate the thickness of the yarn. Chenille sewing needles are ideal. Originally designed to sew upholstery, they're available in fabric stores. Chenille needles are labeled according to the size of the eye. I recommend a collection of every size you can find—they're Annetarsia's secret weapon and they'll simplify your work to an incredible degree. Another option is Susan Bates Finishing Needles, which also have sharp tips and are easy to thread. But, because they are made of thin plastic, they are not as sturdy as chenille needles.

TERMINOLOGY

Although I've tried to keep them to a minimum, there are some terms that make it easier to talk about Annetarsia. The terms will be defined when they're introduced in the following pages, but it's helpful to have them combined here for easy reference.

end allowance: The length, usually 10" (25.5 cm), added to the yarn source to allow for the ends that will need to be buried at the beginning and end of a section. The end allowance is included in the yarn supply calculations.

"in the round" (ITR): The Annetarsia method of working intarsia so that it appears as if it were knitted in rounds, when it has actually been knitted in rows.

loop: The loop of yarn that is moved from the far edge of a section to the near edge and links the last section of a row with the first section of the next row. This loop, which always marks the final section of a row, is critical for the creating the illusion that a piece was worked in rounds.

loop 'n' lock: The action of creating the loop at the end of one row and locking it into place with the first stitch of the next row.

stitches plus rows (S+R): The number of stitches and rows in a section that will be worked with one strand of yarn. The stitches-plus-rows number is used in the yarn supply calculations.

turning point: The end of each right-side and each wrong-side row. The turning point is associated with the edge of a section and will shift to the left or right as the section shifts. Every stitch of every row is worked, but the stitches adjacent to the turning point may need to be slipped from one side of the turning point to the other as the edge of the section shifts.

yarn gauge: The number of inches of yarn required for one knitted (or purled) stitch. The yarn gauge is determined by measuring the length of yarn needed to knit 100 stitches, then dividing that length by 100; the number is typically less than 1" (2.5 cm)/stitch. Yarn gauge is used in the yarn supply calculations.

yarn supply: The amount of yardage needed to knit a color section. The yarn supply is determined by the number of stitches and rows within a section, the number of inches (2.5 cm) of yarn needed to knit one stitch, and the length of the yarn tails at the beginning and end of the section. To account for tension variations, long links, and other unknown factors, the yarn supply calculation is typically rounded up to the next ½ yard (0.45 m). The yarn supply can be a ball, bobbin, butterfly, or loose strand.

READING CHARTS

Charts are an integral part of Annetarsia. They provide a road map of the color sequence on each row and allow you to see how adjacent rows relate to each other.

In general, intarsia and Annetarsia charts are quite simple. The color sections are the focus of the charts, and they're rarely interrupted with increases, decreases, cables, lace, or other stitch manipulations. When shaping is necessary, it tends to be worked in the background and typically within areas of the main color. This is a good thing—we're busy enough keeping track of various yarn supplies without having to decipher stitch manipulations as well.

Annetarsia charts have a couple of useful annotations. Each color section is labeled with a letter (A, B, C, and so on) to indicate the color of the yarn supply needed. If there are multiple sections of the same color, then the letters will be annotated with a number that represents the order in which the yarn supplies are added to the knitting. For example, A-1 will be added first, followed by A-2, which is followed by A-3, and so on. Heavy black lines represent the boundaries between two yarn sources of the same color. In addition, each pattern includes a table listing the sum of stitches plus rows included in each section. These numbers (S+R) are used to calculate the number of yards you'll need for that yarn supply.

Reading charts for Annetarsia is no different than reading charts for other type of knitting. Each row of a chart represents a row of knitting, beginning with the Row 1 at the bottom of the chart and progressing to the last row at the top. Chart rows are read from right to left on right-side rows and from left to right on wrong-side rows. This is true whether you're knitting flat or "in the round" (ITR) because both methods are technically worked in rows. Each box on the chart represents one stitch and the boxes are colored according to the yarn color. Unless otherwise indicated, work all stitches in stockinette (knit on right-side rows; purl on wrong-side rows).

Most aspects of reading charts are exactly the same for working Annetarsia ITR. You'll still work in rows, following the chart from right to left on right-side rows and from left to right on wrong-side rows. You'll still knit every stitch once on every row. *The difference is that each row will end at the edge of a section, not necessarily at the edge of the chart.*

When working flat, the first stitch of every row is the first or last stitch of the chart. When working ITR, the first (and last) stitch of the round will be at the turning point, which coincides with the edge of a section. Because the edge of a section can shift from row to row, the beginning of the row can shift as well, and the edge of the chart will lose its significance. The end of the row will be indicated in your knitting by the loop of yarn that you'll use to work the last section. When you've finished knitting with the loop, it will be time to turn the work and make a new loop to signal the end of the next row.

After you get going, you'll pick up the loop and work the last section without even knowing what you've done. Then you may be startled to find that the yarn is not where it's needed. Just turn the work, make a new loop, and continue on your way.

Before You Begin

To prevent unhappy surprises, examine the chart before you begin knitting Annetarsia. Try to "virtually" knit the motif by reading it from right to left on right-side rows and from left to right on wrong-side rows. Note when color changes occur and whether any look inconveniently placed. Are there long color jumps? Might you want to add another source of yarn or strand behind another color to add a new block of color? Can you change the chart somewhere to make it more convenient to work without affecting the overall look of the motif? Where are new colors added? If you plan to work ITR, do you like where the indicated turning point is, or would you like to move it? Make notes in the margin of the chart to indicate where you expect to have to pay attention to such details so that you're forewarned as you knit.

Motifs are easiest to knit if the yarn for a new color is close to the same place it was on the previous row. For example, diamonds are very easy to knit because the consistent slope of color is a breeze to keep track of.

Beginning with Row 1, examine each stitch of the chart, progressing from row to row as if you were actually knitting the motif.

Row 1

Reading from right to left, observe where new yarn will be added. Are the sections long enough to secure the stitches on the needle? If a section consists of only one or two stitches, you'll want to leave long tails so that those stitches don't

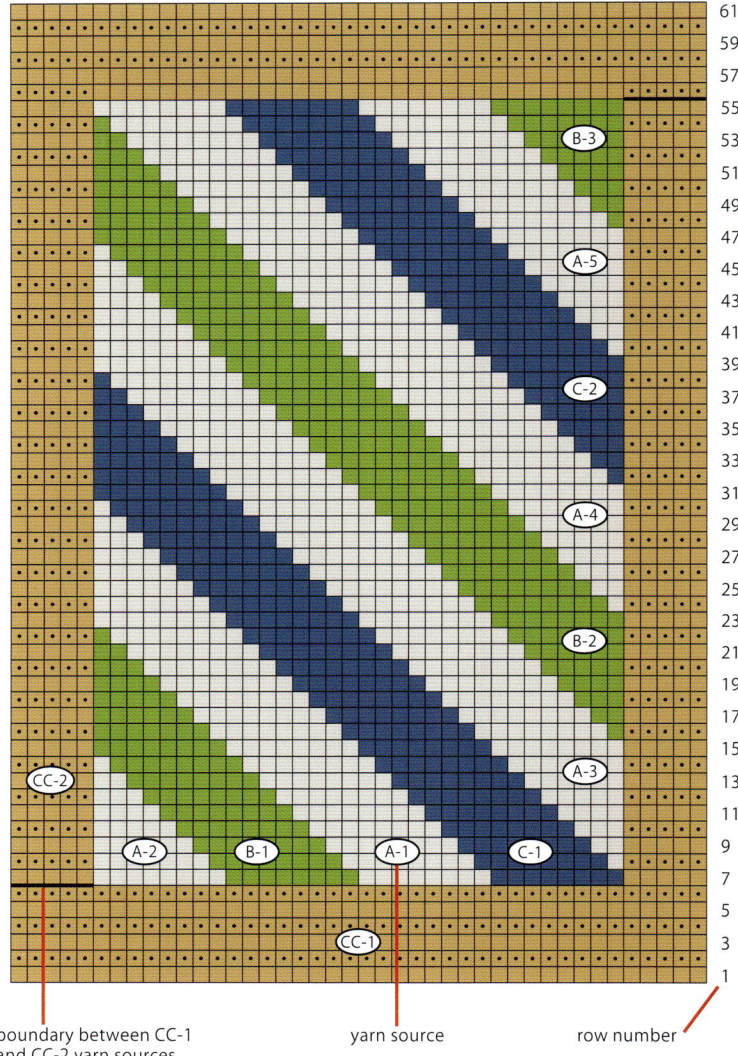

inadvertently pop out of the knitting. How many sections of yarn are needed? Are you comfortable with that number?

Row 2
Regardless of whether you work flat or ITR, you'll have to turn the work to begin an even-numbered row. Reading from left to right, look at how the colors shift from the previous row. An efficient motif will have short color shifts. All of your strands will be fresh, so there will be a lot of ends very close to the needle. Row 2 will solidify the stitches.

Continue to examine odd-numbered rows from right to left and the even-numbered rows from left to right. Make note of when a new section of color will be added. If there's a jump of color along a row, think about whether it would be more efficient to strand the gap or add a new piece of yarn. Above all, remember to look at the motif one stitch at a time because you'll be knitting it one stitch at a time.

Here are a few things that will make a charted motif easiest to knit:

Large Sections of Color
Large sections are easy to knit because you don't have to spend time linking and changing colors.

Lots of Diagonal Lines
Diagonal lines are by far the easiest to knit. The links are elongated by the diagonal, which allows more yarn to help regulate tension.

Gradual Changes in the Boundaries Between Colors
The more gentle the shift in colors (1 or 2 stitches, for eample), the easier it will be to follow the chart. For example, a section that has 14 stitches in the first row, 12 stitches in the second, 10 stitches in the third, and so on, will be easy to knit because there is a consistent decrease of 2 stitches in every row that can be anticipated. A section that has 14 stitches in the first row, 6 stitches in the second, and 2 in the third will be harder to knit because there isn't a predictable change in the number of stitches.

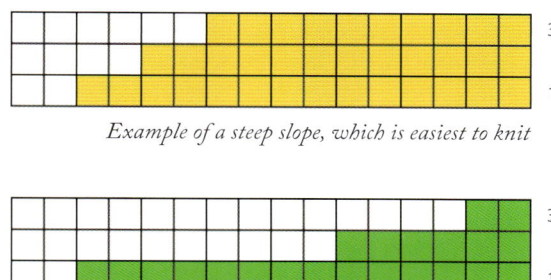

Example of a steep slope, which is easiest to knit

Example of a gradual slope

High Contrast Between Adjacent Colors
The easier it is to see the difference between adjacent yarns, the easier it will be to pick up the correct color as you knit. If the colors are similar in shade, it can be difficult to tell them apart, especially in dim evening light.

Limited Number of New Colors in a Row
It's best to limit the number of new colors in a row because each new yarn destabilizes the work a bit. If there are a lot of new yarns in the same row, the next few rows can make for awkward knitting. You're better off if colors are introduced on different rows.

Keeping Track of Your Place

To keep your place on a chart, place a sticky note, highlighter tape, or a magnet just above the row that you're currently working on. This lets you focus on the stitches in this row and see how they relate to the stitches in the row below. I don't recommend highlighting or crossing off rows that have been worked in case you find a mistake and have re-knit them or refer to them later. Rather, make marks along the side of a chart to indicate rows that have been completed.

If you do lose your place on the chart, simply match your current row to the chart, referring to the rows below as well, if necessary.

To help prevent mistakes (or find them soon after they've been made), it's a good idea to count the stitches in each color section every few rows.

When to Strand a Yarn

There may be times when it's more efficient to strand a color behind its neighbor to use it again on the other side of an intervening color than to cut and join a new yarn source. This is appropriate if there is just one (or two) stitch(es) between two areas of identical color. You might also want to consider stranding if you've finished working a color in one section, but need it again just a few stitches away. If you later need that color in the original location, simply add a new yarn source at that time.

Creating Your Own Chart

Charting your own motifs can be extremely rewarding. You can turn any idea, drawing, or photo into a knittable charted motif. Whether using graph paper or software programs, you'll want to look for the simplest, easiest images to knit. If you stick with a representational motif, instead of an exact replica, you'll be rewarded with a rhythmic and fun knitting experience.

A design or motif may look very pretty and enticing on paper, but that doesn't mean it will be intuitive to knit. It's important to remember that you won't see the picture until you've finished the last row of the chart and stand back from it a bit. Because it's hard to see where you're heading, it's best to stick with simpler motifs that are composed of diagonals and gentle curves that have predictable outlines.

Drawings don't always work this way because it's so easy to add embellishments with a stroke of a pen or click of a mouse. But keep in mind that the realistic ear jutting out from a cat's head will require two strands of new yarn (one for the ear and another for the new background color beside it). These two strands will result in four more tails to deal with when you're done knitting.

What You'll Need

Knitters' Graph Paper

The grid on knitters' graph paper is made to represent the true shape of knitted stitches. It comes in grids to match all standard (and some not-so-standard) gauges. This type of graph paper is most readily available through software programs that allow you to create a printable grid for any gauge.

Colored Pencils

Colored pencils are key for adding color to any motif you've plotted on a chart. My advice is to invest in some good-quality pencils and keep them handy. They're inexpensive, portable, and make you feel like an artist. But they're difficult to erase if you make a mistake, and you may find yourself going through a lot of paper before you finalize a chart.

Charting Software

There are a number of software programs that produce charts for knitting—Intwined, Stitch and Motif Maker, and Excel, to name a few. I started with Intwined, and although I have other programs, I continue to be most comfortable with it. Charting programs allow you to paint by clicking your mouse; you can play with the colors until the design is just right. When you're satisfied, the chart can be printed, saved as program files or PDFs, and inserted into Word documents. Any chart can be copied and modified for a different colorway. But, again, you'll need access to a computer, the software, and a printer. And you'll need time to practice before you become adept at the program.

Designing Your Own Motifs

Annetarsia motifs are representational. This is partially because basic shapes are easier to knit, but also because they're easier to draw. I'm a terrible artist and a lazy knitter, so I like to keep things simple. I look for motifs in magazine ads and pictorials, cookie cutters, and household items. You might also find inspiration from such diverse sources as coloring books, wallpaper, and nature.

Because drawing even the most basic shapes is challenging for me, I trace shapes onto stiff white paper and then cut them out. Whenever I cut out a shape, I save both the positive image (the shape that I cut out) and the negative image (the paper that the shape was removed from).

To plot the chart for a motif, place the negative image on top of your gauge swatch (if your gauge swatch isn't large enough, knit another, bigger one). Starting at the bottom, count how many stitches are at the lower edge of the "window." This represents Row 1 of your chart. Color those stitches in your graph paper. Continue to work up the chart, counting the number of stitches in each row. If there are partial stitches at the edges of the window, you'll have to decide later whether or not to include them on the chart. At this point, only include stitches that are more than 50% visible.

If you're working with square graph paper, be aware that your chart will look out of perspective. But, because you're charting the actual knit stitches, the finished knitting will look like the intended shape. The proportion problem only arises if you draw the motif on the graph paper and knit from that.

In general, I generate my charts in a single color and decide later if I want to add other colors. If you do want to add more color, consider whether you want to do so by knitting it in with the rest of the motif or by adding it later with duplicate stitch or embroidery. Factor in the difficulty of each option, along with how each will appear in the finished piece. If there's no discernable difference, choose whichever method is easiest for you. You may find it helpful to draw directly on the positive image from your tracing to evaluate the effect of the additional color.

Motifs that are easy to knit include those with predictable outlines such as squares, diamonds, circles, and ovals. Try to work with the most simplified motifs possible—plan to add details involving fewer than 20 stitches, such as arms, legs, and ears, with duplicate stitch or embroidery, which will be much easier than managing color sections that are just a few stitches wide. Consider using buttons for eyes.

Example of a circle motif.

Example of a flower motif.

Example of a star motif.

If there's a section that's just one stitch wide, consider stranding the adjacent color behind it instead of joining another source of yarn. Keep in mind that the more yarn sources there are, the more ends you'll have to deal with during the finishing process. But don't be fooled into thinking that the fewer the yarn sources, the better. A far more important factor is how close the strands are to where you'll need them as you knit.

Also, be wary of using colors very similar in value within the same motif. For example, you'll have a hard time keeping track of the correct colors for a leafy tree that includes multiple shades of green. To keep the colors straight, organize them in separate baggies labeled with the color and symbols from the chart.

Swatching

It's helpful to have a large yarn stash available for swatching your motifs. Ideally, you'll want to choose from a range of yarns of similar weight and various colors. I recommend focusing on yarn lines that have large color ranges and clear colors. Machine-washable yarns are good if you want easy care; wool yarns are good if you'd like to spit-splice the ends together.

Like all knitters, I have preferences when it comes to yarn—see page 224 for some of my favorites. I use lots of yarns aside from the ones listed and the search for new ones is a wonderful adventure. As we all know, stashes grow over time.

Watch for opportunities to pick up single skeins, especially ones in new colors—you never know when they'll come in handy for a motif.

A good-sized swatch that uses the yarn and needles you plan for your project is imperative for testing how the colors will interact, as well as for determining your gauge. Knit your swatch at least 6" (15 cm) square, then wash and block it to determine how the yarns will behave in a finished project. This swatch will allow you to evaluate the ease of knitting and the effectiveness of your design. Can you recognize what it is from three feet (0.9 m) away? From ten feet (3.0 m)?

You may find that you'll need to knit multiple swatches as you change the color, size, and number of elements to end up with the ideal combination. Unfortunately, I haven't discovered any shortcuts for this process—in fact, I've had to knit several full-size swatches of many motifs before landing on the right effect.

After you have some experience with charting and swatching, you'll be able to evaluate and design successive charts without knitting every version. You'll still need to swatch, but you may get the effect you want in one or two tries.

For reference, it's useful to knit 6" (15 cm) square swatches from all of the yarns you plan to use. They will then be handy to use when you want to chart a new motif to use with the same yarn and needles.

Making Changes

If you want to change the size or scale of a motif, scan or photocopy it onto a fresh piece of paper. Then enlarge or shrink to the desired size on a photocopier if you're working with a paper copy, or on the computer if you're working with a digital file. Trace the new motif on stiff paper, then use the negative image against your swatch to help produce a new chart.

Motifs can be embellished to create specific items. A circle can be easily turned into a balloon, a ball of yarn, or a peace sign. Don't re-invent the wheel—just turn it into something else.

Take care if you plan to change the colors in a charted motif. If there are many colors involved or if you're switching the placement of colors (for example, if the chart has a red circle on a black background and you want to knit a black circle on a red background), you can easily become confused and grab the wrong color. In these cases, you're better off generating a new chart with the colors you plan to use.

Copyright Issues

Bear in mind that you can come up against copyright issues if you intend to produce someone else's motif for public use (whether or not you'll be paid for it) or if the motif is recognizable as a copyrighted image.

In such cases, you'll need permission from the copyright holder before you can use the image. The holder may refuse under any circumstances, give you limited rights to produce the image, request a licensing fee, or request to see a finished product before deciding. Before making the request, be sure that your presentation is professional and make the best argument possible as to why granting permission to create a knitted motif with their image is in their best interest. Whatever answer they give you, you must abide by it.

The easiest path—both from a knitting and legal perspective—is to only use original ideas or representational (not literal) motifs. For example, if your son really wants Spider-Man on his sweater, ask him to draw his version of the superhero and turn that image into a motif. It will look like Spider-Man to him and it will mean a lot more to both of you.

Photos from my workshop at Wynona Studios.

Chapter 2:
Foundation Workshops

To help you learn the foundations of Annetarsia, let's begin with a couple simple workshops—one with projects to use in the kitchen and another with projects to use in the loo. Designed to give you practical experience on small pieces, these projects don't have to end up a particular size and are useful even if peppered with "mistakes."

I first taught these workshops to fifteen volunteer knitters who gathered at Wynona Studios in Oregon City, Oregon. Their skill levels ranged from beginners who had just learned to knit to experienced knitters who were familiar with complex intarsia designs. All had mastered the technique by the time they bound off their first potholder.

In the Kitchen

Potholders and oven mitts are ideal starting projects for learning Annetarsia. They're large enough to provide good, solid practice and experience, yet small enough for those with limited time and budgets. In this workshop, you'll create potholders while practicing intarsia in stockinette stitch and garter stitch by working flat in rows. I've chosen potholders because they don't have to end up a particular size and most errors will not affect their usefulness. Once you're comfortable working flat, you can move on to an oven mitt while you practice knitting Annetarsia "in the round," or ITR, as I like to call it.

We'll use a forgiving yarn for these projects—a double strand of worsted-weight wool or a single strand of bulky weight wool. Both will create a thick and cushiony fabric that insulates against heat. The projects will be felted, so even if your efforts are a bit rough, it will all be fixed in the wash.

These projects are designed for predominantly wool yarn that knits to a gauge of about 14 stitches and 20 rows to 4" (10 cm) in stockinette stitch. The following yarns are good choices:

Brown Sheep Lamb's Pride Worsted (85% wool, 15% mohair; 190 yd [173 m]/113 g), used double for a pre-felted gauge of 12 stitches and 20 rows = 4" (10 cm).

Knit Picks Wool of the Andes (100% Peruvian Highland wool; 110 yd [100 m]/50 g), used double for a pre-felted gauge of 16 stitches and 20 rows = 4" (10 cm).

Knit Picks Wool of the Andes Bulky (100% wool; 137 yd [125 m]/100 g), used single for a pre-felted gauge of 16 stitches and 20 rows = 4" (10 cm).

Each project requires four colors, one for the border (CC) and three (A, B, and C) for the center. A total of about 175 yards (160 m) of bulky yarn or 350 yards (320 m) of worsted-weight yarn are sufficient to complete all three projects in this workshop.

It's easy to work intarsia in wool because you can use loose strands (which are easier than butterflies or bobbins, as described on page 27) and spit-splice (page 34) them together when more yarn is needed. Begin with an arm's length of yarn; you can simply pull the yarn free when tangles form. When about 10" (25.5 cm) of yarn remains, splice on a slightly longer length. Increase the length in increments until you're comfortable using yarn that's at least as long as your wingspan (the distance between your outstretched arms).

As you progress to longer lengths of yarn, you'll want to wind them into butterflies or onto bobbins. Experiment to see which yarn management style you prefer. There will be a limited number of yarn supplies on your needle at a time, but you will be finishing motifs and adding new ones as you knit.

The diagonal stripes in these projects require from 2 to 16 yards (1.8 to 14.5 m) of yarn. The shorter lengths can be used as loose strands; the longer ones are best wound into butterflies or onto bobbins. As you knit, the yarn supplies will dwindle. As this happens, you can wind the yarn from a bobbin into a butterfly or let a butterfly unwind into a loose strand.

Follow these helpful tips for all of the projects in this workshop, as well as the In the Loo workshop (page 64):

» When you're working with established colors, the links occur between the last stitch of the old color and the first stitch of the new color.

» When adding a new yarn supply, link between the first stitch made with the new yarn and the second stitch.

» The yarn supplies will get smaller as you work and the butterflies or bobbins may tangle with each other. As bobbins become smaller, rewind them into butterflies; as butterflies approach a wingspan in length, unwind them and use them as loose strands.

PROJECT 1: STOCKINETTE-STITCH POTHOLDER WORKED FLAT

This potholder will get you familiar with managing multiple yarns while following a chart. You'll also learn to combine stockinette and garter stitch in the same row as you switch from the garter-stitch border to the stockinette-stitch center, and back again.

Finished Size
About 8" (20.5 cm) wide and 8½" (21.5 cm) long, after felting. Actual size will depend on the degree of felting.

Yarn
Worsted-weight (used double) or bulky weight (used single) wool in four colors: Green for the contrasting border (CC), Brown (A), Natural (B), and Dark Green (C).

Needles
U.S. size 10 (6 mm): straight (or a circular needle used for knitting flat).

Notions
Chenille needle.

Gauge
About 14 stitches and 20 rows = 4" (10 cm) in stockinette stitch, before felting. Exact gauge is not important and will depend on the yarn used.

Tips
» On right-side rows, all stitches are knitted and the yarn will be at the back of the work. At the boundaries between the border and center section, place the old color over the new color, then pick up the new yarn from under the old to lock the old yarn in place.

» On wrong-side rows, the border yarn will be in the back of the work, but you'll need to bring the yarn to the front of the work in order to purl the center section. Bring the border

STOCKINETTE-STITCH POTHOLDER CHART

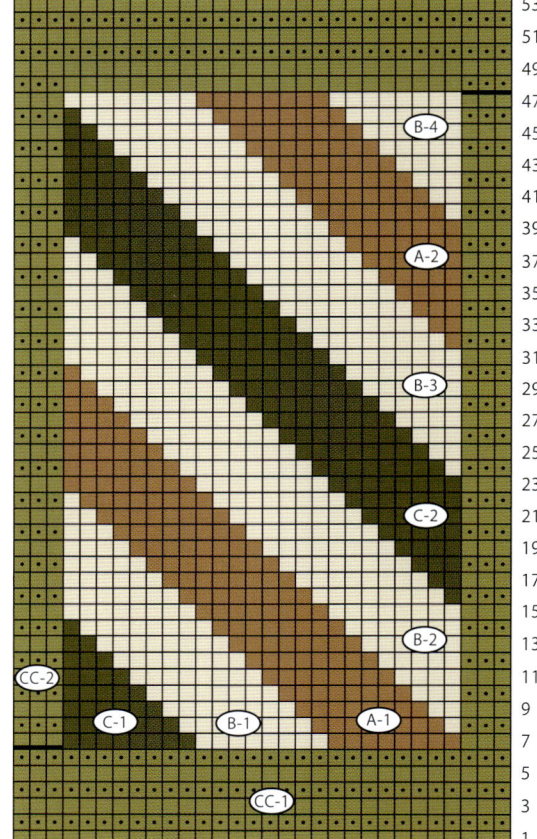

30 sts

- With CC, knit on RS
- With CC, knit on WS
- With A, knit on RS, purl on WS
- With B, knit on RS, purl on WS
- With C, knit on RS, purl on WS
- Boundary between yarn sources

yarn between the needles (to avoid making an inadvertent yarnover), place the border yarn over the new yarn, then pick up the new yarn from under the old to lock the old yarn in place.

» The number of stitches in the partial stripes at the edges will always total 8. For example, if there are 5 stitches of a section on the right edge, there will be 3 stitches of a section on the left edge, for a total of 8 stitches.

Instructions

Set-up: With the contrasting border color (CC-1), use the method of your choice to CO 30 sts.

Work according to the Stockinette-Stitch Potholder chart (page 50) as follows:

Rows 1–6: Knit all sts.

Row 7: (RS) Following the chart from right to left, k3 with CC-1. Leaving a 5" (12.5 cm) tail hanging in the back of the work, k1 with A-1, place CC-1 over A-1, k1 with A-1 to lock in CC-1, k6 with A-1 (8 sts A-1 total). Drop A-1 to the back of the work. Leaving a 5" (12.5 cm) tail hanging in the back of the work, k1 with B-1, place A-1 over B-1, k1 with B-1 to lock in A-1, k6 with B-1. Drop B-1 to the back of the work. Leaving a 5" (12.5 cm) tail hanging in the back of the work, k1 with C-1, place B-1 over C-1, k1 with C-1 to lock in B-1, k6 with C-1. Drop C-1 to the back of the work. To finish, k1 with CC-2, leaving a tail as for the other colors, place C-1 over CC-2, k2 with CC-2 (see tip at right).

Row 8: (WS) K3 with CC-2, bring CC-2 to the front of the work between the needles, place CC-2 over C-1, bring C-1 from under CC-2 to link the yarn, p7 with C-1. Place C-1 over B-1, bring B-1 from under C-1 to link the yarn, p8 with B-1. Place B-1 over A, bring A from under B-1 to link

Row 7 Tip: On this first row of color pattern, you'll work one stitch with the new color (Photo 1) before linking the two yarns (Photo 2). Linking the yarns between the first and second stitches only happens when a new color is introduced (Photo 3).

Work one stitch in the new color.

Bring the old color over the new, then work one more stitch with the new color.

Two stitches are on the right needle and the old yarn is locked between the first and second stitch, viewed from wrong side.

the yarn, p8 with A, then drop A. To add a new source of B, leave a tail, p1 with B-2, place B-2 over CC-1 to link. Bring CC-1 to the back of the work between the needles, k3 with CC-1.

> **Tip:** When you're working with established colors, the links occur between the last stitch of the old color and the first stitch of the new color.

Row 9: (RS) K3 with CC-1, place CC-1 over B-2, pull B-2 from under CC-1, k2 with B-2. Place B-2 over A-1, pull A-1 from under B-2, k8 with A-1. Place A-1 over B-1, pull B-1 from under A-1, k8 with B-1. Place B-1 over C-1, pull C-1 from under B-1, k6 with C-1. Place C-1 over CC-2, pull CC-2 from under CC-1 to link, k3 with CC-2.

Row 10: (WS) K3 with CC-2, bring CC-2 to the front of the work between the needles. Place CC-2 over C-1, bring C-1 from under CC-2 to link, p5 with C-1. Place C-1 over B-1, bring B-1 from under C-1 to link, p8 with B-1. Place B-1 over A-1, bring A-1 from under B-1 to link, p8 with A-1. Place A-1 over B-2, bring A-1 from under B-2 to link, p3 with B-2. Place B-2 over CC-1 to link, bring CC-1 to the back of the work between the needles, k3 with CC-1.

Row 11: (RS) K4 with CC-1, place CC-1 over B-2, pull B-2 from under CC-1, k4 with B-2. Place B-2 over A-1, pull A-1 from under B-2, k8 with A-1. Place A-1 over B-1, pull B-1 from under A-1, k8 with B-1. Place B-1 over C-1, pull C-1 from under B-1, k6 with C-1. Place C-1 over CC-2, pull CC-2 from under CC-1 to link, k3 with CC-2.

Row 12: (WS) K3 with CC-2, bring CC-2 to the front of the work between the needles. Place CC-2 over C-1, bring C-1 from under CC-2 to link, p3 with C-1. Place C-1 over B-1, bring B-1 from under C-1 to link, p8 with B-1. Place B-1 over A-1, bring A-1 from under B-1 to link, p8 with A-1. Place A-1 over B-2, bring A-1 from under B-2 to link, p5 with B-2. Place B-2 over CC-1 to link, bring CC-1 to the back of the work between the needles, k3 with CC-1.

Stockinette-Stitch Potholder right side (unfelted).

Stockinette-Stitch Potholder wrong side (unfelted).

Row 13: (RS) K2 with CC-1, place CC-1 over B-2, pull B-2 from under CC-1, k6 with B-2. Place B-2 over A-1, pull A-1 from under B-2, k8 with A-1. Place A-1 over B-1, pull B-1 from under A-1, k8 with B-1. Place B-1 over C-1, pull C-1 from under B-1, k6 with C-1. Place C-1 over CC-2, pull CC-2 from under CC-1 to link, k3 with CC-2.

Row 14: (WS) K3 with CC-2, bring CC-2 to the front of the work between the needles. Place CC-2 over C-1, bring C-1 from under CC-2 to link, p1 with C-1. Place C-1 over B-1, bring B-1 from under C-1 to link, p8 with B-1. Place B-1 over A-1, bring A-1 from under B-1 to link, p8 with A-1. Place A-1 over B-2, bring A-1 from under B-2 to link, p7 with B-2. Place B-2 over CC-1 to link, bring CC-1 to the back of the work between the needles, k3 with CC-1.

Row 15: (RS) K3 with CC-1, place CC-1 over B-2, pull B-2 from under CC-1, k8 with B-2. Place B-2 over A-1, pull A-1 from under B-2, k 8 with A-1. Place A-1 over B-1, pull B-1 from under A-1, k 8 with B-1. Place B-1 over CC-2, pull CC-2 from under B-1 to link, k3 with CC-2.

Rep Rows 8–15 for pattern, changing colors according to the chart.

Continue through Row 53 of the chart, working odd-numbered (right side) rows from right to left and even-numbered (wrong side) rows from left to right. Because felting will cause the piece to shrink more in the vertical direction than the horizontal, the piece will be rectangular instead of square when it comes off the needles.

Finishing

BO all sts. Use the chenille needle to bury the ends into the links (page 36). To felt, machine wash (using the appropriate amount of detergent for the size of the load) on the regular cycle in hot water. Remove from washing machine promptly to prevent creases from forming and lay flat to dry.

Stockinette-Stitch Potholder right side (felted).

Stockinette-Stitch Potholder wrong side (felted).

PROJECT 2: GARTER-STITCH POTHOLDER WORKED FLAT

This potholder will help you learn how to work Annetarsia in garter stitch. The fabric isn't exactly reversible, but it's close enough for most purposes. The two sides certainly are more similar than the two sides of the Stockinette-Stitch Potholder. Because there are typically more rows to the inch (2.5 cm) in garter stitch than in stockinette, the Garter-Stitch Potholder needs more rows worked if you wish to match the length of the stockinette potholder. Just keep following the pattern as established to desired length.

Finished Size
About 8" (20.5 cm) wide and 8" (20.5 cm) tall, after felting. Actual size will depend on the degree of felting.

Yarn
Worsted-weight (used double) or bulky weight (used single) wool in four colors: Dark green for the contrasting border (CC), Natural (A), Green (B), and Brown (C).

Needles
U.S. size 10 (6 mm): straight (or a circular needle used for knitting flat).

Notions
Chenille needle.

Gauge
About 14 stitches and 20 rows = 4" (10 cm) in garter stitch, before felting. Exact gauge is not important and will depend on the yarn used.

Tips
» There is no "right" or "wrong" side. Depending on where new yarn is added, the tail can be on either side of the work. When it is time to bury the ends, you can decide if you want to move them all to one side, or bury them randomly on both sides.

Garter-Stitch Potholder right side (unfelted).

Garter-Stitch Potholder wrong side (unfelted).

Garter-Stitch Potholder right side (felted).

Garter-Stitch Potholder wrong side (felted).

» Every stitch of every row is knitted; when you turn your work, the yarn supplies will be on the side facing you. When you reach a new color, bring the new yarn supply to the back of the work between the needles to avoid making a yarnover. After moving the yarn, work the next stitch with the appropriate color according to the chart.

» If you need a new color before that color appears on the left needle, pull the needed strand over to where you're working. Bring the yarn between needles to the back of the work, then work the next stitch in the new color. This will create a visible link or "running stitch." It is not a mistake!

» Move yarn to the back of the work between the needles to avoid making a yarnover and increasing the number of stitches. Count your stitches often and if you notice that you've made a yarnover, just drop it off the needle and the yarn will smooth itself out.

» The number of stitches in the partial stripes at the edges will always total 8. For example, if there are 5 stitches of a section on the right edge, there will be 3 stitches of a section on the left edge, for a total of 8 stitches.

Instructions

Set-up: With the contrasting border color (CC-1), use the method of your choice (I used the long-tail method) to CO 30 sts.

Work according to the Garter-Stitch Potholder (page 56) chart as follows:

Rows 1–6: Knit all sts.

Row 7: (RS) Following the chart from right to left, k3 with CC-1. Leaving a 5" (12.5 cm) tail hanging in the back of the work, k1 with A-1, place CC-1 over A-1, k1 with A-1 to lock in CC-1, k6 with A-1 (8 sts A-1 total). Drop A-1 to the back of the work. Leaving a 5" (12.5 cm) tail hanging in the back of the work, k1 with B-1, place A-1 over B-1, k1 with B-1 to lock in A-1, k6 with B-1. Drop B-1 to the back of the work. Leaving a 5" (12.5 cm) tail hanging in the back of the work, k1 with C-1, place B-1 over C-1, k1 with C-1 to lock in B-1, k6 with C-1 (8 sts total C-1). Drop C-1 to the back of the work. To finish, k1 with CC-2, leaving a tail as for the other colors, place C-1 over CC-2, then k2 with CC-2.

> **Tip:** Note that this Row 7 is exactly the same as Row 7 for the Stockinette-Stitch Potholder on page 51.

Row 8: (WS) K3 with the CC-2, bring C-1 to the back of the work between the needles. Place CC-2 over C-1, pick up C-1 from under CC-2 to link, k7 with C-1. *Bring B-1 to the back of work between the needles and in front of the last C-1 st on the left needle tip, place C-1 over B-1 to link the yarn, k8 with B-1.

Rep from *, changing colors according to the chart, ending with 8 sts of A-1—4 CC-1 sts will remain unworked. To add C-2, leave a 5" (12.5 cm) tail, k1 with C-2. Bring CC-1 to the back of the work between the needles, place C-2 over CC-1 to link, k3 with CC-1.

Row 9: (RS) K3 with CC-1, place CC-1 over C-2, pull C-2 from under CC-1 to link, k2 with C-2. Place C-2 over A-1, pull A-1 from under C-2, k8 with A-1. Place A-1 over B-1, pull B-1 from under A-1, k8 with B-1. Place B-1 over C-1, pull C-1 from under B-1, k6 with C-1. Place CC-2 over C-1, pull C-1 from under CC-2, k3 with CC-2.

Row 10: (WS) K3 with CC-2, bring C-1 to the back of the work between the needles. Place CC-2 over C-1, pick up C-1 from under CC-2 to link, k5 with C-1. *Bring B-1 to the back of work between the needles and in front of the last C-1 st on the left needle tip. Place B-1 over C-1 to link, k8 with B-1.

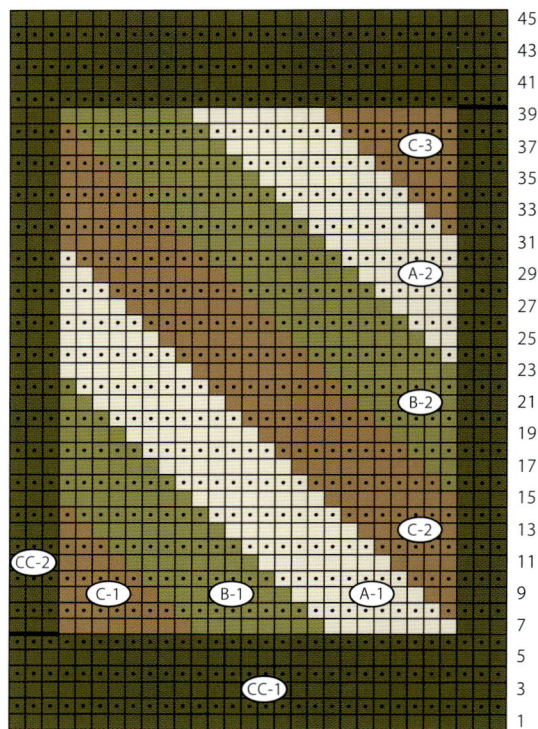

GARTER-STITCH POTHOLDER CHART

30 sts

- With CC, knit on RS
- With CC, knit on WS
- With A, knit on RS
- With A, knit on WS
- With B, knit on RS
- With B, knit on WS
- With C, knit on RS
- With C, knit on WS
- Boundary between yarn sources

Rep from *, following the colors as charted and ending with 3 sts of C-2. Bring CC-1 to the back of the work, place C-2 over CC-1 to link, k3 with CC-1.

Row 11: (RS) K3 with CC-1, place CC-1 over C-2, pull C-2 from under CC-1 to link, k4 with C-2. Place C-2 over A-1, pull A-1 from under C-2, k8 with A-1. Place A-1 over B-1, pull B-1 from under A-1, k8 with B-1. Place B-1 over C-1, pull C-1 from under B-1, k4 with C-1. Place CC-2 over C-1, pull C-1 from under CC-2, k3 with CC-2.

Row 12: (WS) K3 with CC-2, bring C-1 to the back of the work between the needles, place CC-2 over C-1, pick up C-1 from under CC-2 to link, k3 with C-1. *Bring B-1 to the back of work between the needles and in front of the last C-1 st on the left needle tip. Place B-1 over C-1 to link, k8 with B-1.

Rep from *, following the colors as charted and ending with 5 sts of C-2. Bring CC-1 to the back of the work, place C-2 over CC-1 to link, k3 with CC-1.

Row 13: (RS) K3 with CC-1, place CC-1 over C-2, pull C-2 from under CC-1 to link, k6 with C-2. Place C-2 over A-1, pull A-1 from under C-2, k8 with A-1. Place A-1 over B-1, pull B-1 from under A-1, k8 with B-1. Place B-1 over C-1, pull C-1 from under B-1, k2 with C-1. Place CC-2 over C-1, pull C-1 from under CC-2, k3 with CC-2.

Row 14: (WS) K3 with CC-2, bring C-1 to the back of the work between the needles. Place CC-2 over C-1, pick up C-1 from under CC-2 to link, k1 with C-1. *Bring B-1 to the back of work between the needles and in front of the last C-1 st on the left needle tip, place B-1 over C-1 to link, k8 with B-1.

Rep from *, following the colors as charted and ending with 7 sts of C-2. Bring CC-1 to the back of the work, place C-2 over CC-1 to link, k3 with CC-1.

Bring working yarn from front to back, between needles, to work the first stitch of a new color section.

A running stitch is made by moving the new color from the front to the back in front of a stitch of the old color.

The pattern appears slightly different on each side of this garter-stitch scarf.

Row 15: (RS) K3 with CC-1, place CC-1 over C-2, pull C-2 from under CC-1 to link, k8 with C-2. Place C-2 over A-1, pull A-1 from under C-2, k8 with A-1. Place A-1 over B-1, pull B-1 from under A-1, k8 with B-1. Place CC-2 over B-1, pull B-1 from under CC-2, k3 with CC-2.

Continue in this manner through Row 45 of the chart, working odd-numbered (right side) rows from right to left and even-numbered (wrong side) rows from left to right.

Finishing

BO all sts. Use the chenille needle to bury the ends into the links (page 36). To felt, machine wash (using the appropriate amount of detergent for the size of the load) on the regular cycle in hot water. Remove from washing machine promptly to prevent creases from forming and lay flat to dry.

The running stitches are visible where the colors shift to the right.

Largish loops are visible on the other side where the colors appear to move to the left.

The pattern changes when the stripes change direction.

PROJECT 3: OVEN MITT WORKED "IN THE ROUND"

You're now ready to master Annetarsia "in the round," or ITR, as I call it. This oven mitt will teach you the foundations and give you a chance to become familiar reading a chart while working "in the round."

Finished Size
About 12" (30.5 cm) circumference and 12½" (31.5 cm) tall, after felting. Actual size will depend on the degree of felting.

Yarn
Worsted-weight (used double) or bulky weight (used single) wool in four colors: Green for the contrasting border (CC), Dark Green (A), Brown (B), and Natural (C).

Needles
U.S. size 10 (6 mm): set of 4 or 5 double-pointed (dpn), two circular needles, or a long circular for "magic loop."

Notions
Ring marker; locking marker; tapestry needle; chenille needle.

Gauge
About 14 stitches and 20 rows = 4" (10 cm) in stockinette stitch, before felting. Exact gauge is not important and will depend on the yarn used.

Tips

» Each stripe contains 7 stitches.

» When changing from one double-pointed needle to another, snug up the first stitch on the new needle to tighten it and prevent a ladder from forming between needles. (You can also reduce ladders by working with two circular needles or one long circular in the magic-loop method.)

» The stripes shift along the diagonal according to the chart. This means that the turning point (the beginning or end of each row) will also shift along the diagonal. After Row 1, the

Oven Mitt right side (unfelted on left, felted on right).

Oven Mitt wrong side (unfelted on left, felted on right).

edge of the chart will no longer coincide with the beginning and end of the rows.

» The turning point will be between the A-1 and C-2 stripes. On wrong-side rows, the loop will always be in A-1; on right-side rows, the loop will always be in C-2.

» At the end of every row, there should be 7 stitches in each color section. If you have more or fewer stitches, look for a dropped stitch, a color shift that was worked in the wrong diagonal direction, or a missed color shift.

» Remember that loop 'n' lock is the action of creating the loop at the end of one row and locking it into place with the first stitch of the next row.

Instructions

Set up: With the contrasting border color (CC), use the method of your choice (I used the long-tail method) to CO 42 sts. Place a marker and join for working in rnds, being careful not to twist sts.

Rnd 1: Purl.

Rnd 2: Knit.

Rep Rnds 1 and 2 two more times—3 garter ridges on each side. Knit 1 more rnd, then cut the border yarn.

You can remove the marker at this point because the loop will indicate the last stripe of each "round."

Work according to the Oven Mitt chart (page 61) as follows:

Row 1: (RS) Work as for stockinette intarsia to the end of color C-2. The yarn you need is on the other side of the next stripe (A-1). Turn the work, pick up A-1 and pull it from the right to where you just finished knitting, place it over the strand of C-2 you just worked with, then pick up C-2 from under A-1 to "loop 'n' lock" the yarn.

Row 2: (WS) Because you're facing the wrong side of the work, you'll purl this row. Slip the next A-1 st (the first st knitted on the previous row) purlwise from the right needle tip onto the left needle tip without working it. If you haven't done so already, pick up A-1 from the right edge of the A-1 stripe, carry it over, and place it over the strand of C-2 that you used at the end of the previous row. Purl the slipped A-1 st with C-2, then purl the next 6 sts with C-2—the strand of A-1 that you carried over to lock into C-2 has formed a loop of yarn. That loop marks the last section of Row 2 that will be worked—the end of the row.

*Place C-2 over B-2, then bring B-2 from under C-2 and p7 with B-2. Rep from *, changing colors according to the chart and ending with 7 sts of B-1—you'll be at the A-1 loop. Drop B-1 through the A-1 loop, pull out enough of the A-1 strand to work with comfortably, and p7 with A-1 to finish the row. Gently tug on the A-1 yarn source to remove any remaining slack in the loop and any evidence of the beginning of the row. Turn the work.

Row 3: (RS) Slip the next A-1 st purlwise from the left needle tip onto the right needle tip without working it. Pick up C-2 from the right edge of the C-2 stripe, carry it over, and place it over the strand of A-1 that you used at the end of the previous row to "loop 'n' lock" the yarn.

Skip the slipped A-1 st, then k7 with A-1 (there will be 8 sts of A-1 on the needle, but the slipped st will be worked with C-2 at the end of this row). Notice that the strand of C-2 that you carried over to lock with A-1 has formed a new loop of yarn.

*Place A-1 over B-1, then bring B-1 from under A-1 and k7 with B-1. Rep from *, changing colors according to the chart and ending with 7 sts of B-2—you'll be at the C-2 loop. Drop B-2 through the loop, pull out enough of the C-2 strand to work with comfortably, and k7 with C-2 to finish the row. Gently tug on the C-2 yarn source to remove any remaining slack in the loop and any evidence of the beginning of the row. Turn the work.

Shift the colors one st every row in this manner to form spirals according to the chart for 30 more rows.

Shape Thumb Gusset

Pick any stripe to be the thumb. You will work the thumb with this single color. No intarsia! On the next 2 right-side rows, knit into the front and back of the same stitch (kf&b) two times in this stripe as follows:

Row 1: (RS) Kf&b, k4, kf&b, k1—9 sts in thumb stripe.

Row 2: (WS) Purl all sts in the colors as they appear.

Row 3: (RS) Kf&b, k6, kf&b, k1—11 sts in thumb stripe.

Row 4: (WS) Purl all sts in the colors as they appear.

OVEN MITT CHART

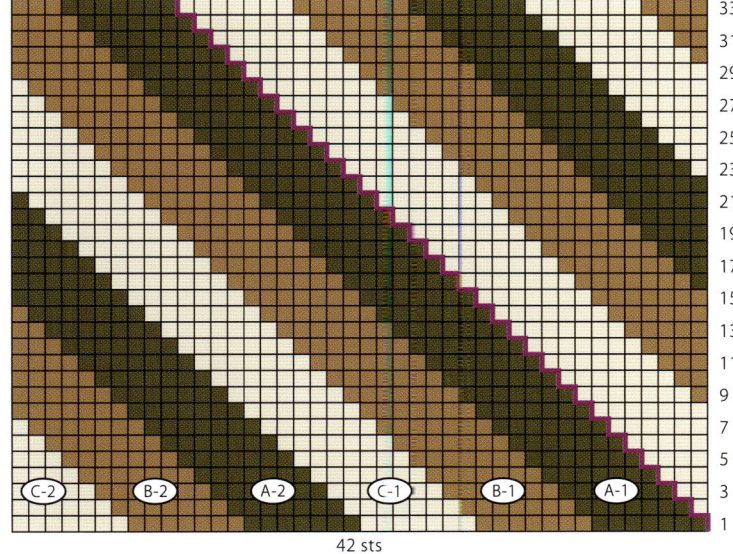

Next row: (RS) Place 11 thumb sts on waste-yarn holder. These sts will be worked later for the thumb.

Join the rem 35 sts for working "in the round" and continue in spiral pattern as established for about 14 rows until piece measures 3" (7.5 cm) from the thumb. You can add or subtract rows here for a longer or shorter hand.

Shape Top

Continuing to spiral every row, as established, dec 1 st in each stripe every right-side row as follows:

Row 1: (RS) *K1, k2tog, k4; rep from * for each stripe—30 sts rem; 6 sts in each stripe.

Row 2: (WS) Purl, maintaining 6 sts per stripe.

Rows 3 and 4: Work even in stripe pattern.

Row 5: *K1, k2tog, k3; rep from * for each stripe—25 sts rem; 5 sts in each stripe.

Row 6: Purl, maintaining 5 sts per stripe.

Rows 7 and 8: Work even in stripe pattern.

Row 9: *K1, k2tog, k2; rep from * for each stripe—20 sts rem; 4 sts in each stripe.

Row 10: Purl, maintaining 4 sts per stripe.

Rows 11 and 12: Work even in stripe pattern.

Row 13: *K1, k2tog, k1; rep from * for each stripe—15 sts rem; 3 sts in each stripe.

Row 14: Purl, maintaining 3 sts per stripe.

Row 15: *K1, k2tog; rep from * for each stripe—10 sts rem; 2 sts in each stripe.

Cut yarn, leaving an 8" (20.5 cm) tail. Thread tail onto a chenille needle and draw through rem sts, pull tight to close hole, and secure on WS.

Thumb

Carefully remove waste yarn from 11 thumb sts and place these sts on dpns so that there are 4 sts on Needle 1, 4 sts on Needle 2, and 3 sts on Needle 3. Join yarn in the same color and, with Needle 3, pick up and knit 2 sts from the base of the thumb—13 thumb sts total.

Place a marker and join for working in rnds. Knit 12 rnds—thumb measures about 2½" (6.5 cm) from joining rnd.
You can add or subtract rows for a longer or shorter thumb.

Decrease for Top

Rnd 1: *K1, k2tog; rep from * to last st, k1—9 sts rem.

Rnd 2: *K1, k2tog; rep from *—6 sts rem.

Cut yarn, leaving an 8" (20.5 cm) tail. Thread tail onto a tapestry needle and draw through rem sts, pull tight to close hole, and secure on WS.

Finishing

Turn the mitt inside out and use chenille needle to bury the ends into the links (page 36). To felt, machine wash (using the appropriate amount of detergent for the size of the load) on the regular cycle in hot water. Remove from washing machine promptly to prevent creases from forming, and lay flat to dry.

Tips for Working in the Round

You're bound to get confused when learning Annetarsia "in the round." Follow these simple "rules" to keep on track.

» Annetarsia "in the round" involves knitting one row, then purling the next, just as for knitting flat. Loops of yarn are made to link the rows to create a seamless tube.

» When shifting a motif in a diagonal direction, you'll slip (don't work the stitch) the first stitch of the row to move the motif to the left; you'll also slip the last stitch worked from the right needle tip to the left needle tip, and then knit that stitch as the first stitch of the new row to move motif to the right.

» After working with the loop, you'll make a new loop and lock it in place with the working yarn.

» There may be lots of *stitches*, but there will always be one, and only one, *loop* on the needle.

» The loop marks the last section of the row.

» The loop is always the same color as the section it covers (the color needs to match because you'll work those stitches with the loop).

» The loop is made from the section to your right as you face the work, ready to start a row. Whether you knit or purl, you'll move away from the loop.

In the Loo

For this workshop, we'll use worsted-weight cotton. Both bulky and strong, it holds up beautifully to vigorous washing and scrubbing. Cotton yarn cannot be spit-spliced and is more challenging to bury into the links, so it's a bit more difficult to manage than wool.

This workshop will teach you how to estimate how much yarn is needed for a color section, so that you can measure yarn supplies accurately. This process requires a bit of math and measuring time, but will make yarn management much easier.

Don't be discouraged if your first effort is lumpy or if you find working with the yarn difficult. If you get frustrated, return to working with wool to regain your confidence, then pick up the cotton project again. After you finish one, cast on for another, and keep making washcloths until you're satisfied with the result. You'll end up with a pile of washcloths that are equally useful, even if they have mistakes. Take pride in how your skill improved with each one and be assured that your future projects will go smoothly.

The projects in this workshop are designed for predominantly cotton yarn to produce thick and thirsty fabrics. The projects shown here were worked with Brown Sheep Cotton Fleece (80% cotton, 20% merino wool; 215 yd [196 m]/100 g) and KnitPicks Dishie (100% cotton; 190 yd [174 m]/100 g).

Each project requires five colors: one for the contrasting border and four colors for the central stripes. You'll need a total of about 44 yards (40 m) of the contrasting border color and 19 yards (17.5 m) of each of the four central colors to knit all three projects. Turn to page 25 for details on how to determine the amount of yarn needed for each color.

Follow these helpful tips for this workshop:

» Knit a 100-stitch swatch to determine your yarn gauge (page 25).

» The yarn amounts provided are based on a yarn gauge of 0.80. If the yarn from your 100-stitch swatch measures between 75" and 85" (between 190 and 216 cm), you can use the lengths specified below. If, however, your strand is shorter than 75" (190 cm), you'll probably end up using less yarn than I've specified. If, on the other hand, your strand is longer than 85" (216 cm), you'll probably need more yarn.

PROJECT 1: STOCKINETTE-STITCH WASHCLOTH WORKED FLAT

This washcloth will get you familiar with working with cotton.

Finished Size
About 8" (20.5 cm) wide and 7" (18 cm) long.

Yarn
Brown Sheep Cotton Fleece (80% cotton, 20% merino wool; 215 yd [196 m]/100 g): about 28 yd [25.6 m] Beige for contrasting border (CC), 21½ yd [19.6 m] Natural (A), 10½ yd [9.6 m] Green (B), and 11¼ yd [9.6 m] Blue (C).

Needles
U.S. size 6 (4 mm): straight (or a circular needle used for knitting flat).

Notions
Chenille needle.

Gauge
About 24 stitches and 32 rows = 4" (10 cm) in stockinette stitch. Exact gauge is not important but will affect the finished size.

Tips

» The two yarn supplies for the border (CC-1 and CC-2) are 14 yards (12.8 m) each, which is too long to use efficiently as loose strands. Unless you want to cut the yarn into smaller lengths and weave in the ends, wind them into butterflies (page 29), onto large bobbins, or use small balls contained in a yarn bowl.

» The border stitches are worked in garter stitch (knit on all rows).

» The motif stitches are worked in stockinette stitch (knit on right-side rows; purl on wrong-side rows).

» The numbers of stitches in the stripes on the outer edges of the chart change each row. But the sum of the number of stitches in the edge sections will always total 8.

Instructions

Set-up: With CC-1, use the method of your choice (I used the long-tail method) to CO 42 sts.

Work according to Stockinette-Stitch Washcloth chart as follows:

Rows 1–6: Knit all sts.

Prepare yarn supplies as described on page 67.

Row 7: (RS) Following the chart from right to left, k5 with CC-1. *Add C-1 by knitting 1 stitch, leaving a 5" (12.5 cm) tail at the back of work. Place CC-1 over C-1, bring C-1 from under CC-1 and k1 with C-1 to lock in CC-1, k6 with C-1 (8 sts total of C-1). Drop C-1 to the back of the work.

Rep from * for A-1, B-1, A-2, and CC-2 as indicated on the chart.

> **Tip:** On this first row of color pattern, you'll work one stitch with the new color before linking the two yarns. Linking the yarns between the first and second stitches only happens when a new color is introduced.

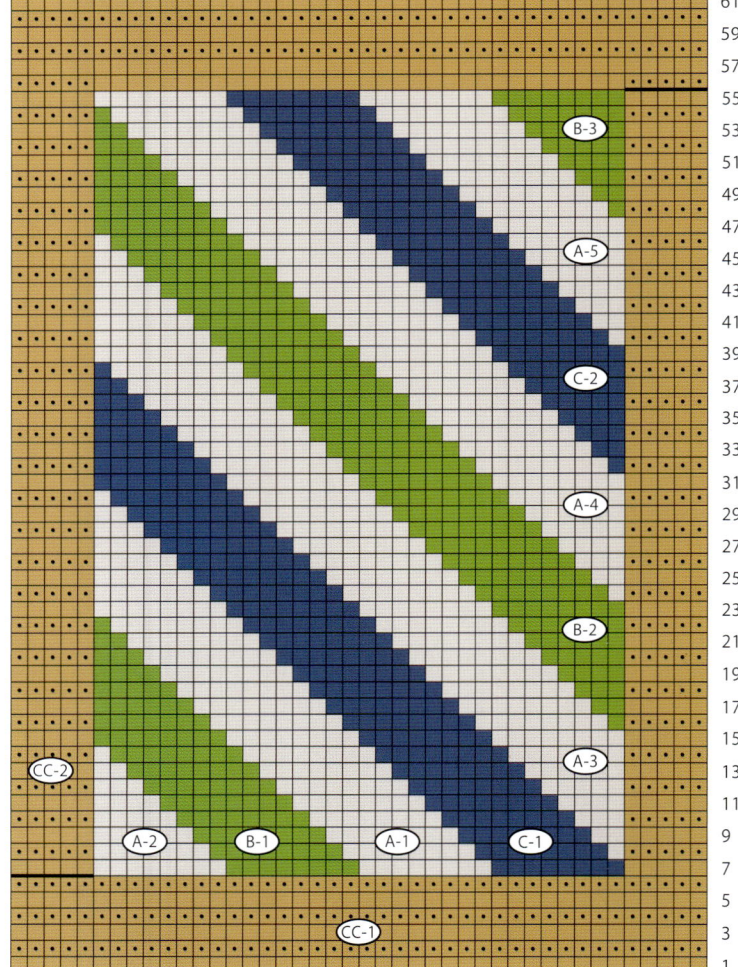

STOCKINETTE-STITCH WASHCLOTH CHART

42 sts

- ▨ With CC, knit on RS
- ▫ With CC, knit on WS
- ☐ With A, knit on RS, purl on WS
- ▧ With B, knit on RS, purl on WS
- ▨ With C, knit on RS, purl on WS
- — Boundary between yarn sources

YARN PREPARATION

Cut the yarns into the following lengths, noting that there are at least two lengths of every color. The lengths given here are based on the number of stitches and rows in a section and a yarn gauge of C.80 (see page 26 for details). You'll need the first six lengths on the first row of Annetarsia knitting; the remaining six lengths will be added at different times. You can cut and wind the remaining six lengths now or wait until they're needed. Store the prepared yarn supplies in a zip-top baggie to prevent them from tangling before you have a chance to use them.

CC-1: 14 yd (12.8 m)

C-1: 6 yd (5.5 m)

A-1: 4½ yd (4.1 m)

B-1: 3 yd (2.7 m)

A-2: 1¼ yd (1.1 m)

CC-2: 14 yd (12.8 m)

A-3: 7 yd (6.4 m)

B-2: 7 yd (6.4 m)

A-4: 6 yd (5.5 m)

C-2: 4¼ yd (3.9 m)

A-5: 3 yd (2.7 m)

B-3: 1¼ yd (1.1 m)

Row 8: (WS) Following the chart from left to right, k5 with CC-2, bring CC-2 to the front of the work. Place CC-2 over A-2 to link, p7 with A-2. *Place A-2 over B-1, p8 with B-1.

Rep from * for each section as charted, ending with one stitch of C-1 left on the left needle tip. Add new strand of A-3, to start this new color section. You may secure this stitch with a slipknot if desired. Place A-3 over CC-1 to link. Bring CC-1 to the back of the work, k5 with CC-1.

> **Tip:** When you're working with established colors, the links occur between the last stitch of the old color and the first stitch of the new color.

Row 9: (RS) Following the chart from right to left, k5 with CC-1, place CC-1 over A-3 to link, k2 with A-3. *Place A-3 over C-1 to link, k8 with C-1.

Changing colors according to the chart, rep from *, ending with 6 sts of A-2. Bring CC-2 to the back of work, place A-2 over CC-2, and k5 with CC-2. The first colored section A-3 will have 2 sts, the last section (A-2) will have 6 sts. When added together, the first and last sections should always total 8 sts.

Row 10: (WS) K5 with CC-2, bring yarn to front, place CC-2 over A-2, p5 with A-2. Place A-2 over B-1, p8 with B-1. Continue to work according to chart, ending with 3 sts of A-3. Place A-3 over CC-1 to link, bring CC-1 to the back of the work, k5 with CC-1.

Row 11: (RS) K5 with CC-1. Place CC-1 over A-3 to link, k4 with A-3. *Place A-3 over C-1 to link, k8 with C-1.

Changing colors according to the chart, rep from *, ending with 4 sts of A-2. Place A-2 over CC-2, k5 with CC-2. The first colored section (A-3) will have 4 sts, the last section (A-2) will have 4 sts.

Row 12: (WS) K5 with CC-2, bring yarn to front, place CC-2 over A-2, p3 with A-2. Place A-2 over B-1, p8 with B-1. Continue to work according to chart, ending with 5 sts of A-3. Place A-3 over CC-1 to link, bring CC-1 to the back of the work, k5 with CC-1.

Row 13: (RS) K5 with CC-1. Place CC-1 over A-3 to link, k6 with A-3. *Place A-3 over C-1 to link, k8 C-1.

Changing colors according to the chart, rep from *, ending with 2 sts of A-2. Place A-2 over CC-2, k5 with CC-2. The first colored section (A-3) will have 6 sts, the last section (A-2) will have 2 sts.

Row 14: (WS) K1 with CC-2, bring yarn to front. Place CC-2 over A-2, p1 with A-2. Place A-2 over B-1, p8 with B-1. Continue to work according to chart, ending with 7 sts A-3. Place A-3 over CC-1 to link, bring CC-1 to the back of the work, k5 with CC-1.

Row 15: (RS) K5 with CC-1. Place CC-1 over A-3 to link, k8 with A-3. *Place A-3 over C-1 to link, k8 with C-1.

Changing colors according to the chart, rep from *, ending with 8 sts of B-1. Place B-1 over CC-2, k5 with CC-2. All sections inside the border will have 8 sts.

Repeat Rows 8–15 for pattern, adding and ending colors as indicated by chart.

Continue in this manner through Row 61 of the chart, working odd-numbered (right side) rows from right to left and even-numbered (wrong side) rows from left to right.

Finishing

BO all sts. Use the chenille needle to bury the ends into the links (page 36). Hold fabric firmly between your fingers as you pull the needle through the links, to guide the needle smoothly through the fibers. Machine wash and machine dry.

Stockinette-Stitch Washcloth right side.

Stockinette-Stitch Washcloth wrong side.

PROJECT 2: GARTER-STITCH WASHCLOTH WORKED FLAT

This washcloth uses the same chart as the Stockinette-Stitch Washcloth on page 65, so the yarn amounts are the same. But because this washcloth is worked entirely in garter stitch (all stitches are knitted every row), it will be shorter in length than the stockinette version. This is because, all other things being equal, there are more rows per inch (2.5 cm) in stockinette stitch than in garter stitch. If you'd like this washcloth to be the same length as the other, continue working diagonal stripes as established until you reach the desired length. Be aware that doing so will require more yarn.

Finished Size
About 8" (20.5 cm) wide and 6" (15 cm) tall.

Yarn
Brown Sheep Cotton Fleece (80% cotton, 20% merino wool; 215 yd [196 m]/100 g): about 28 yd [25.6 m] Beige for contrasting border (CC), 21½ yd [19.6 m] Natural (A), 10½ yd [9.6] Green (B), and 11¼ yd [10.3 m] Blue (C).

Needles
U.S. size 6 (4 mm): straight (or a circular needle used for knitting flat).

Notions
Chenille needle.

Gauge
About 24 stitches and 32 rows = 4" (10 cm) in stockinette stitch. Exact gauge is not important but will affect the finished size.

Garter-Stitch Washcloth right side.

Garter-Stitch Washcloth wrong side.

Tips

» All stitches are knitted; when you turn your work, the yarn supplies will be on the side facing you. Yarn supplies are moved to the back of the work when you get to them, or when you need to work with that color.

» The yarn tails can be on either face of the work; there is no distinct right or wrong side of the fabric.

» If you need a new color before that color appears on the left needle, pull the needed strand over to where you're working. Bring the yarn between needles to the back of the work, then work the next stitch in the new color. This will create a visible link or "running stitch." It is not a mistake!

» Move yarn to the back of the work between the needles to avoid making a yarnover and increasing the number of stitches. Count your stitches often and if you notice that you've made a yarnover, just drop it off the needle and the yarn will smooth itself out.

» The number of stitches in the partial stripes at the edges will always total 8 stitches. For example, on Row 12 of the chart, there are 5 stitches of A-2 at the right edge and 3 stitches of A-1 on the left edge.

Instructions

Set-up: With CC-1, use the method of your choice (I used the long-tail method) to CO 42 sts.

Work according to Garter-Stitch Washcloth chart (page 71) as follows:

Rows 1–6: Knit all sts.

Prepare yarn supplies as described at right.

YARN PREPARATION

Cut the yarns into the following lengths, noting that there are at least two lengths of every color. You'll need the first six lengths on the first row of Annetarsia knitting; the remaining six lengths will be added at different times. You can cut and wind the remaining six lengths now or wait until they're needed. Store the prepared yarn supplies in a zip-top baggie to prevent them from tangling before you have a chance to use them.

CC-1: 14 yd (12.8 m)

C-1: 6 yd (5.5 m)

A-1: 4½ yd (4.1 m)

B-1: 3 yd (2.7 m)

A-2: 1¼ yd (1.1 m)

CC-2: 14 yd (12.8 m)

A-3: 7 yd (6.4 m)

B-2: 7 yd (6.4 m)

A-4: 6 yd (5.5 m)

C-2: 4¼ yd (3.9 m)

A-5: 3 yd (2.7 m)

B-3: 1¼ yd (1.1 m)

GARTER-STITCH WASHCLOTH CHART

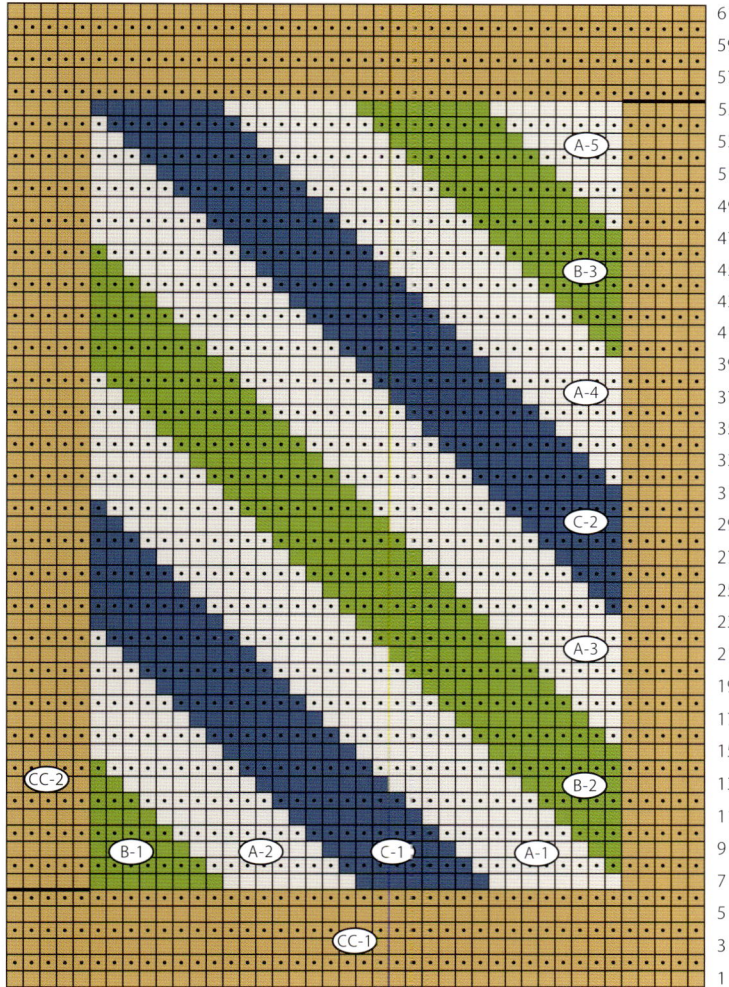

42 sts

- ☐ With CC, knit on RS
- ⊡ With CC, knit on WS
- ☐ With A, knit on RS
- ⊡ With A, knit on WS
- ☐ With B, knit on RS
- ☐ With B, knit or WS
- ☐ With C, knit on RS
- ☐ With C, knit on WS
- — Boundary between yarn sources

Row 7: (RS) Following the chart from right to left, k5 with CC-1. *Add A-1 by knitting 1 st, leaving a 5" (12.5 cm) tail at the back of work. Place CC-1 over A-1, bring A-1 from under CC-1, then k1 with A-1 to lock in CC-1, k6 with A-1 (8 sts total of A-1). Drop A-1 to the back of the work.

Rep from * for C-1, A-2, B-1, and CC-2 as indicated on the chart.

Tip: Note that this Row 7 is exactly the same as Row 7 for the Stockinette-Stitch Washcloth on page 66.

Row 8: (WS) Following the chart from left to right, k5 with CC-2, bring B-1 to the back of work. Place CC-2 over B-1 to link, k7 with B-1. *Bring A-2 to back, moving it in front of the 8th st of B-1 on the left needle. Place B-1 over A-2, k8 with A-2.

Rep from * for each section, ending with one stitch of A-1 on the left needle tip. Add a new strand of B-2, leaving a 5" (12.5 cm) tail at the back of work. To start the new color section, k1 with B-2 (you may secure this stitch with a slipknot if desired). Place B-2 over CC-1 to link, k5 with CC-1.

Row 9: (RS) K5 with CC-1. Bring B-2 to the back of work. Place CC-1 over B-2 to link, k2 with B-2. *Bring A-1 to the back, place B-2 over A-1 to link, k8 with A-1.

Rep from * for C-1, A-2, B-1 (ending with 6 sts of B-1), and CC-2 as indicated on the chart.

Row 10: (WS) K5 with CC-2. Bring B-1 to the back of work, place CC-2 over B-1 to link, k5 with B-1. *Bring A-2 to the back, moving it in front of the 6th st of B-1 on the left needle tip. Place B-1 over A-2, k8 with A-2.

Rep from * for each section, ending with 3 sts of B-2. Place B-2 over CC-1 to link, k5 with CC-1.

Row 11: (RS) K5 with CC-1. Bring B-2 to the back of work. Place CC-1 over B-2 to link, k4 with B-2. *Bring A-1 to the back, place B-2 over A-1 to link, k8 with A-1.

Rep from * for C-1, A-2, B-1 (ending with 4 sts of B-1), and CC-2 as indicated on the chart.

Row 12: (WS) K5 with CC-2. Bring B-1 to the back of work, place CC-2 over B-1 to link, k3 with B-1. *Bring A-2 to the back, moving it in front of the 4th st of B-1 on the left needle tip. Place B-1 over A-2, k8 with A-2.

Rep from * for each section, ending with 5 sts of B-2. Place B-2 over CC-1 to link, k5 with CC-1.

Row 13: (RS) K5 with CC-1. Bring B-2 to the back of work. Place CC-1 over B-2 to link, k6 with B-2. *Bring A-2 to the back, place B-2 over A-2 to link, k8 with A-2.

Rep from * for C-1, A-1, B-1 (ending with 2 sts of B-1), and CC-2 as indicated on the chart.

Row 14: (WS) K5 with CC-2. Bring B-1 to the back of work, place CC-2 over B-1 to link, k3 with B-1. *Bring A-2 to the back, moving it in front of the 4th st of B-1 on the left needle tip. Place B-1 over strand of A-2, k8 with A-2.

Rep from * for each section, ending with 5 sts of B-2. Place B-2 over CC-1 to link, k5 with CC-1.

Row 15: (RS) K5 with CC-1. Bring B-2 to the back of work. Place CC-1 over B-2 to link, k8 with B-2. *Bring A-1 to the back, place B-2 over A-1 to link, k8 with A-1.

Rep from * for C-1, A-2 (ending with 8 sts of A-2), and CC-2 as indicated on the chart.

Repeat Rows 8–15 for pattern, adding and ending colors as indicated by chart.

Continue in this manner through Row 61 of the chart, or length desired, working odd-numbered (right side) rows from right to left as for Row 7 and working even-numbered (wrong side) rows from left to right as for Row 8.

Finishing

BO all sts. Use the chenille needle to bury the ends into the links (page 36). Hold fabric firmly between your fingers as you pull the needle through the links, to guide the needle smoothly through the fibers. Machine wash and machine dry.

PROJECT 3: SOAP BAG WORKED "IN THE ROUND"

This little soap bag gives you another chance to try Annetarsia "in the round," or ITR. Keep in mind that the chart is deceptive and it appears that you'll need to add new colors as you go. But, in reality, the stripes wind around the work in a spiral. There will be always be the same four yarn sources, one for each stripe.

Finished Size
About 8" (20.5 cm) around and 5" (12.5 cm) long to eyelet row; base measures 3" (7.5 cm) wide and 1" (2.5 cm) deep.

Yarn
Brown Sheep Cotton Fleece (80% cotton, 20% merino wool; 215 yd [196 m]/100 g): about 16½ yd [15 m] Natural (A and C), 8¼ yd (7.5 m) Green (B), and 8¼ yd (7.5 m) Blue (D), plus 8¼ yd (7.5 m) Beige (E) for the base.

Needles
U.S. size 6 (4 mm): set of 4 or 5 double-pointed (dpn), two circular needles, or a long circular for "magic loop."

Notions
Chenille needle; size F/5 (3.75 mm) crochet hook.

Gauge
About 24 stitches and 32 rows = 4" (10 cm) in stockinette stitch. Exact gauge is not important but will affect the finished size.

Tips
» Each stripe consists of 8 stitches.

» Each of the four stripes has the same number of stitches and rows and, therefore, same S+R number.

» Yarn should be wound into butterflies or onto bobbins for ease of management.

Soap Bag untied.

Soap Bag tied.

» When changing from one double-pointed needle to another, snug up the first stitch on the new needle to tighten it and prevent a ladder from forming between needles. (You can also reduce ladders by working with two circular needles or one long circular in the magic-loop method.)

» The stripes shift along the diagonal according to the chart. This means that the turning point (the beginning and end of each row) will also shift along the diagonal. After Row 1, the edge of the chart will no longer coincide with the beginning and end of the rows.

» The turning point will be between the A and D stripes. On wrong-side rows, the loop will always be in D; on right-side rows, the loop will always be in A.

» At the end of every row, there should be 8 stitches in each color section. If you have more or fewer stitches, look for a dropped stitch, a color shift that was worked in the wrong diagonal direction, or a missed color shift.

» Remember that loop 'n' lock is the action of creating the loop at the end of one row and locking it into place with the first stitch of the next row.

Instructions

Base

With your chosen base color (E), use the e-wrap (also called the backward-loop) method to CO 12 sts on one dpn.

Work back and forth in garter st for 8 rows—4 garter ridges on each side of the work.

Body

Prepare yarn supplies as described at right.

With the same supply of E and a second dpn, pick up and knit 4 sts (1 st in each garter ridge) along the selvedge of the base; with a third dpn, pick up and knit 12 sts from the loops along the CO edge; with a fourth dpn, pick up and knit 4 sts (1 st in each garter ridge) along the other selvedge—32 sts total.

> **YARN PREPARATION**
>
> Cut the yarns into the following lengths, noting that they're all the same. You'll need all four lengths for the body of the bag on the first row of Annetarsia knitting.
>
> **A:** 8¼ yd (7.5 m)
>
> **B:** 8¼ yd (7.5 m)
>
> **C:** 8¼ yd (7.5 m)
>
> **D:** 8¼ yd (7.5 m)
>
> **E:** 8¼ yd (7.5 m)

With a fifth dpn, join for working in rnds, and knit 1 rnd. Cut E, leaving a 5" (12.5 cm) tail.

Work Annetarsia ITR according to Soap Bag Worked "in the Round" chart (page 75) as follows:

Row 1: (RS) Following the chart from right to left and leaving a 5" (12.5 cm) tail hanging in the back of the work, *k1 with A, place tail of E over A to lock E in place, bring A from under E and k7 with A.

Leaving a 5" (12.5 cm) tail of each new color, rep from * for B, C, and D, ending with 8 sts of D. Turn the work.

Row 2: (WS) Because you're facing the wrong side of the work, you'll purl this row. Slip the next A st (the first stitch knitted on the previous row) purlwise from the right needle tip onto the left needle tip without working it. Pick up A from the right edge of the A stripe, bring it over to where you're working, and place it over the strand of D that you used at the end of the previous row. Pick up D from under A, purl the slipped A st with D, then continue to purl the next 7 sts with D—the strand of A that was carried over to lock with D has formed a loop of yarn.

*Place D over C, then bring C from under D and p8 with C.

Rep from *, changing colors according to the chart and ending with 8 sts of B—you'll be at the A loop. Drop B through the A loop, pull out enough of the A strand to work with comfortably, and p8 with A to finish the row. Gently tug on the A strand to remove any remaining slack in the loop and any evidence of the beginning of the row. Turn the work.

Row 3: (RS) Slip the next A st purlwise from the left needle tip onto the right needle tip without working it. Pick up D from the right edge of the D stripe, bring it over, and place it over the strand of A that you used at the end of the previous row to "loop 'n' lock" the yarn.

Skip the slipped A st, then k8 with A (there will be 9 sts of A on the needle, but the slipped st will be worked with D at the end of this row). Note that the strand of D that you carried over to lock with A has formed a new loop of yarn.

*Place A over B, then bring B from under A and p8 with B.

Rep from *, changing colors according to chart and ending with 8 sts of C—you'll be at the D loop. Drop C through the loop of D, pull out enough D to work with comfortably, and p8 D to finish the row. Gently tug on the D yarn source to remove any remaining slack in the loop and any evidence of the beginning of the row. Turn the work.

Shift the colors one stitch every row in this manner to form spirals according to the chart until the piece measures 4" (10 cm) from the pick-up rnd, ending with a wrong-side row.

Eyelet rnd: (RS) Maintaining stripe pattern as established, *k1, [k2tog, yo] 3 times, k1; rep from * to end of row.

In stockinette, maintain stripe pattern as established for 1½" (3.8 cm) more, ending in a WS row.

Finishing

With RS facing, BO all sts (or work the optional picot BO as described below). Trim ends of working yarns to 5" (12.5 cm). Use the chenille needle to bury the ends into the links.

Optional Picot BO (worked in rnds)

Knit 3 rnds with base color (E).

Next row: *(K1, p1, k1, p1) into the same st, lift the first 3 sts over the 4th and off the needle, BO 3 sts as usual, slip the last st worked back onto the left needle tip; rep from * until all sts have been bound off.

Tie

With crochet hook and the color of your choice, work a crochet chain 16" to 18" (40.5 to 45.5 cm) long. Thread through eyelets and knot the ends.

SOAP BAG WORKED "IN THE ROUND" CHART

32 sts

☐ With A (C), knit on RS, purl on WS
☐ With B, knit on RS, purl on WS
■ With D, knit on RS, purl on WS
▮ Turning point

DETOURS AND HOW TO FIX THEM

I prefer to think of unexpected events in knitting as detours, rather than mistakes. Detours can be frustrating, inconvenient, and cost us time and effort. Sometimes a detour is just that, which can be very annoying. But every now and then you'll find yourself in a new and unexpected spot that teaches you something.

Detours can be expected whenever you learn something new. Before you embark on a full project, it is a good idea to sit down and knit some swatches. Swatches are never a waste of time. I used to say "rarely" a waste of time, but I've become convinced that this is one of those times where the word "never" is appropriate. I've learned something from every swatch I've ever knitted, even if it was only to reinforce that I had been absolutely right about my assumptions and hadn't needed the swatch at all. It never hurts to get some positive reinforcement!

If you're nervous about any aspect of intarsia, then, by all means, begin with a swatch (or several). You'll learn from your detours without compromising a project. Use leftover yarn that you enjoy working with, but no longer have enough of for a full-scale project. You'll put the yarn to good use and it just might turn into a coaster or pillow.

Let's take a look at the most common detours associated with Annetarsia.

Omitted Links

It is fairly common to omit a link at a color change. Even though you could swear that every single time you placed the old color over the new, then picked up the new from under the old, there will be times when you find something that looks like a buttonhole at some of the color boundaries. Generally, this happens on just the right or wrong side of the piece because some people have more difficulty making links on the knit side; others have more difficulty on the purl side. Even experienced intarsia knitters will occasionally miss a link.

If you miss links repetitively, you can produce an attractive fabric by using it as a design element or some terrific, strong buttonholes! But if you'd rather not go in that direction, there are two solutions.

Solution 1
When you link the yarn, look to make sure that the new yarn holds the old yarn snug against the work. Check to see that a line of links forms on the wrong side. With practice, this will become second nature and you'll no longer have to check every link.

Solution 2
When burying in the ends, slip your needle into each edge of the hole to sew it together on the wrong side of the work.

When you forget to link, you get something that looks like a buttonhole between color boundaries.

Close the holes created by missed link when you bury the ends.

Missed or Repeated Chart Row

It is surprisingly easy to lose your place on a chart. If your row marker (such as a sticky note or magnet) slips, you'll find yourself missing or repeating a row.

Solution 1: An Ounce of Prevention

» Pay attention to two rows when knitting: the row you're on and the one directly below it. The colors on the chart should line up identically with the colors on your needle, as well as the colors in the row below the needle.

» Count the stitches in each section every few rows and compare them to the chart. The faster you discover you have made an error—er, detour—the easier it will be to fix.

» Make a note along the side of the chart to indicate when you've finished a row. This will help prevent you from working the same row twice.

» Double check that you're following the chart from right to left on even-numbered (right side) rows and from left to right on odd-number (wrong-side) rows.

Solution 2: A Pound of Cure

» Evaluate how the motif will be affected if you just work the next row as it should be, or make a small alteration in the next row to get back on track.

» Un-knit until you get to a row that matches the chart. Un-knitting stitch by stitch is the easiest method. In general, you should avoid ripping intarsia out unless completely starting over, or bailing on a design completely. Ripping out intarsia gets messy very quickly due to the links and yarn supplies.

» Place a locking marker at the spot that does not match the chart, and continue working the chart as specified. After a few rows (or when you finish the piece), go back and correct the marked stitches with duplicate stitch.

The circled white stitch should be red.

Correct the wrong color stitch by duplicate stitching over it with the right color.

All fixed!

Place a needle in the correct stitches above the section of wrong color.

Pull out the entire strand of incorrect yarn.

Thread the strand through the link on the other side.

Wrong Color Used

This is usually a very minor issue. Generally, it happens when you're working with several shades of a color in dim light. Such a detour will rarely affect the motif noticeably, and you can consider it a design element.

Solution 1: An Ounce of Prevention

If you're using colors that are very similar to each other, store them carefully so that when you reach for a new yarn strand, you're guided by something other than color. For example, color A can be wound onto a bobbin and color B can be wound into a yarn butterfly. Store them in different types of baggies, or mark the bags labeled with the color names. Just make sure that you are guided by something other than the color so that you don't add the wrong one to the knitting in error.

Solution 2: A Pound of Cure

If the mistake does matter and you really want to substitute the intended color, you can un-knit just that section if, and only if, the ends haven't been buried yet.

Step 1. If the yarn to be replaced is encased in knitting, thread a holder through the stitches just above the section. If desired, thread another holder through the stitches just below it as well (Photo 1).

Step 2. Pull out the entire strand of the incorrect yarn. This will create a sizable hole in your knitting, with loops at the end of each row to work as your links (Photo 2). Mark these loops with contrast yarn.

Step 3. With the right side facing, knit the stitches off the lower needle with the proper color and, at the end of each "row," thread the strand through the link.

Step 4. With the wrong side facing, purl these stitches, then thread the strand through the link on the other side (Photo 3).

Repeat Steps 3 and 4 until all of the links have been connected.

Note: If you had knitted a row (or more) above the section that needed correcting, use the Kitchener stitch to join the two sets of stitches together.

Solution 3

If the ends were buried before you noticed the wrong color, you can use duplicate stitch to cover the errant stitches with the correct color. This will make for a slightly thickened fabric in that spot, but it's usually insignificant and you'll eventually forget about it.

Forgot to Shift a Color

Knit the next row exactly as it should be, leaving the errant row(s) alone, but place a locking marker in that location so you'll remember to come back to it (this type of detour often blends in with the rest of the knitting). When you've finished knitting, use duplicate stitch as needed to match the chart. In many cases, you can use a nearby end of yarn for the duplicate stitch, before burying it into the links.

"Missing" Stitches at Motif Edges

If you pull the new yarn too tightly when picking it up from under the old, the last stitch worked with that yarn will shrink in response. If the link doesn't have enough yarn, it will steal it from the adjacent stitch and that stitch will effectively disappear.

Solution 1

Always keep the links as loose as possible. While I've seen many links that are too tight, I've rarely seen one that's too loose. This is especially true when you're linking from a stitch that is below the needle that was worked in the previous row. Because the stitch is not held on the needle, there is nothing to prevent it from being pulled too tightly. When linking in such a situation, pull the working yarn upward from the stitch on the needle to slightly enlarge the stitch below it. This will give that stitch enough extra length to be pulled slightly for the link without shrinking.

In the example to the right (Photo 1), the yellow yarn is coming from the non-working needle, and is secure. When you pull the yellow strand for linking, the needle will prevent it from affecting the tension of the work.

But in the next example (Photo 2), the blue yarn comes from a stitch that is in the row below the needle. When you pull the blue strand for linking, there's nothing to prevent you from pulling the yarn so hard that thestitch "disappears."

The yellow yarn on the non-working needle is secured by the needle and cannot be pulled too tightly.

Pulling too hard on the blue yarn will cause the last knitted stitch to nearly disappear. Disappearing stitch is outlined in green.

Lift up on the old color (yellow) to enlarge the stitch below it (blue).

Relaxed link as viewed from the right side (outlined in green).

Relaxed link as viewed from the wrong side.

To prevent tightening the stitch, lift up with the old color (yellow) to enlarge the stitch below it (blue) before linking the colors (Photo 3).

When links are relaxed, the stitches will have the chance to expand and stretch the same as other stitches (Photos 4 and 5).

Solution 2
When you bury the ends, you can tighten up loose links by running the needle through the loose plies and tacking it to the fabric below.

There are Two Loops

If you find that there are two loops on your needles, you probably forgot to drop the old yarn through the loop on the last row. This will create a "false loop" of the old yarn, which will be the first loop you'll get to in the row.

Solution
Undo the butterfly or bobbin (if you're using one) of the first loop that you come to. Simply pull the strand loose from the link to free it. Re-wrap the bobbin or butterfly, link as usual with the previous section, and work to the true loop. When you get to the true loop, drop your yarn supply through the loop, work with the loop as usual, then continue on your way.

The Turning Point is at an Awkward Position

If the turning point is at an inconvenient place, you can shift its location. Ideally, the turning point should coincide with fairly consistent vertical or diagonal boundary between two sections of color. If there are large jogs in the boundary, then the turning point and the associated loop can become awkward to manage. If your turning point has run into such a situation, you'll probably want to shift it to another place where there is a diagonal or vertical line. To do so, simply use the color stranding technique (as for Fair Isle knitting) to move the yarn across the back of the work to where you'd rather start the next row, and then turn the work and begin the new row from that point.

The important thing to remember is that every stitch in every row needs to be worked. Where the turning point is on every row does not matter, as long as you keep track of where you are. As the knitter, you have complete freedom to move this point—you're not tethered to the edge of the chart.

Sunriver Scarf (page 166)

Oaks Park Socks (page 180)

Blue Moon Shawl (page 138)

Timberline Hat and Mitts (page 116)

Chapter 3:
Projects

Now that you've practiced Annetarsia and are comfortable with the techniques in the workshops, it's time to put your skills to use in larger projects.

For the projects that follow, I've chosen basic patterns that aren't particularly challenging so that you can concentrate on incorporating Annetarsia techniques without worrying about fussy construction details. Most of the projects were designed well before I decided to write a book—they originated from my trying something new and writing a pattern to test whether it was possible. The Astoria Socks (page 98) and Dizzy Scarf (page 86) started out as swatches that evolved into successful projects. For my first Annetarsia garment, the Columbia Suit (page 158), I simply added motifs into a garment that I'd knitted once before and loved: Sally Melville's "Not Mrs. Doubtfire's Suit." I hope you'll do the same with my technique—transform another pattern by adding your own Annetarsia motifs. Choose "in the round" or flat knitting, combine stranded knitting and intarsia at will, and take control of your colorwork.

Based on what happened when other knitters test-knitted my designs, I encourage you to use my projects for springboards for your own creations. For example, as knitters often do, Marcia Weinert changed pretty much everything about the Astoria Sock pattern (page 98) to create a design that was so different and wonderful that it deserved its own name—the Willamette Valley Socks (page 172).

Bobbie Hodges went bat-crazy creating new motifs for Namanu Shawl (page 132), resulting in the Tawanka variation (page 150). I had the pleasure of test-knitting Bobbie's ideas and had so much fun that I knitted two of my own bat shawls. Bobbie also made a stunning variation of the Dizzy scarf (page 86) by placing random zigs and zags throughout her knitting. Val McPherson wanted to use maple leaf motifs in the same shawl, which led to her Seneca Maples Variation (page 146). I'm looking forward to seeing many other creative versions of this versatile pattern!

No matter how proficient a knitter you may be, Annetarsia will take some practice. That's why I've concentrated on simple shapes that allow you to concentrate on managing multiple yarn supplies and linking the yarns at color changes. If you find yourself getting frustrated, knit another small project from Chapter 1 for a refresher of the basics. It's good to take the role of a beginner again and to challenge yourself. Before long, you'll be proficient with something that you may have considered quite impossible. And that's a pretty great accomplishment!

Dizzy Scarf

The Dizzy scarf is the result of wondering what would happen if I worked intarsia in garter stitch. I wound some black and white butterflies, cast on 30 sts, started swatching, and fell in love. Annetarsia garter stitch creates a flat, fairly reversible fabric. This is a wonderful stash-buster pattern, as different yarns can be used for each stripe. The knitting is fun, rhythmic, highly addictive, and requires no pattern after you have the technique down and the stripes established.

The scarf is named after Dizzy T. Sheep and the Dizzy Sheep Groupies, a Ravelry community that has been extremely kind to me. One skein of Cascade 220 in each color will make 4 scarves, so we split ours up into kits.

The Cascade 220 color range is large enough that not all of the colors will be available at all times. The colors listed are the ones we used, but substitutions are part of the fun!

WHAT YOU'LL NEED TO KNOW

Annetarsia garter stitch, page 54.

Calculating yarn gauge, page 26.

Managing multiple yarn supplies, page 25.

Reading charts, page 39.

Burying ends, page 36.

Skill Level
Advanced beginner.

Finished Measurements
About 6½" (16.5 cm) wide and 64" (162.5 cm) long.

Yarn
Cascade Yarns Cascade 220 (100% Peruvian Highland wool; 220 yd [201 m]/100 g): #8010 Natural; (A), #2401 Burgundy (B), #2450 Mystic Purple (C), #8892 Azure (D), #2429 Ireland (E), #9465B Cognac (F), #2410 Purple (G), and #2452 Turtle (H), 55 yd (50.2 m) each.

Note: One skein of each color is enough to make four scarves.

Needles
U.S. size 7 (4.5 mm): straight.

Adjust needle size if necessary to obtain correct gauge.

Notions
Locking stitch markers; chenille needle.

Stitch and Row Gauge
24 sts and 32 rows/rnds = 4" (10 cm) in garter st, after blocking.

Yarn Gauge
0.83.

Take time to check stitch, row, and yarn gauges.

Notes
» Knit all stitches in Annetarsia garter stitch.

» Knit until you run out of yarn, or until desired length.

» The end allowance (page 38) for this project is 15" (38 cm), as the diagonal links in garter stitch take more yarn than in stockinette.

Wow! A scarf named after me and the Dizzy Sheep Groupies! And by the very talented Anne Berk! I am so honored.

Oh, let me introduce myself! For those that don't know me, I am Dizzy T. Sheep, your fuzzy, clover devouring, and occasionally mischievous mascot extraordinaire. *That mischievous part has yet to be proven, by the way.* I run a different sort of yarn and fiber shop at DizzySheep.com, where we offer the Daily Dizzy Deal, $1 Dizzy Shipping, and other super discounts on a growing selection of fabulous yarn, fiber, and accessories.

My stock room is always open to satisfy your knitting, crocheting, spinning, and other crafty needs. Whether it's a bad day at the office that can only be remedied by something soft and squishy or you need comfort after waking up from a nightmare where a fiber-loving cat slurped up your entire stash like it was a clover milkshake, we've got you covered. We also share stories to brighten your day in our Blaaag, including the adventures of myself, Nameless Alpaca, a very unfuzzy gargoyle named Fred, and many others. Also, be sure to say "hi" on Ravelry in our Dizzy Sheep Groupies group, which is a wonderful community of fun and supportive individuals affectionately referred to as Dizzyites. Ultimately, our goal is to make the world a happier, fuzzier place, one knitter at a time. And eat lots of clover.

Now, you might ask why Anne would name a scarf after me. I remember it well…*[cue music and fade to flashback]*

It all started in 2012 with a weekend get-together at my place with some of the Dizzyites. Anne graciously accepted an invitation to come and teach a class on her new intarsia method. It was a wonderful experience for all.

Somewhere between Anne's awesome workshop presentation, the Dizzyites' amazing knitting talents, the 29-minute scarf challenge (that Anne completed in 19), and the opening of a warm liter of Faygo Rock & Rye (complete with a shower of sweet, red soda), everyone got invited to participate in this book—and did!

Check it out—my image is on the patterns that the Dizzyites knitted or designed. And keep an eye out for Fred; he's around here somewhere. He wandered off earlier to plan his next invention and was mumbling something about bats.

For this official version of the Dizzy Scarf, my expert staff at the House of Dizzy, a.k.a., The Village Yarn & Fiber Shop in East Rochester, New York, selected colors that reflect the endearing cast of characters and icons from the DizzySheep.com website. I love the selection. But enough about me, let's get back to this wonderful scarf!

Happy times at the House of Dizzy.

Nameless Alpaca, Dizzy Sheep, and Fred the Gargoyle.

YARDAGES NEEDED

The yarn amounts given here are based on the yarn and gauge specified and a yarn gauge of 0.83, and include 15" (38 cm) added for tails to be woven in. If your gauge or yarn gauge is different, knit a swatch and work your individual calculations (page 26) to determine the amount of yarn you'll need.

You'll need about 55 yd (50.3 m) of each color for eight pattern repeats (eight stripes of each color). Wind eight butterflies of about 7 yd (6.4 m) each. A few stripes at the beginning and end of the scarf will share a butterfly; all other stripes will have their own butterfly.

For a longer scarf, plan to use more yarn.

This is left as an exercise for the student — I've always wanted to say that. And about now Anne is probably regretting asking me to comment on this pattern.

Row 2 (right side).

Row 2 (wrong side).

SCARF

Prepare yarn supplies as described above.

With A, CO 30 sts.

Row 1: (RS) K6 with A, *k1 with B, bring A over B to link yarns, k5 with B; rep from *, changing colors every 6 sts.

Row 2: (diagonal shifts to right) Following Dizzy Scarf chart (page 91) from left to right, knit the first section with the last color worked, working 1 fewer st than on the previous row, *move the next color in the sequence from front to back of work between the needles, place the old color over the new color, pull the new color from under the old, k6 with the new color; rep from * until 1 st rem, then add new color and k1.

Row 3: (diagonal shifts to left): Following chart from right to left, knit the first section with the last color worked, working the same number of sts as on previous row, *move the next color in the sequence from front to back of work between the needles, k1 in old color, bring the new color over the old color, k5 with the new color; rep from * to end of row.

Place a locking marker at the beginning of the next row to designate it as Row 1 in case you get lost. Remember that Row 1 moves to the left on the RS; Row 2 moves to the right on the RS.

Rep Rows 2 and 3, shifting the diagonal 1 st every row and adding new yarn supplies as needed, until scarf is the desired length or you run out of yarn. BO all sts.

Note: For detailed row-by-row instructions, refer to the Garter-Stitch Potholder on page 54.

FINISHING

Use chenille needle to bury all loose ends into links.

And now the most important part: put the scarf on, find the nearest mirror, admire your beautiful creation, decide to keep it and not to give it away as the gift you intended, go back to the beginning and enjoy creating another one. Well, that's what I would do, and I'm never wrong!

DIZZY SCARF CHART

30 sts

- ☐ With A, knit on RS and WS
- ▨ With B, knit on RS and WS
- ▨ With C, knit on RS and WS
- ▨ With D, knit on RS and WS
- ▨ With E, knit on RS and WS
- ▨ With F, knit on RS and WS
- ▨ With G, knit on RS and WS
- ▨ With H, knit on RS and WS

Rose City Hat

Portland, Oregon is known as the Rose City. It's also known for a lot of gray days! The deep rose color and steel gray of the Malabrigo yarn used in this hat are a very good representation of our city.

Combining lace and small cables "in the round," this pattern is for the intermediate Annetarsia knitter who is confident with the ITR technique and is ready to incorporate other stitch patterns into a project. The lace pattern shown here is Wasp Wings, from *A Second Treasury of Knitting Patterns* by Barbara Walker. This hat is a fun and quick knit that provides lots of opportunity for creative expression—choose your own stitch patterns to make the hat truly your own.

WHAT YOU'LL NEED TO KNOW

Annetarsia "in the round" (ITR), page 12.

Calculating yarn gauge, page 26.

Managing multiple yarn supplies, page 25.

Reading charts, page 39.

Burying ends, page 36.

Skill Level
Intermediate.

Finished Measurements
About 19" (48.5 cm) brim circumference.

Yarn
Malabrigo Silky Merino (50% silk, 50% baby merino; 150 yd [137 m]/50 g): #400 Rupestre (A) and #429 Cape Cod Gray (B), 1 skein each.

Needles
U.S. size 4 (3.5 mm): 16" (40 cm) circular (circ) and set of 4 or 5 double-pointed (dpn).

Adjust needle size if necessary to obtain correct gauge.

Notions
Markers (m); stitch holders or waste yarn; chenille needle.

Stitch and Row Gauge
26 sts and 32 rows/rnds = 4" (10 cm) in St st, after blocking;

26 sts and 32 rnds = 4" (10 cm) in patt, after blocking.

Yarn Gauge
0.55.

Take time to check stitch, row, and yarn gauges.

HAT

Prepare yarn supplies as described at right.

With B and circ needle, CO 120 sts.

Place marker (pm) and join for working in rnds, being careful not to twist sts.

Set-up rnd: *With B, [k2, p2] 2 times; with A, [k2, p2] 3 times; rep from * to end of rnd.

Adding a new yarn supply for each color and working Annetarsia ITR (see Special Abbreviations), cont in k2, p2 rib as established until piece measures 1½" (3.8 cm) from CO, ending with a RS row.

Inc row: (WS) *With A, k6, M1 (see Special Abbreviations), k6; with B, p4, M1, p4; rep from * 5 more times—132 sts.

Maintaining 13 sts in A sections and 9 sts in B sections, work intarsia lace pattern ITR according to Rose City Hat chart (page 96) or written instructions as foll:

Row 1: (RS) *With B, k2, RT (see Special Abbreviations), sl 1, LT (see Special Abbreviations), k2; with A, p3, k2tog, yo, k1, p1, k1, yo, ssk, p3; rep from * 5 more times. Turn work.

Row 2: (WS) Loop 'n' lock (see Special Abbreviations). *With A, k3, p3, k1, p3, k3, with B, p9; rep from * 5 more times. Turn work.

SPECIAL ABBREVIATIONS

ITR: The method of working Annetarsia in rows that appear as if it was worked in rounds.

M1 (make 1): Use the left needle tip to lift the horizontal strand between the two needles from front to back, placing it on the left needle. Knit this lifted strand through the back loop to increase 1 stitch.

loop 'n' lock: Pull yarn from the last section worked on the previous row. Lock it into place with the first stitch of the next row to form a loop.

RT (right twist): K2tog but leave these sts on left needle tip, knit first st again, and then drop both sts off the needle.

LT (left twist): Working around the back of the first st, insert needle into the back of the second st and knit this st, then knit the first st and drop both sts off the needle.

k1tbl: Knit 1 stitch through the back loop to twist it.

YARN PREPARATION

The yarn amounts given here are based on the yarn and gauge specified and a yarn gauge of 0.55, and include 10" (25.5 cm) added for tails to be woven in. If your gauge or yarn gauge is different, knit a swatch and work your individual calculations (page 25) to determine the amount of yarn you'll need.

Prepare six butterflies for each color block (stripe) as follows:

15 yd (14 m) of A and 11 yd (10 m) of B for 9 pattern repeats each.

16 yd (14.6 m) of A and 11½ yd (10.5 m) of B for 10 pattern repeats each.

For a longer, slouchier hat, plan to use more yarn.

Row 3: Loop 'n' lock. *With B, k1, RT, k1, sl 1, k1, LT, k1; with A, p2, [k2tog, yo] 2 times, p1, [yo, ssk] 2 times, p2; rep from * 5 more times. Turn work.

Row 4: Loop 'n' lock. *With A, k2, p3, k1tbl (see Special Abbreviations), k1, k1tbl, p3, k2; with B, p9; rep from * 5 more times. Turn work.

Row 5: Loop 'n' lock. *With B, RT, k2, sl 1, k2, LT; with A, p1, [k2tog, yo] 2 times, p3, [yo, ssk] 2 times; rep from * 5 more times. Turn work.

Row 6: Loop 'n' lock. *With A, k1, p3, k1tbl, k3, k1tbl, p3, k1; with B, p9; rep from * 5 more times. Turn work.

Row 7: Loop 'n' lock. *With B, k4, sl 1, k4; with A, p1, yo, sl 1, k2tog, pass slipped st over decreased st and off the needle, yo, p5, yo, ssk, sl last st worked to left needle tip, pass second st on left needle tip over the first and off the needle, return sl st to right needle tip, yo, p1; rep from * 5 more times. Turn work.

Row 8: Loop 'n' lock. *With A, k1, [k1tbl, p1] 2 times, k3, [p1, k1tbl] 2 times, k1; with B, p9; rep from * 5 more times. Turn work.

Repeat Rows 1–8 eight more times for beanie fit; nine more times for slouchy fit—piece measures about 9" (23 cm) from top of ribbing for beanie; 10" (25.5 cm) from top of ribbing for slouchy fit.

Shape Crown

Changing to dpn when there are too few sts to fit comfortably on circ needle, dec as foll:

Row 1: (RS) Loop 'n' lock. *With B, k2, k2tog, sl 1, ssk, k2; with A, p3, k2tog, yo, k1, p1, k1, yo, ssk, p3; rep from * 5 more times—120 sts rem. Turn work.

Row 2: (WS) Loop 'n' lock. *With A, k3, p3, k1, p3, k3; with B, p7; rep from * 5 more times. Turn work.

Row 3: Loop 'n' lock. *With B, k1, k2tog, sl 1, ssk, k1; with A, p2, [k2tog, yo] 2 times, p1, [yo, ssk] 2 times, p2; rep from * 5 more times—108 sts rem. Turn work.

Row 4: Loop 'n' lock. *With A, k2, p3, k1tbl, k1, k1tbl, p3, k2; with B, p5; rep from * 5 more times. Turn work.

Row 5: Loop 'n' lock. *With B, k2tog, sl 1, ssk; with A, p1, [k2tog, yo] 2 times, p3tog,

ROSE CITY HAT CHART

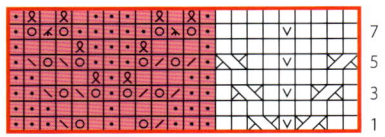

22-st repeat

- With A, knit on RS, purl on WS
- With A, purl on RS, knit on WS
- With A, yo
- With A, k2tog
- With A, ssk
- With A, k1tbl on WS
- With A, sl 1, k2tog, pass slipped st over
- With A, ssk, sl ssk st to LHN, pass 2nd st on LHN over 1st st and return sl st to RHN
- With B, knit on RS, purl on WS
- With B, sl 1 purlwise with yarn in back
- Pattern repeat
- RT (See Special Abbreviations)
- LT (See Special Abbreviations)

Portland, Oregon

ALTERNATIVE VARIATIONS

If this hat does not get you compliments…

Gold and Tan Version: knitted by Evelyn Mondo with Rowan Summerspun #110 (Holborn) and SMC Extra Soft Merino Cotton #05611 (Caramel).

…you need new friends!

Green Version: knitted by Sarah Reilly with Rowan Felted Tweed #152 (Watery) and #184 (Celadon).

[yo, ssk] 2 times, p1; rep from * 5 more times—84 sts rem. Turn work.

Row 6: Loop 'n' lock. *With A, k1, p3, k1tbl, k1, k1tbl, p3, k1; with B, p3; rep from * 5 more times. Turn work.

Row 7: Loop 'n' lock. *With B, sl 2 as if to k2tog, k1, pass 2 slipped sts over; with A, p1, yo, sl 1, k2tog, pass 2 slipped sts over, yo, p3tog, yo, ssk, sl last st worked to left needle tip, pass 2nd st on left needle tip over the first and off the needle, return sl st to right needle tip, yo, p1; rep from * 5 more times—60 sts rem. Turn work.

Row 8: Loop 'n' lock. *With A, k1, k1tbl, p1, k3, p1, k1tbl, k1; with B, p1; rep from * 5 more times. Do not turn work.

Cut all strands of B, leaving 5" (12.5 cm) tails. Isolate the strand of A from the first section of the row, then cut other strands of A, leaving 5" (12.5 cm) tails. Tuck ends into the center of the knitting to keep them out of the way.

Pm and cont in rnds with a single strand of A as foll:

Rnd 1: *Ssk (rem st of B with first st of A), p2, k3, p3tog; rep from * 5 more times—42 sts rem.

Rnd 2: Purl.

Rnd 3: *P2tog; rep from * to end of rnd—21 sts rem.

Cut A, leaving a 10" (25.5 cm) tail.

FINISHING

Thread tail on a tapestry needle, pull through rem sts, and pull tight to close hole.

Use chenille needle to bury all loose ends into links.

Astoria Socks

Astoria is a coastal town where the Columbia River meets the Pacific Ocean. The Astoria Column stands 600 feet (183 meters) above sea level and offers beautiful views of the coastline. Constructed in 1926, it has a spiral design that is echoed in these socks.

This project is designed to be a first "in the round" (ITR) sock project. The diagonals to the left are identical to the ones knitted in the beginning workshops and will be familiar. If you want to do something different for the second sock, knit the swirls in the opposite direction. Bust your stash by working each stripe a different color, or vary the color patterning to your whim.

WHAT YOU'LL NEED TO KNOW

Annetarsia "in the round" (ITR), page 12.

Calculating yarn gauge, page 26.

Managing multiple yarn supplies, page 25.

Reading charts, page 39.

Burying ends, page 36.

Skill Level
Advanced beginner.

Finished Measurements
About 7½ (8½, 9½)" (19 [21.5, 24] cm) foot circumference and 8¼" (21 cm) long from back of heel to tip of toe.

Socks shown measure 8½" (21.5 cm) in foot circumference.

Yarn
Miss Babs Yummy Toes Fingering (100% superwash merino; 133 yd [122 yd]/1.3 oz.): Oyster (MC), Nori (A), Russet Shadows (B), 1 skein each.

Needles
U.S. size 2 (2.75 mm): two 24" (61 cm) circular (circ; see Notes).

Adjust needle size if necessary to obtain correct gauge.

Notions
Marker (m); chenille needle.

Stitch and Row Gauge
7.5 sts and 9 rows = 1" (2.5 cm) in St st after blocking.

Yarn Gauge
0.44.

Take time to check stitch, row, and yarn gauges.

NOTES

» You can substitute a 32" (81 cm) circular needle for the "magic-loop" method, or use double-pointed needles. Be aware that yarn butterflies tend to catch on the ends of double-pointed needles.

» Wrong-side (purl) rows will always be worked in the same color sequence as the previous row; colors shift on right-side (knit) rows only.

» Be sure to follow the correct chart for your size and direction of swirl.

YARDAGES NEEDED FOR ASTORIA CHARTS

Based on a yarn gauge of 0.44, you'll need about 20 yd (18.3 m) of yarn for each stripe, which amounts to about 20–25 wraps around the hand. Two to three butterflies will be needed for each stripe, depending on the size of the butterflies.

SPECIAL ABBREVIATIONS

Loop 'n' lock: Pull yarn from the last section worked on the previous row, then lock it into place with the first stitch of the next row to form a loop.

LEG

Prepare yarn supplies as described at left.

With MC and using a stretchy method, CO 56 (64, 72) sts.

Place marker (pm) and join for working in rnds, being careful not to twist sts.

Work in k1, p1 ribbing until piece measures 1½" (3.8 cm) from CO.

Cut MC, leaving a 5" (12.5 cm) tail. Remove marker.

Work Annetarsia ITR as foll:

Set-up row: (RS; Row 1 of right- or left-leaning chart for your size; page 102) *K7 (8, 9) with A, k7 (8, 9) with MC, k7 (8, 9) with B, k7 (8, 9) with MC; rep from * once more. Turn work.

Next row: (WS; Row 2 of chart) Loop 'n' lock (see Special Abbreviations), purl to end, working each st in the same color as the previous row. Turn work. Loop 'n' lock.

Following the chart for your size, work through Row 16 (18, 20), then continue in swirl pattern as established until piece measures 7" (18 cm) from CO, ending with a WS row.

HEEL

Note: The heel is worked in short-rows on 21 (24, 27) sts that span three stripes of color. Work as established to the beginning of the stripe where you'd like the heel to begin. For the sock shown, the heel is worked on a red (B) stripe sandwiched between 2 white (MC) stripes.

Place a locking marker to mark the beginning of the row. Turn work.

Work short-rows back and forth on the 21 (24, 27) heel sts in two sections as foll.

First Half

Short-Row 1: K20 (23, 26), wrap next st, turn work.

Short-Row 2: P19 (22, 25), wrap next st, turn work.

Short-Row 3: Knit to 1 st before wrapped st, wrap that st, turn work.

Short-Row 4: Purl to 1 st before wrapped st, wrap that st, turn work.

Rep Short-Rows 3 and 4 until there are 7 (8, 9) unwrapped sts in the center of the heel (the sts of the middle stripe).

Second Half

Short-Row 1: K7 (8, 9) center sts, knit the first wrapped st tog with its wrap, wrap the next st (it will now be double wrapped), turn work.

Short-Row 2: Purl to the first wrapped st, purl the wrapped st tog with its wrap, wrap the next st for double-wrap, turn work.

Short-Row 3: Knit to the first wrapped st, knit the wrapped st tog with its wrap, wrap the next st for double-wrap, turn work.

Rep Short-Rows 2 and 3 until all of the wrapped sts have been worked—all 21 (24, 27) heel sts have been worked.

Work to the locking marker at the end of the row, turn work.

FOOT

Next row: Loop 'n' lock. Cont in swirl patt as previously established until foot measures 5½ (6, 7)" (14 [15, 18] cm) from the back of the heel or until it reaches the tip of your little toe, ending with a wrong-side row.

TOE

Arrange sts on needles with half of the sts on one needle for the sole and the other half on another needle for instep, so that the sock can lie flat. Pm to indicate beg of rnd.

Wrap a stitch at the turning point, remembering to link the old yarn over the new yarn before wrapping.

On wrong side, purl wrap together with its wrapped stitch.

Finished working purl stitch and wrap together, as seen from right side.

Complete heel as seen from the wrong side. Line of double-wrapped stitches created from the short-row is visible.

SIZE SMALL RIGHT LEANING CHART

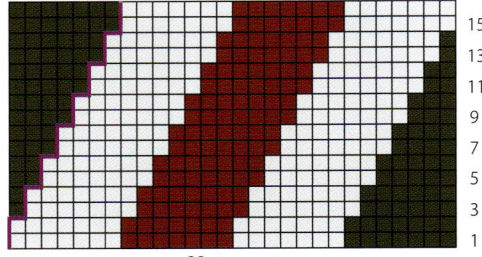

28-st repeat

SIZE SMALL LEFT LEANING CHART

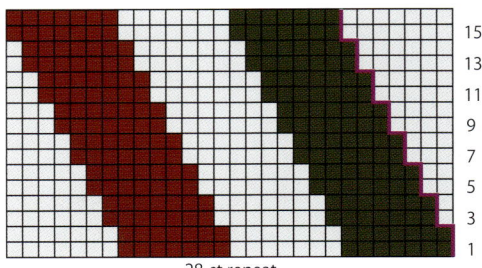

28-st repeat

SIZE MEDIUM RIGHT LEANING CHART

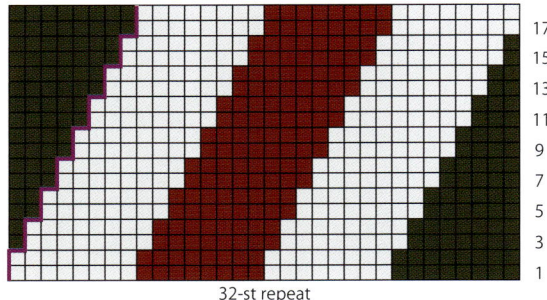

32-st repeat

SIZE MEDIUM LEFT LEANING CHART

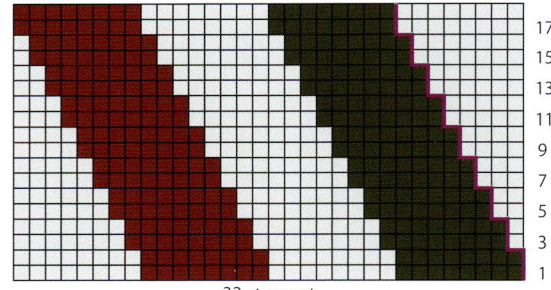

32-st repeat

SIZE LARGE RIGHT LEANING CHART

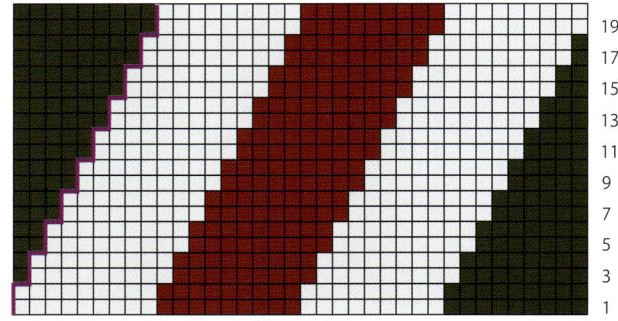

36-st repeat

SIZE LARGE LEFT LEANING CHART

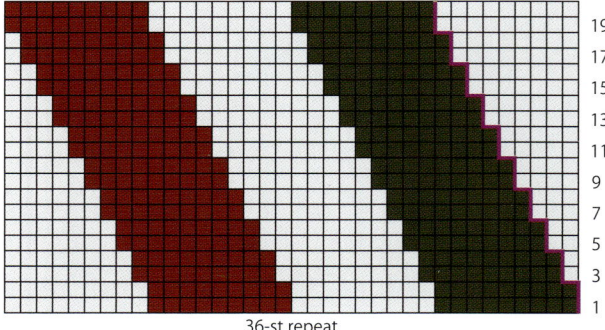

36-st repeat

- ☐ With MC, knit on RS, purl on WS
- ■ With A, knit on RS, purl on WS
- ■ With B, knit on RS, purl on WS
- | Turning Point

Continue to turn work, loop 'n' lock as established. Shift colors 1 st each row as established, work decs to follow the direction of the spiral (k2tog for a right-leaning spiral; ssk for a left-leaning spiral) as foll.

Left-Leaning Spiral

Row 1: (RS; dec in A stripes only) *With A, k1, ssk, k4 (5, 6); with MC, k7 (8, 9); with B, k7 (8, 9); with MC k7 (8, 9); rep from * once—2 sts decreased; 54 (60, 70) sts rem.

Row 2 and all WS rows: Purl, maintaining colors as they appear.

Row 3: (dec in MC stripes only) *With A, k6 (7, 8); with MC, k1, ssk, k4 (5, 6); with B, k7 (8, 9); with MC, k1, ssk, k4 (5, 6); rep from * once more—4 sts decreased; 50 (56, 66) sts rem.

Row 5: (dec in B stripes only) *With A, k6 (7, 8); with MC, k6 (7, 8); with B, k1, ssk, k4 (5, 6); with MC, k6 (7, 8); rep from * once—2 sts decreased; 48 (54, 64) sts rem.

Row 7: (dec in A stripes only) *With A, k1, ssk, k3 (4, 5); with MC, k5 (6, 7); with B, k5 (6, 7); with MC, k5 (6, 7); rep from * once—2 sts decreased; 46 (52, 62) sts rem.

Row 9: (dec in MC stripes only) *With A, k5 (6, 7); with MC, k1, ssk, k3 (4, 5); with B, k5 (6, 7); with MC, k1, ssk, k3 (4, 5); rep from * once—4 sts decreased; 42 (48, 58) sts rem.

Row 11: (dec in B stripes only) *With A, k5 (6, 7); with MC, k5 (6, 7); with B, k1, ssk, k3 (4, 5); with MC, k5 (6, 7); rep from * once—2 sts decreased; 40 (46, 56) sts rem.

Right-Leaning Spiral

Work to the beg of the first MC stripe after turning work and making loop.

Row 1: (RS; dec in A stripes only) *With MC, k7 (8, 9); with A, k4 (5, 6), k2tog, k1; with MC, k7 (8, 9); with B, k7 (8, 9); rep from * once—2 sts decreased; 54 (60, 70) sts rem.

Row 2 and all WS rows: Purl, maintaining colors as they appear.

Row 3: (dec in MC stripes only): *With MC, k4 (5, 6), k2tog, k1; with A, k6 (7, 8); with MC, k4 (5, 6), k2tog, k1; with B, k7 (8, 9); rep from * once—4 sts decreased; 50 (56, 66) sts rem.

Row 5: (dec in B stripes only) *With MC, k6 (7, 8); with A, k6 (7, 8); with MC, k6 (7, 8); with B, k4 (5, 6), k2tog, k1; rep

from * once—2 sts decreased; 48 (54, 64) sts rem.

Row 7: (dec in A stripes only) *With MC, k6 (7, 8); with A, k3 (4, 5), k2tog, k1; with MC, k6 (7, 8); with B, k6 (7, 8); rep from * once—2 sts decreased; 46 (52, 62) sts rem.

Row 9: (dec in MC stripes only) *With MC, k3 (4, 5), k2tog, k1; with A, k5 (6, 7); with MC, k3 (4, 5), k2tog, k1; with B, k6 (7, 8); rep from * once—4 sts decreased; 42 (48, 58) sts rem.

Row 11: (dec in B stripes only) *With MC, k5 (6, 7); with A, k5 (6, 7); with MC, k5 (6, 7); with B, k3 (4, 5), k2tog, k1; rep from * once—2 sts decreased; 40 (46, 56) sts rem.

Both Spirals

Maintaining swirl patt as established, dec 1 st from each stripe (8 sts decreased per row) every RS row as established (ssk for left-leaning swirls; k2tog for right-leaning swirls) 3 (4, 5) times—16 (14, 16) sts rem.

FINISHING

Divide sts between two needles so that there are 8 (7, 8) sts on each needle. With MC threaded on a tapestry needle, use the Kitchener st to graft the sts tog.

Use chenille needle to bury all loose ends into links.

Finished toe, wrong side.

Finished toe, right side.

Astoria Column

ALTERNATIVE VARIATIONS

These folks avoid that terrible, dreaded foot condition…

Prevent bland feet! Knit yourself a pair of these!

Pink and Gray Variation: knitted by Jodi Houlihan with Holiday Yarns Flock Sock Sock Yarn in Cheeky and Charcoal.

Pink and Teal Variation: knitted by Marcie Shapiro with Regia Angora Merino #07080 (Fuchsia), #07083 (Petrol), and #07075 (Ecru). Knitted with a Star Toe in one color, then establishing swirl pattern from there.

Purple and Teal Variation: knitted by Laura Mondo with Plymouth Happy Feet #0014, #0011, and #1249.

Cannon Beach and Seaside Pillows

The yarn was the inspiration for this pillow design. Pediboo is a bouncy, soft yarn that promised to be an irresistible pillow. Yarn packs with coordinating colors are available from Frog Tree Yarn, which is very convenient when you need several colors. The soft pale colors in this particular color group reminded me of the Oregon Coast—Cannon Beach and Seaside are two of my favorite coastal towns.

You can make one pillow with a different charted pattern on each side, but you'll only be able to see one motif at a time. The yarn pack contained enough yarn for several pillows, so I knitted the backs in solid colors and made a separate pillow from each chart.

Whether you select yarns from stash, or search for the perfect yarn to accent your décor, you'll end up with a unique statement.

WHAT YOU'LL NEED TO KNOW

Linking yarn, page 31.

Calculating yarn gauge, page 26.

Managing multiple yarn supplies, page 25.

Reading charts, page 39.

Burying ends, page 36.

Skill Level
Beginner to intermediate.

Finished Measurements
About 12" (30.5 cm) wide and 12" (30.5 cm) tall.

Yarn
Frog Tree Yarns Pediboo 3-ply, (80% washable merino wool, 20% bamboo viscose, 255 yd [233 m]/100 g): #1100 White (A), #1137 Blue (B), #1196 Light Green (C), #1134 Light Blue (D), #1182 Lavender (E), and #1146 Green (F), 1 skein each.

Needles
U.S. size 2 (2.75 mm): straight.

Adjust needle size if necessary to obtain correct gauge.

Notions
Two 12" (30.5 cm) square pillow forms; tapestry needle; chenille needle.

Stitch and Row Gauge
28 sts and 40 rows = 4" (10 cm) in St st, after blocking.

Yarn Gauge
0.48.

Take time to check stitch, row, and yarn gauges.

YARN PREPARATION

Prepare butterflies or loose strands for each block as follows. The yarn amounts given here are based on the yarn and gauge specified and a yarn gauge of 0.48, and include 10" (25.5 cm) added for tails to be woven in. If your gauge or yarn gauge is different, knit a swatch and work your individual calculations (page 26) to determine the amount of yarn you'll need.

Note: Strand lengths have been averaged for ease of measurement. Some will be longer than actually needed for the project.

Yarn supplies of less than 2 yd (1.83 m) can be worked as single strands.

Cannon Beach Pillow Front: Yardages Needed

Color Block	Number Needed	S+R	Yards (Meters)
A-1	4	27	¾ (0.68)
C-1	4	98	1½ (1.25)
A-2	4	84	1½ (1.25)
E-1	4	206	3 (2.74)
A-3	4	144	2¼ (2.06)
D-1	4	314	4½ (4.11)
A-4	4	204	3 (2.74)
F-1	4	430	6 (5.49)
A-5	4	228	3¼ (2.97)
B-1	2	764	10½ (9.60)
A-6	2	389	5½ (5.03)
C-2	2	593	8¼ (7.54)
A-7	2	269	3¾ (3.43)
E-2	2	386	5½ (5.03)
A-8	2	149	2¼ (2.06)
D-2	2	161	2½ (2.29)
A-9	1	59	1 (0.91)

Cannon Beach Pillow Back: Yardages Needed

150 yd (137 m)

Seaside Pillow Front: Yardages for Color A

Color Block	Number Needed	S+R	Yards (Meters)
A-1	1	756	10¼ (9.37)
A-2	4	211	3 (2.74)
A-3	1	815	11¼ (10.29)
A-4	15	76	1¼ (1.14)
A-5	5	13	½ (0.46)
A-6	24	77	1¼ (1.14)
A-7	6	274	4 (3.66)

Seaside Pillow Front: Yardages Needed for Other Color Blocks

Color Block	Number Needed	S+R	Yards (Meters)
1	1 of B	48	1 (0.91)
	2 of C		1 (0.91)
	1 of D		1 (0.91)
	1 of E		1 (0.91)
	1 of F		1 (0.91)
2	2 of B	32	¾ (0.68)
	2 of C		¾ (0.68)
	6 of E		¾ (0.68)
3	1 of B	56	1 (0.91)
	2 of C		1 (0.91)
	3 of D		1 (0.91)
	1 of E		1 (0.91)
	3 of F		1 (0.91)
4	4 of B	137	2 (1.83)
	4 of C		2 (1.83)
	4 of D		2 (1.83)
	4 of E		2 (1.83)
	8 of F		2 (1.83)
5	2 of B	39	¾ (0.68)
	2 of C		¾ (0.68)
	2 of D		¾ (0.68)
	4 of E		¾ (0.68)
	2 of F		¾ (0.68)

FRONT

Prepare yarn supplies as described on page 108.

With A and using the long-tail method, CO 86 sts.

Purl 1 WS row.

Work Rows 1–122 of Cannon Beach chart (page 110) or Rows 1–120 of Seaside chart (page 112).

With A, knit 1 row.

With WS facing, BO all sts purlwise.

BACK

Notes for the back:

» If you choose to knit the back in a solid color, you'll need a second ball of that color.

» If you'd rather use up the leftovers from all colors, you can knit horizontal or diagonal stripes in any or all of the colors, follow the chart for the other pillow, or repeat the same chart.

» Solid-color knitting may result in a slighter tighter gauge than intarsia knitting. If you want the front and back to have the same gauge, you may need to adjust the needle size used for the back to match the gauge for the front.

» It's not necessary to have the same gauge for the pillow front and back. The important factor is having the identical number of stitches and rows for both pieces. They will seam together perfectly with the mattress stitch and the back will stretch over the pillow form for a beautiful result.

FINISHING

With chenille needle, bury all loose ends into the links.

Wet-block pieces by giving them a bath in warm water and rinse-free wool wash for at least 30 minutes. Roll in a clean, dry towel to remove excess moisture, then lay flat and pin to 12" (30.5 cm) square. Let air-dry completely before removing pins.

With the color of your choice threaded on a tapestry needle, use the mattress stitch to sew three sides of the pillow. Insert pillow form, then sew remaining side, or use single crochet for a removable seam if you wish to be able to remove the form for easy laundering.

CANNON BEACH CHART ROWS 1-61

86 sts

☐ With A, knit on RS, purl on WS
■ With B, knit on RS, purl on WS
■ With C, knit on RS, purl on WS
■ With D, knit on RS, purl on WS
■ With E, knit on RS, purl on WS
■ With F, knit on RS, purl on WS
— Boundary between yarn sources

ROWS 62-121

86 sts

111

SEASIDE CHART ROWS 1-60

- □ With A, knit on RS, purl on WS
- ■ With B, knit on RS, purl on WS
- ■ With C, knit on RS, purl on WS
- ■ With D, knit on RS, purl on WS
- ■ With E, knit on RS, purl on WS
- ■ With F, knit on RS, purl on WS
- — Boundary between yarn sources

ROWS 61-120

86 sts

ALTERNATIVE VARIATIONS

Manzanita Variation: Knitting a chart with different sized yarn and needles is the easiest way to change the size of an intarsia project. Making a larger pillow is as easy as choosing a bulkier yarn and larger needle size. This project was knitted with the Cannon Beach chart (page 110) but on the center 86 rows and 66 sts, using luxurious hand-dyed variegated yarn for a nicely distinctive effect.

Yarn: Blue Moon Fiber Arts De-vine (100% merino wool; 225 yd [205 m]/8 oz [226 g]): Debra Anna (Purple; A), 90 yd (82.3 m), Retroid (Green; B), 189 yd (173 m).

Berocco Chunky Vintage (50% acrylic, 40% wool, 10% nylon; 130 yd [119 m]/100 g): #6167 Dewberry (C), 190 yd (175 m), used for the solid-color back.

Needles: U.S. size 10½ (6.5 mm): straight.

Stitch and Row Gauge: 13 sts and 17 rows = 4" (10 cm) in St st, after blocking.

Yarn Gauge: Blue Moon Fiber Arts De-vine: 1.10. Berocco Chunky Vintage: 1.00.

Finished Measurements: 19" (48.2 cm) square.

Manzanita Variation sample knitted by Deb Jaworowicz.

Lincoln City Variation: Changing to worsted-weight yarn and only 2 colors creates a completely different pillow.

Yarn: Frog Tree Yarns Pediboo worsted (80% washable merino wool, 20% bamboo viscose, 182 yd [166 m]/100 g): #1325 Orange (A), #1340 Dark Gold (B), 1 skein each.

Needles: U.S. size 6 (4.25 mm): straight.

Stitch and Row Gauge: 20 sts and 26 rows = 4" (10 cm) in St st, after blocking.

Yarn Gauge: 0.70.

Finished Measurements: About 12" (30.5 cm) square.

Lincoln City Variation sample knitted by Anne Berk.

Cannon Beach

Timberline Hat and Mitts

The Oregon mountains are snowcapped most of the year and are popular with skiers and hikers. This hat-and-mitt set is worked in the argyle motif, which is among my favorites—in large part because it's so easy to knit. Knitted in worsted-weight yarn, these accessories are a fast and satisfying introduction to Annetarsia ITR that will be welcome on any mountain expedition. The yarn, Brown Sheep Lanaloft, comes in a wide range of colors, with plenty to choose from.

WHAT YOU'LL NEED TO KNOW

Annetarsia "in the round" (ITR), page 12.

Calculating yarn gauge, page 26.

Managing multiple yarn supplies, page 25.

Reading charts, page 39.

Burying ends, page 36.

Skill Level
Advanced beginner.

Finished Measurements
Hat: About 25" (63.5 cm) brim circumference.

Mitts: About 9" (23 cm) hand circumference and 10" (25.5 cm) long from cast-on to bind-off.

Yarn
Brown Sheep Lanaloft Worsted (100% wool; 160 yd [146 m]/100 g): LL75 Garland (MC), LL60 Feather Gold (A), and LL45 Manhattan Mist (B) 1 skein each; LL01 Cottage White (AC), 5 yd (4.6 m).

Needles
U.S. size 8 (5 mm): set of 4 or 5 double-pointed (dpn).

You may substitute 24" (61 cm) circular (circ) to work with the magic-loop method for the mitts and 16" (40.5 cm) circular for hat.

Adjust needle size if necessary to obtain correct gauge.

Notions
Markers (m); stitch holders or waste yarn; chenille needle; pom-pom maker (optional).

Stitch and Row Gauge
16 sts and 24 rows/rows = 4" (10 cm) in St st, after blocking.

Yarn Gauge
0.76.

Take time to check stitch, row, and yarn gauges.

Notes
The accent color (AC) diagonal lines are worked in duplicate stitch after the hat and mitts are complete. When working the chart, work the AC color squares in the background color over which they appear.

SPECIAL ABBREVIATIONS

Loop 'n' lock: Pull a loop of the yarn at the end of the row, then lock it into place with the first stitch of the next row.

M1 (make 1): Use the left needle tip to lift the horizontal strand between the two needles from front to back, placing it on the left needle. Knit this lifted strand through the back loop to increase 1 stitch.

YARN PREPARATION

Prepare butterflies or loose strands for each block as follows. The yarn amounts given here are based on the yarn and gauge specified and a yarn gauge of 0.76, and include 10" (25.5 cm) added for tails to be woven in. If your gauge or yarn gauge is different, knit a swatch and work your individual calculations (page 26) to determine the amount of yarn you'll need. Yarn supplies of less than 2 yd (1.83 m) can be worked as single strands.

Yardages Needed for Hat

Color Block	Number Needed	S+R	Yards (Meters)
A diamonds	6	100	2½ (2.25)
B diamonds	6	100	2½ (2.25)
MC	12	100	2½ (2.25)
Accent lines (AC)	12	36	1 (0.91)

Yardages Needed for Mitts

Color Block	Number Needed	S+R	Yards (Meters)
A diamonds	2	200	4½ (4.11)
B diamonds	2	200	4½ (4.11)
MC	4	200	4½ (4.11)
Accent lines (AC)	add as needed		1 (0.91)

MITTS (MAKE 2)

Prepare yarn supplies as described on page 118.

Note: Use yarn from the skein for the CO and cuff.

With dpn and MC, CO 36 sts. Place marker (pm) and join for working in rnds, being careful not to twist sts.

Work in k2, p2 rib for 20 rnds.

Knit 1 rnd, then remove marker.

Working Annetarsia ITR, work Timberline chart (page 121) as foll, working the AC diagonal lines with the background color (the correct color will be added with duplicate st later):

Row 1: (RS) *K4 with MC, k1 with A, k8 with MC, k1 with B, k4 with MC; rep from * once, pm for thumb, k3 with MC (1 st rem before first st of A on Row 1). Turn work (this becomes the turning point). Place locking marker if desired to mark beg of row.

Row 2: (WS) Loop 'n' lock (see Special Abbreviations), purl according to Row 2 of chart, slipping thumb marker, omitting the AC diagonal lines, and adding new sources of MC between the diamond motifs.

Row 3: (begin thumb incs; work all thumb sts in MC) Work as charted to thumb m, sl m, M1 (see Special Abbreviations), pm for end of thumb sts, work to turning point, turn work— 1 thumb st between markers for thumb.

Row 4: Loop 'n' lock, work as charted to first thumb m, sl m, with MC, purl to next m, sl m, work in charted patt to turning point, turn work.

Rows 5 and 6: Work even as charted.

Inc row: (RS) Loop 'n' lock, work as charted to m, sl m, M1 with MC, knit to next m, M1, sl m, work as charted to turning point, turn work—3 thumb sts between markers.

Rep Inc row every 4th row 5 more times, ending with a RS row—49 sts; 13 thumb sts between markers.

Next row: (WS) Loop 'n' lock, work as charted to m, remove m, place 13 thumb sts onto waste yarn or holder, remove m, work as charted to turning point, turn work—36 sts rem.

Cont even on 36 sts until Row 36 of Timberline chart has been completed.

Pm to indicate beg of rnd. Working with the single strand of MC, knit 1 rnd.

Work in k1, p1 rib for 9 rnds, or desired length to cover fingertips.

BO all sts in patt.

Thumb

With MC, pick up and knit 3 sts along gap at base of thumb, then k13 held thumb sts—16 sts total. Pm and join for working in rnds.

Knit 8 rnds.

Work in k1, p1, rib for 3 rnds.

BO all sts in patt.

Finishing

With AC threaded on a tapestry needle, work duplicate sts to form diagonal lines on chart.

Use chenille needle to bury all loose ends in links.

HAT

Prepare yarn supplies as described on page 118.

Note: Use yarn from the skein for the CO and ribbing.

With MC and dpn or 16" (40.5 cm) circ needle, CO 100 st. Place marker (pm) and join for working in rnds, being careful not to twist sts.

Work in k2, p2 rib for 21 rnds.

Turning ridge: Purl 1 rnd.

Inc rnd: [P12, M1 (see Special Abbreviations)] 8 times, purl to end—108 sts.

Knit 1 rnd.

Working Annetarsia ITR, work Timberline chart as foll, working the AC diagonal lines with the background color (the correct color will be added with duplicate st later):

Row 1: (RS) K4 with MC, *k1 with A, k8 with MC, k1 with B, k8 with MC; rep from * to last 7 sts, k7 with MC (1 st rem before first st of A on Row 1). Turn work (this becomes the turning point).

Place locking marker on the work, if needed, to mark beg of row.

Note: Remember, the end of the row will move with the edge of the diamond motif, *not* with the edge of the chart.

Row 2: (WS) Loop 'n' lock (see Special Abbreviations), purl according to Row 2 of chart, omitting the AC diagonal lines and adding new sources of MC between the diamond motifs.

Cont in this manner through Row 18 of chart.

Border

With MC only, knit 1 rnd, then purl 2 rnds.

Crown

Knit 4 rnds with MC.

Dec Rnd 1: [K11, k2tog] 8 times, knit to end—100 sts rem.

Work even in St st (knit every rnd) until piece measures 7" (18 cm) from turning ridge.

Dec Rnd 2: [K23, k2tog] 4 times—96 sts rem.

Changing to dpn when there are too few sts to fit comfortably on circ needle, cont as foll:

Dec Rnd 3: *K2, k2tog; rep from * to end—72 sts rem.

Next rnd: Knit.

Rep the last 2 rnds once more—48 sts rem.

Dec Rnd 4: *K2tog; rep from * to end—24 sts rem.

Rep the last rnd 2 more times—6 sts rem.

Cut yarn, leaving a 12" (30.5 cm) tail. Thread tail on a tapestry needle, pull through rem sts, and pull tight to close hole.

Finishing

With AC threaded on a tapestry needle, work duplicate st to form diagonal lines as shown on chart.

Use chenille needle to bury all loose ends into links.

Fold the ribbing to the inside of the hat along the turning ridge and tack in place, if desired.

Soak hat in water for 30 minutes, squeeze out the water, and place over a bowl to air-dry.

Make pompom as desired and secure to top of hat, burying ends on the inside of hat.

TIMBERLINE CHART

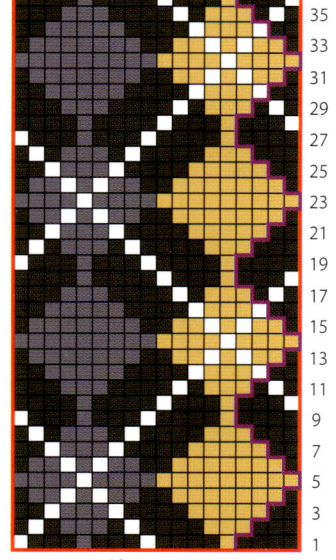

18-st repreat

■ With MC, knit on RS, purl on WS
■ With A, knit on RS, purl on WS
■ With B, knit on RS, purl on WS
☐ With AC, duplicate st
▢ Pattern repeat
| Turning point

Multnomah Coat

The Columbia Gorge of Oregon contains the magnificent Multnomah Falls. The vertical lines of the falls are contrasted by the horizontal counterpoint of the bridge that spans the river. These contrasting lines are echoed in the plaid motif of this coat.

I love to wear sweater coats. In fact, after finishing the Columbia Suit (page 158), I immediately set out to use the same Toots Le Blanc yarn for the drop-shoulder coat you see here. I acquired every color that I could, and then worked for months on designing motifs. I swatched repeatedly to create a quick and enjoyable knit with flattering lines.

The edging is from Anna Zilboorg's "Tina's Sweater" pattern published by Blue Moon Fiber Arts. It's a delightful change from ribbing and adds weight and swing to the coat.

> **WHAT YOU'LL NEED TO KNOW**
>
> Linking yarn, page 31.
>
> Calculating yarn gauge, page 26.
>
> Managing multiple yarn supplies, page 25.
>
> Reading charts, page 39.
>
> Burying ends, page 36.

Skill Level
Advanced beginner.

Finished Measurements
About 42" (106.5 cm) chest circumference and 38" (96.5 cm) long.

Yarn
Toots LeBlanc Jacob/Alpaca Worsted, (50% alpaca, 50% wool; 250 yd [228 m]/ 6 oz): Fawn (A) and Ivory (B), 3 skeins each; Medium Brown (C), Dark Brown (D), and Black (E), 1 skein each.

Needles
U.S. sizes 7 (4.5 mm) and 6 (4 mm): straight.

Adjust needle size if necessary to obtain correct gauge.

Notions
Ten ⅞" (2.2 cm) buttons; tapestry needle; chenille needle; buttonhole thread in matching color.

Stitch and Row Gauge
20 sts and 28 rows = 4" (10 cm) in St st on larger needles, after blocking.

Yarn Gauge
0.85.

Take time to check stitch, row, and yarn gauges.

Notes
» The gauge for this yarn changes significantly with blocking, which fluffs the fibers and tightens the gauge. A blocked swatch is crucial to the final result, especially if you use unprocessed wool. Only trust your blocked gauge!

» One size fits most. If you need to significantly widen or narrow back and front pieces, add or subtract sts in the solid-color sections on each side.

SPECIAL STITCHES

Anna Zilboorg Border Pattern (multiple of 3 sts + 2)

Row 1: (RS) Sl 1 purlwise, *k1, wrapping yarn twice around needle; rep from * to last st, k1.

Row 2: Sl 1 purlwise, *sl 3 purlwise, dropping extra wraps, sl the 3 sts back to left needle tip, [k1, p1, k1] in these 3 sts tog; rep from * to last st, p1.

Rows 3 and 4: Knit.

One-Row Buttonhole (from Barbara Walker's Second Treasury of Knitting Patterns)

Step 1: Work across row to where buttonhole is to start.

Step 2: Bring yarn to front, sl 1 st purlwise from the left to the right needle tip, bring yarn to back and drop it there (yarn is left hanging and is not used in Steps 3 and 4).

Step 3: *Sl 1 st purlwise from left to right needle tip, then pass the first st over it; rep from * 2 more times— 3 sts BO.

Step 4: Return the last st onto the left needle tip and turn work.

Step 5: With yarn left hanging, use the cable method to CO as follows: *insert the right needle tip knitwise between the first and second sts on the left needle tip, wrap yarn as usual around right-hand needle and draw up a loop between these two sts, place this loop onto the left needle tip to create a new st; rep from * until 4 sts have been CO (one more st than was BO). Before placing the last loop onto the left needle tip, bring yarn to front to form a dividing strand between the last 2 sts. Turn work.

Step 6: Sl the first st from the left to the right needle tip, then pass the fourth CO st over it and work to end of row.

SPECIAL ABBREVIATIONS

M1 (make 1): Use the left needle tip to lift the horizontal strand between the two needles from front to back, placing it on the left needle. Knit this lifted strand through the back loop to increase 1 stitch.

Multnomah Falls

YARN PREPARATION

Prepare butterflies for each color block as follows. The yarn amounts given here are based on the yarn and gauge specified and a yarn gauge of 0.85, and include 10" (25.5 cm) added for tails to be woven in. If your gauge or yarn gauge is different, knit a swatch and work your individual calculations (page 26) to determine the amount of yarn you'll need.

Note: All A and E sections can be worked with the yarn from the skein.

Yarn supplies of less than 2 yd (1.83 m) can be worked as single strands.

Yardages Needed for Back

Color Block	Number Needed	S+R	Yards (Meters)
A-1	2	255	6¼ (5.71)
D-1	6	84	2¼ (2.06)
B-1	32	42	1¼ (1.14)
C-1	8	147	3¾ (3.43)
E-1	4	357	8¾ (8.00)
D-2	9	147	3¾ (3.43)
A-2	3	357	8¾ (8.00)

Yardages Needed for Each Pocket

Color Block	Number Needed	S+R	Yards (Meters)
A-8	2	231	5¾ (5.26)
D-1	2	184	4½ (4.11)
B-3	4	21	¾ (0.68)
C-1	2	147	3¾ (3.43)
B-1	4	42	1¼ (1.14)
E-6	1	231	5¾ (5.26)

Yardages Needed for Each Front

Color Block	Number Needed	S+R	Yards (Meters)
A-3	1	120	3 (2.74)
D-3	1	60	1¾ (1.60)
B-1	27	42	1¼ (1.14)
C-1	3	147	3¾ (3.43)
D-4	1	48	1½ (1.37)
E-2	3	168	4¼ (3.89)
D-5	3	105	2¾ (2.51)
D-6	3	84	2¼ (2.06)
A-4	3	168	4¼ (3.89)
C-2	1	107	2¾ (2.51)
E-3	1	115	3 (2.74)
D-7	1	48	1½ (1.37)
A-5	1	45	1¼ (1.14)

Yardages Needed for Each Sleeve

Color Block	Number Needed	S+R	Yards (Meters)
A-6	1	270	6¾ (6.17)
D-4	1	48	1½ (1.37)
B-2	12	419	10¼ (9.37)
C-1	2	147	3¾ (3.43)
D-1	1	84	2¼ (2.06)
D-8	1	96	2½ (2.29)
E-4	1	378	9¼ (8.46)
D-9	1	93	2½ (2.29)
D-2	1	147	3¾ (3.43)
D-10	1	112	3 (2.74)
A-7	1	378	9¼ (8.46)
C-3	2	98	2½ (2.29)
E-5	1	422	10¼ (9.37)

BACK

Prepare yarn supplies as described on page 125.

With A and larger needles, CO 122 sts.

Work in k1, p1 rib for 2 rows.

Work Rows 1–4 of Anna Zilboorg Border patt (see Special Stitches) 8 times— 32 patt rows total.

Dec row: (RS) K1, k2tog, *k5, k2tog; rep from * to end—104 sts rem.

Next row: (WS) Purl—piece measures 5½" (14 cm) from CO.

Begin intarsia as foll:

Set-up row: (RS) K27 with A, k50 with B, k27 with A.

Next row: (WS) Purl, maintaining colors as established and linking to join colors.

Work intarsia in St st as established until piece measures 22" (56 cm) from CO, ending with a WS row.

Next row: (RS) Cut A. K27 with B, work Back chart sts 1–22 twice, then sts 23–28 once, k27 with B.

Cont in St st and intarsia, work Rows 1–33 of Back chart, then rep Rows 6–33 two more times, then work Rows 34–59

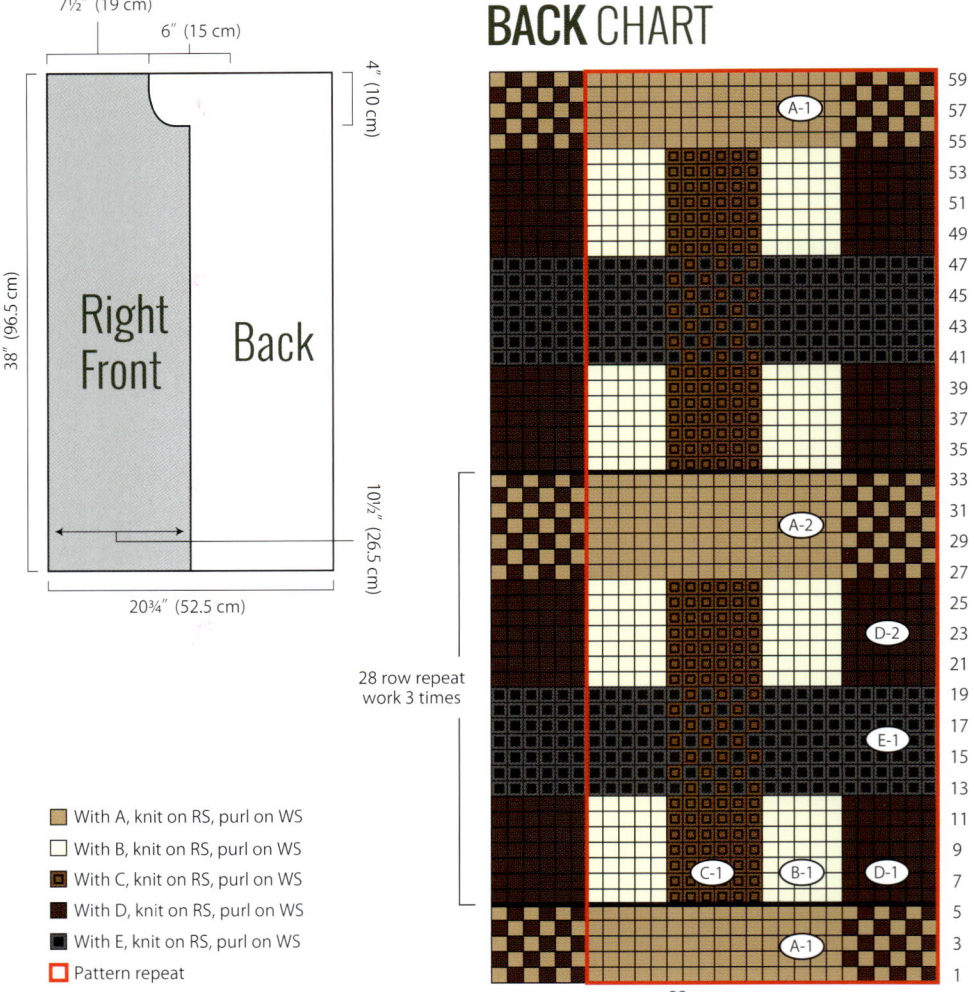

once—piece measures 38" (96.5 cm) from CO.

BO all sts purlwise on WS with A-1.

RIGHT FRONT

With A and larger needles, CO 62 sts.

Work in k1, p1 rib for 2 rows.

Work Rows 1–4 of Anna Zilboorg Border patt 8 times.

Dec row: (RS) K1, k2tog, [k4, k2tog, k5, k2tog] 4 times, k7—53 sts rem.

Next row: (WS) Purl—piece measures 5½" (14 cm) from CO.

Begin intarsia as foll:

Set-up row: (RS) K23 with A, k30 with B.

Next row: (WS) Purl, maintaining colors as established and linking to join colors.

Work intarsia in St st as established until piece measures 22" (56 cm) from CO, ending with a WS row.

Next row: (RS) Work Row 1 of Right Front chart (page 128) over 23 sts, then k30 with A.

Work Rows 1–59 of Right Front chart.

BO all sts purlwise on WS with A-5.

LEFT FRONT

With A and larger needles, CO 62 sts.

Work in k1, p1 rib for 2 rows.

Work Rows 1–4 of Anna Zilboorg Border patt 8 times.

Dec row: (RS) K1, k2tog, [k4, k2tog, k5, k2tog] 4 times, k7—53 sts rem.

Next row: (WS) Purl—piece measures 5½" (14 cm) from CO. Cut A.

Begin intarsia as foll:

Set-up row: (RS) K30 with B, k23 with A.

Next row: (WS) Purl, maintaining colors as established and linking to join colors.

Work intarsia in St st as established until piece measures 22" (56 cm) from CO, ending with a WS row.

Next row: (RS) K30 with A, work Left Front chart (page 128) over 23 sts.

Work Rows 1–59 of Left Front chart.

BO all sts purlwise on WS with A-5.

RIGHT FRONT CHART

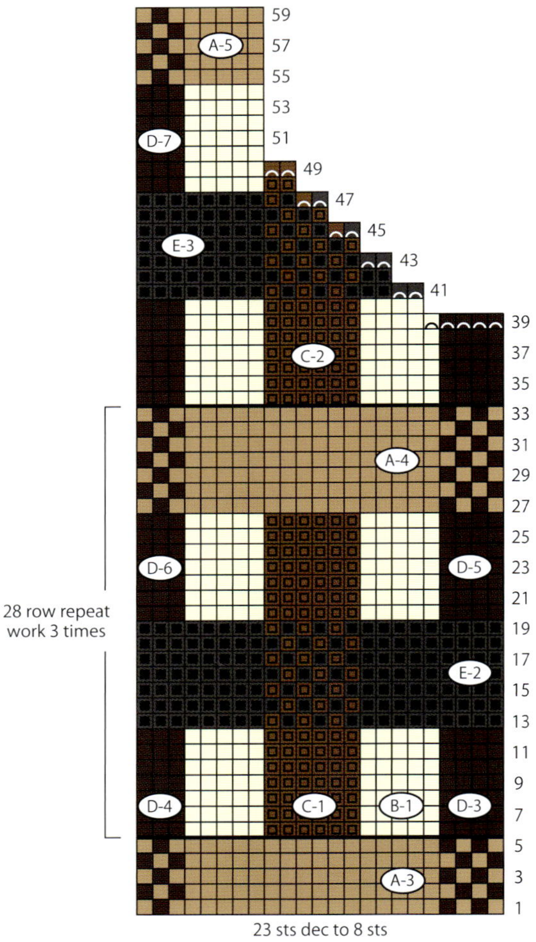
A-5
D-7
E-3
C-2
A-4
D-6
D-5
E-2
D-4
C-1
B-1
D-3
A-3
28 row repeat work 3 times
23 sts dec to 8 sts

LEFT FRONT CHART

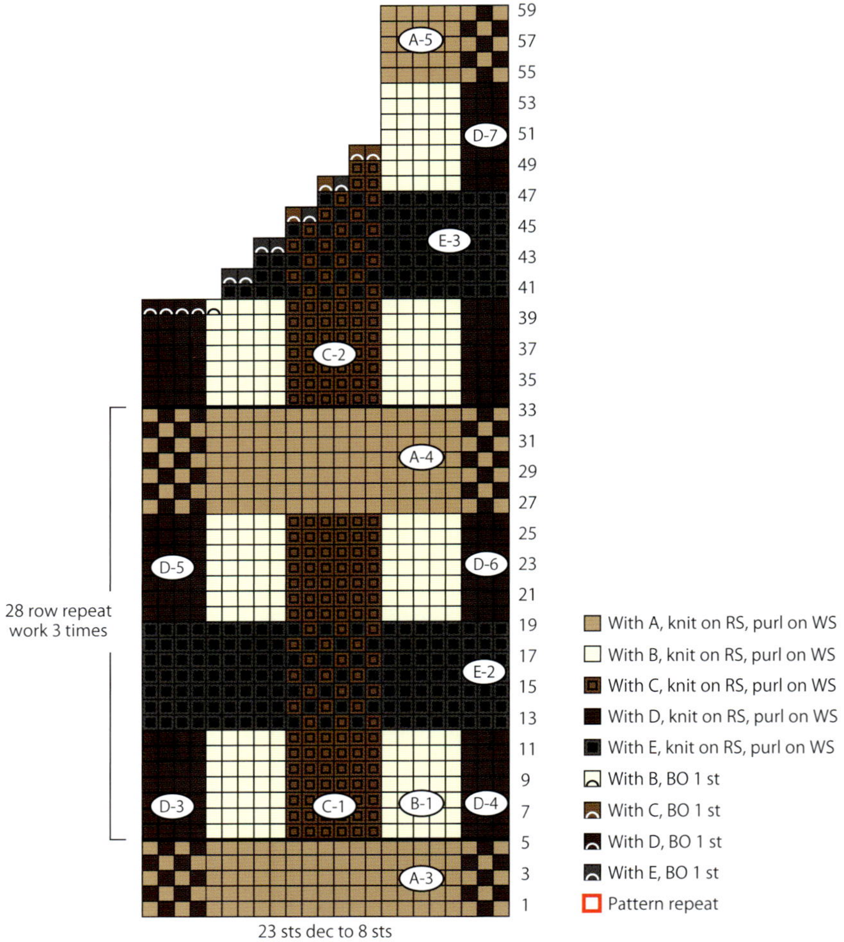
A-5
D-7
E-3
C-2
A-4
D-5
D-6
E-2
D-3
C-1
B-1
D-4
A-3
28 row repeat work 3 times
23 sts dec to 8 sts
With A, knit on RS, purl on WS
With B, knit on RS, purl on WS
With C, knit on RS, purl on WS
With D, knit on RS, purl on WS
With E, knit on RS, purl on WS
With B, BO 1 st
With C, BO 1 st
With D, BO 1 st
With E, BO 1 st
Pattern repeat

SLEEVES

Note: Sleeve shaping is introduced while charted pattern is in progress; read all the way through the following sections before proceeding.

With A and larger needles, CO 52 sts.

Work in k1, p1 rib for 1 row.

Inc row: (WS) K1, use the make-1 (M1) method (see Special Abbreviations) to inc 1 st, work in rib as established to end—53 sts.

Work Rows 1–4 of Anna Zilboorg Border patt once.

Beg with a WS row, work Rows 1–47 of Sleeve chart (page 130)—61 sts.

At the same time, beg on Row 34 of chart, inc 1 st each end of needle as foll:

Inc row: (RS) K2, M1, work to last 2 sts, M1, K2—2 sts increased.

Inc 1 st each end of needle in this manner every 4th row 23 more times.

Also at the same time, after Sleeve chart is completed, establish intarsia for upper sleeve as foll (cut all yarns from the Sleeve motif).

Right Sleeve Only

Set-up row: (RS) K27 with B, k6 with D, k28 with A.

Cont color blocks as established, working incs as established until there are 101 sts and piece measures 19" (48.5 cm) from CO, ending with a WS row.

BO all sts knitwise on RS with colors as established.

Left Sleeve Only

Set-up row: (RS) K27 with A, k6 with D, k28 with B.

Continue color blocks as established, working incs as established until there are 101 sts and piece measures 19" (48.5 cm) from CO, ending with a WS row.

BO all sts knitwise on RS with colors as established.

SLEEVE CHART

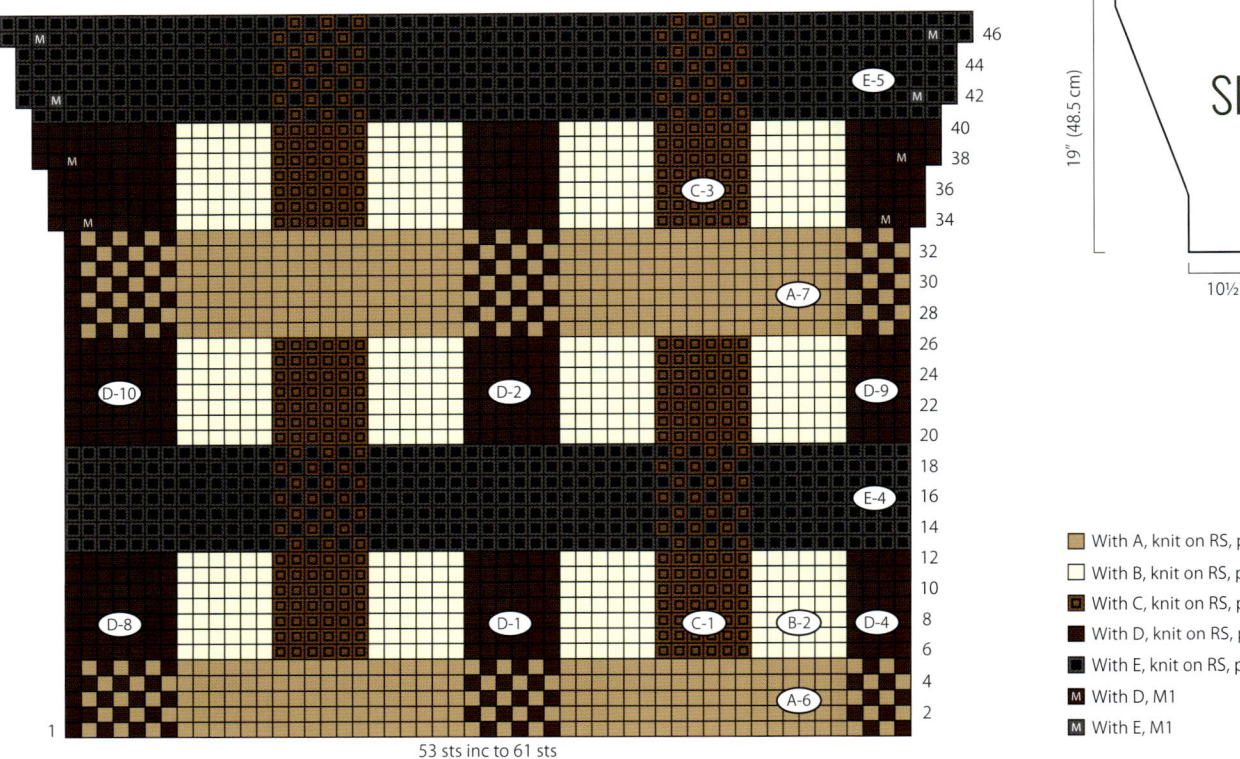

FINISHING

Pockets (make 2)

With A and larger needles, CO 32 sts.

Work Rows 1–36 of Pocket chart (page 131).

With B, work 5 rows in k1, p1 ribbing, ending with a RS row. With WS facing, BO all sts in patt.

Wet-block pieces by giving them a bath in warm water and rinse-free wool wash for at least 30 minutes. Roll in clean, dry towel to remove excess moisture, lay flat, and pin to schematic measurements. Allow to air-dry completely before removing pins.

Right Front (Buttonhole) Band

With C, smaller needles, and RS facing, pick up and knit 22 sts evenly spaced along the border section, then about 3 sts for every 4 rows along the St st section—180 sts total.

Knit 4 rows.

Buttonhole row: (WS) K10, [work one-row buttonhole (see Special Stitches), k12] 8 times, work one-row buttonhole, knit to end—9 buttonholes total.

Knit 5 rows.

BO all sts knitwise.

Left Front (Button) Band

With C, smaller needles, and RS facing, pick up and knit 3 sts for every 4 rows along the St st section, then 22 sts along the border section—180 sts total.

Knit 10 rows.

BO all sts knitwise.

Collar

With A threaded on a tapestry needle, sew shoulder seams.

With C, smaller needles, and RS facing, pick up and knit 6 sts along right front buttonhole band, 20 sts along the right front neck edge, 1 st at the shoulder seam, 28 sts along back BO edge, 1 st at shoulder seam, 20 sts along the left front neck edge, and 6 sts along the left front button band—82 sts total.

Work in k1, p1 rib until piece measures 1½" (3.8 cm) from pick-up row, ending with a RS row.

Note: There is no buttonhole in the collar. The 10th button on the button band is for decoration only.

With WS facing, BO all sts in rib patt.

With chenille needle, bury in all loose ends into links and seams.

Center the sleeve tops on the shoulder seams, sew them to body with A. Use the mattress st to sew side and sleeve seams.

Holding one strand of C tog with one strand of button thread, sew buttons onto button band, opposite buttonholes. Sew the 10th button on the collar for decorative purposes only.

Try on coat and position pockets for desired placement, then pin in place on right and left front. With A threaded on a tapestry needle, use a running stitch to sew pockets in place.

POCKET CHART

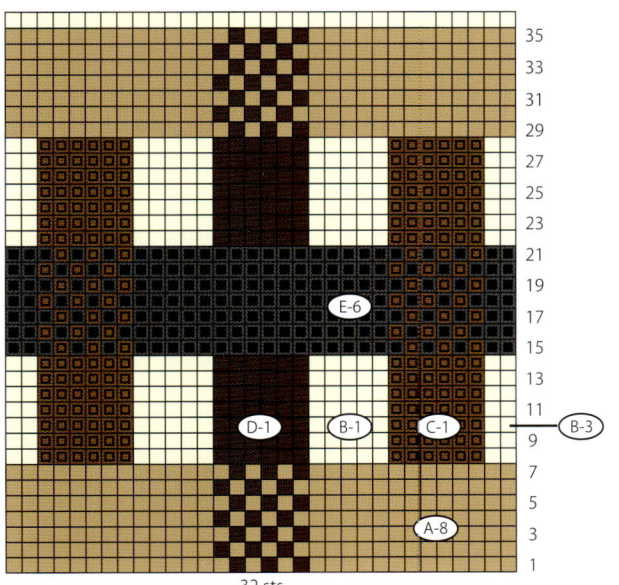

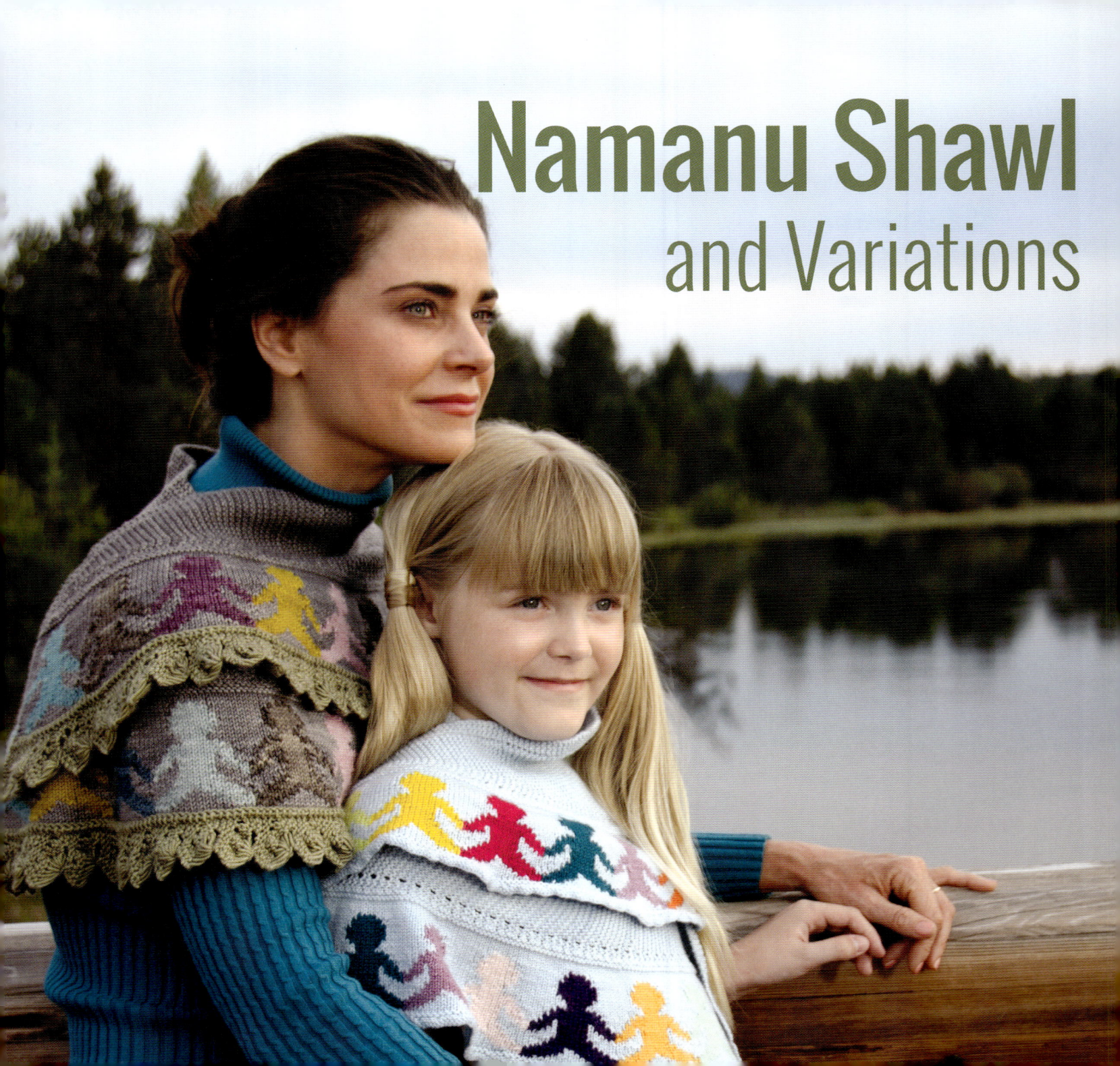
Namanu Shawl
and Variations

Namanu Shawl

Camp Namanu, nestled in the foothills of Mt Hood, has been a Northwest tradition for youth since 1924. A warm and inviting environment, Namanu inspires and encourages all who enter. Lifelong friendships are made, an appreciation of nature is developed, and new skills are learned.

The opportunity for creative design in the border of this basic garter-stitch crescent-shaped shawl captures the feeling of excitement that Namanu campers and staff experience every day. After I designed the original "paper doll" version, contributors devised their own motifs, which are included here. It just takes a little creativity to develop a unique motif, and the versatile design works with a wide variety of yarns, offering plenty of room for customization.

WHAT YOU'LL NEED TO KNOW

Linking yarn, page 31.

Stranded knitting (*Seneca Maples and Tawanka Variations* only).

E-wrap cast-on (*Tawanka and Sandy Hook Variations* only).

Pick up and knit.

Calculating yarn gauge, page 26.

Managing multiple yarn supplies, page 25.

Reading charts, page 39.

Burying ends, page 36.

Skill Level
Advanced beginner.

Finished Measurements
About 48" (122 cm) long and 12" (30.5 cm) tall.

Yarn
Simply Socks Yarn Company Simply Sock Yarn Solids, (80% wool, 20% nylon; 175 yd [160 m]/ 50 g): #632 Icicle (MC), 3 skeins; 125 yd (114 m) total of contrasting colors for 27 doll motifs at 4½ yd (4.1 m) per doll.

Needles
U.S. size 3 (3.25 mm): straight or 16" (40.5 cm) circular (circ) for body and 32" to 47" (81.5 to 119.5 cm) circ for border.

Adjust needle size if necessary to obtain correct gauge.

Notions
Chenille needle.

Stitch and Row Gauge
28 sts and 48 rows = 4" (10 cm) in garter st, after blocking; 28 sts and 36 rows = 4" (10 cm) in St st, after blocking.

Yarn Gauge
0.48.

Take time to check stitch, row, and yarn gauges.

*Namanu shawl is on the right and the Sandy Hook Variation is on the left.

NOTES

» To widen shawl, work more repeats of Rows 1–4 in the center section. Each 4-row repeat will add 1 eyelet and about 3 stitches to the border. For example, 3 repeats will add 3 eyelets, 6 garter ridges, and 10 stitches to the border stitch count.

» For a loose border edge, pick up stitches with a size 4 (3.5 mm) needle, then continue with a size 3 (3.25 mm) needle.

SPECIAL ABBREVIATIONS

w&t (wrap and turn): Bring yarn between needles to the front of the work. Slip 1 stitch purlwise from left to right needle tip. Bring yarn between needles to the back of the work, wrapping the slipped stitch. Turn work. Move the slipped stitch from the left needle tip to the right needle tip, and then bring the yarn between the needles to the back of work to complete wrapping the stitch.

Work to the end of the row as instructed. On the next row, knit the wrapped stitch, ignoring the wrap, which will be hidden in the garter stitch.

kfb: Knit into the front and back of the same stitch to increase 1 stitch.

SHAWL BODY

With MC, CO 1 st.

Initial Set-up

Row 1: Kfb (see Special Abbreviations)—2 sts.

Row 2: Kfb, k1—3 sts.

Row 3: Kfb, k2—4 sts.

Row 4: K3, yo, k1—5 sts.

Row 5: Kfb, k4—6 sts.

Row 6: K3, yo, k1, yo, k2—8 sts.

Short Increase Section

Row 7: Knit.

Row 8: K3, yo, k2tog, knit to end.

Row 9: Knit.

Row 10: K3, yo, k2tog, knit to last 2 sts, yo, k2—1 st increased; 1 eyelet at the tip and 1 eyelet on the inc edge.

Rep the last 4 rows 31 more times, then rep Rows 7 and 8 once more—40 sts; 33 eyelets along inc edge (plus 1 at the tip).

Short-Row Increase Section

Note: Row 1 begins at the same edge as the simple knit rows (all odd-numbered rows). Working in short rows, you'll turn the work in the middle of this row and therefore you won't get to the other edge until Row 3.

Row 1: K14, w&t (see Special Abbreviations).

Row 2: Knit to last 2 sts, yo, k2—1 st increased.

Row 3: Knit.

Row 4: K3, yo, k2tog, knit to end.

Row 5: K24, w&t.

Rows 6, 7, and 8: Rep Rows 2, 3, and 4.

Row 9: K32, w&t.

Rows 10, 11, and 12: Rep Rows 2, 3, and 4.

Row 13: Knit.

Row 14: K3, yo, k2tog, knit to last 2 sts, yo, k2—1 st increased.

Rows 15 and 16: Rep Rows 3 and 4.

Rep these 16 rows 3 more times—56 sts; 49 eyelets along inc edge (plus 1 eyelet at the tip).

Center Section

Row 1: Knit.

Row 2: K3, yo, k2tog, knit to last 4 sts, k2tog, yo, k2.

Row 3: Knit.

Row 4: K3, yo, k2tog, knit to end.

Rep these 4 rows 29 more times, then rep Rows 1 and 2 once more—80 eyelets along inc edge (plus 1 at the tip).

Note: To widen shawl, repeat Rows 1–4 to the desired length. Each rep will add 1 eyelet and about 3 stitches to the border stitch count. For example, adding 3 repeats will add 3 eyelets, 6 garter ridges, and 10 sts to the border stitch count.

Short-Row Decrease Section

Row 1: K32, w&t.

Rows 2 and 3: Knit.

Row 4: K3, yo, k2tog, knit to last 6 sts, [k2tog] 2 times, yo, k2—1 st decreased.

Row 5: K24, w&t.

Rows 6, 7, and 8: Rep Rows 2, 3, and 4.

Row 9: K14, w&t.

Rows 10, 11, and 12: Rep Rows 2, 3, and 4.

Row 13: Knit.

Row 14: K3, yo, k2tog, knit to end.

Rows 15 and 16: Rep Rows 3 and 4.

Rep these 16 rows 3 more times—40 sts rem; 96 eyelets along inc edge (plus 1 at the tip).

Short Decrease Section

Row 1: Knit.

Row 2: K3, yo, k2tog, knit to end.

Row 3: Knit.

Row 4: K3, yo, k2tog, knit to last 6 sts, [k2tog] 2 times, yo, k2—1 st decreased.

Rep these 4 rows 29 more times—10 sts rem; 126 eyelets along inc edge (plus 1 at the tip).

Final Decrease

Row 1: Knit.

Row 2: K3, yo, [k2tog] 2 times, knit to end—9 sts rem.

Row 3: Knit.

Row 4: K3, yo, [k2tog] 3 times—7 sts rem.

Row 5: K4, k2tog, k1—6 sts rem.

Row 6: K1, yo, [k2tog] 2 times, k1—5 sts rem.

Row 7: K1, [k2tog] 2 times—3 sts rem.

Row 8: K1, k2tog—2 sts rem.

Row 9: K2tog—1 st rem.

Transfer rem st to longer circ needle in preparation to pick up sts for the border.

BORDER

Pick-up row: Pick up and knit (by inserting needle from front to back into the garter bump at the edge of each garter ridge) 5 sts for every 3 garter ridges along curved edge as foll: *[pick up and knit 1 st, yo] 2 times, pick up and knit 1 st; rep from * to end of curved edge—about 425 sts.

Row 1: (WS) Knit, inc 15 sts evenly spaced—440 sts.

Note: If you don't have 440 sts, inc (kfb) or dec (k2tog) evenly spaced as needed over the next 3 rows to reach 440 sts.

Row 2, 3, and 4: Knit.

Row 5: K3, purl to last 3 sts, k3.

Row 6: Knit.

Row 7: K3, purl to last 3 sts, k3.

Prepare yarn supplies as described at right.

Work Rows 1–27 of Doll chart (page 137), keeping first and last 3 sts in garter st for border.

Cont with MC only.

Next row: (WS) K3, purl to last 3 sts, k3.

Knit 2 rows.

Edging

Row 1: (RS) Knit.

Row 2: K3, *k2, work (k1, yo, k1) into next st; rep from * to last 3 sts, k3—728 sts (the exact number is not crucial; this is simply to inc for a loose, lightly ruffled edge).

Row 3: Knit.

BO all sts purlwise.

YARN PREPARATION

The yarn amounts given here are based on the yarn and gauge specified and a yarn gauge of 0.48, and include 10" (25.5 cm) added for tails to be woven in. If your gauge or yarn gauge is different, knit a swatch and work your individual calculations (page 26) to determine the amount of yarn you'll need.

The yarn supplies needed for MC-1 and MC-3 are quite large; you could split these into two butterflies if desired. Yarn supplies of less than 2 yd (1.83 m) can be worked as single strands.

Yardages Needed for Doll Chart

Color Block	Number Needed	S+R	Yards (Meters)
MC-1	1	199	3 (2.70)
CC-1	27	132	2¼ (2.00)
MC-2	26	144	2 (1.80)
MC-3	1	199	3 (2.70)
MC-4	54	35	¾ (0.68)
CC-2	27	90	2 (1.80)
CC-3	27	16	½ (0.50)
MC-5	27	37	1 (0.91)
CC-4	27	26	¾ (0.68)

EDGING NOTE

The edging is knit from the top down, so the motif will also be knit from the top down. The dolls are knit from head to toe, so that they will be oriented correctly when worn. Remember this for all shawls knit with this pattern.

FINISHING

Use chenille needle to bury all loose ends into links.

Machine wash on hand-wash setting, then machine-dry until just damp.

Pin onto a flat surface with WS facing up and lightly press with a steam iron, if using wool. Allow to air-dry completely before removing pins. If yarn is not machine washable, hand-wash, roll into towels to remove excess moisture, and then proceed with pinning, ironing, and air-drying.

DOLL CHART

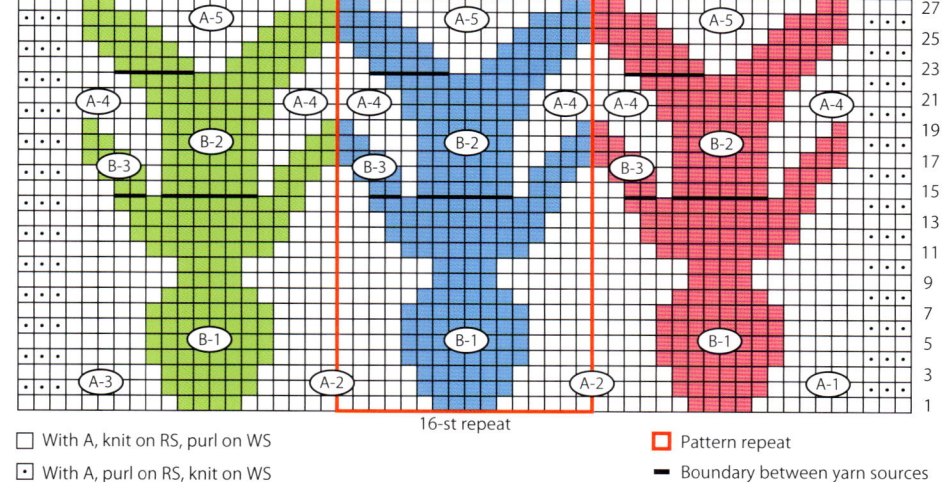

16-st repeat

☐ With A, knit on RS, purl on WS
⊡ With A, purl on RS, knit on WS
▇ ▇ ▇ With B, knit on RS, purl on WS

☐ Pattern repeat
— Boundary between yarn sources

Blue Moon Variation

The Namanu shawl was so much fun to knit that I wanted to knit a second version. I asked Tina Newton of Blue Moon Fiber Arts if she could suggest a colorway. Instead, she wondered if I'd accept a new idea for a motif. She thought the phases of the moon would be beautiful and helped me select the perfect yarn for the project. The result is this lovely shawl.

Skill Level
Advanced beginner.

Finished Measurements
About 48" (122 cm) long and 12" (30.5 cm) tall.

Yarn
Blue Moon Fiber Arts Lightweight (100% superwash merino; 405 yd [370 m]/ 5.5 oz): My Blue Heaven (MC), 2 skeins; Inspired by Light (CC), 1 skein.

Needles
U.S. Size 3 (3 mm): straight or 16" (40.5 cm) circular (circ) for body and 32" to 47" (81.5 to 120 cm) circ for border.

Adjust needle size if necessary to obtain correct gauge.

Notions
Chenille needle.

Stitch and Row Gauge
28 sts and 48 rows = 4" (10 cm) in garter st, after blocking; 28 sts and 36 rows = 4" (10 cm) in St st, after blocking.

Yarn Gauge
0.51.

Take time to check stitch, row, and yarn gauges.

SHAWL BODY

With MC, CO 1 st.

Work as for Namanu Shawl (page 132)—1 st rem.

BORDER

Pick-up row: Pick up and knit (by inserting needle from front to back into the garter bump at the edge of each garter ridge) 5 sts for every 3 garter ridges along curved edge as foll: *[pick up and knit 1 st, yo] 2 times, pick up and knit 1 st; rep from * to end of curved edge—425 sts.

Row 1: (WS) Using kfb, increase sts evenly to 440 sts. If you find that you don't have 440 sts, inc (kfb) or dec (k2tog) as needed over the next 3 rows, to reach 440 sts. Spread inc/dec evenly through work.

Row 2, 3, and 4: Knit.

Row 5: K3, purl to last 3 sts, k3.

Row 6: Knit.

Row 7: K3, purl to last 3 sts, k3.

Prepare yarn supplies as described at right.

Work Rows 1–24 of Blue Moon chart (page 141), keeping first 3 and last 3 sts in garter st for border.

Cont with MC only.

YARN PREPARATION

The yarn amounts given here are based on the yarn and gauge specified and yarn gauge of 0.51, and include 10" (25.4 cm) added for tails to be woven in. If your gauge or yarn gauge is different, knit a swatch and work your individual calculations (page 26) to determine the amount of yarn you'll need. Yarn supplies of less than 2 yd (1.83 m) can be worked as single strands.

Yardages Needed for Blue Moon Chart

Color Block	Number Needed	S+R	Yards (Meters)
MC-1	2	240	3¾ (3.43)
CC-1	8	194	3 (2.75)
MC-2	8	190	3 (2.75)
CC-2	8	168	2¾ (2.50)
MC-3	8	168	2¾ (2.50)
CC-3	8	131	2¼ (2.06)
MC-4	8	193	3 (2.75)
CC-4	8	50	1 (0.91)
MC-5	4	238	3¾ (3.42)
MC-6	6	224	3½ (3.20)
CC-5	3	304	4½ (4.11)

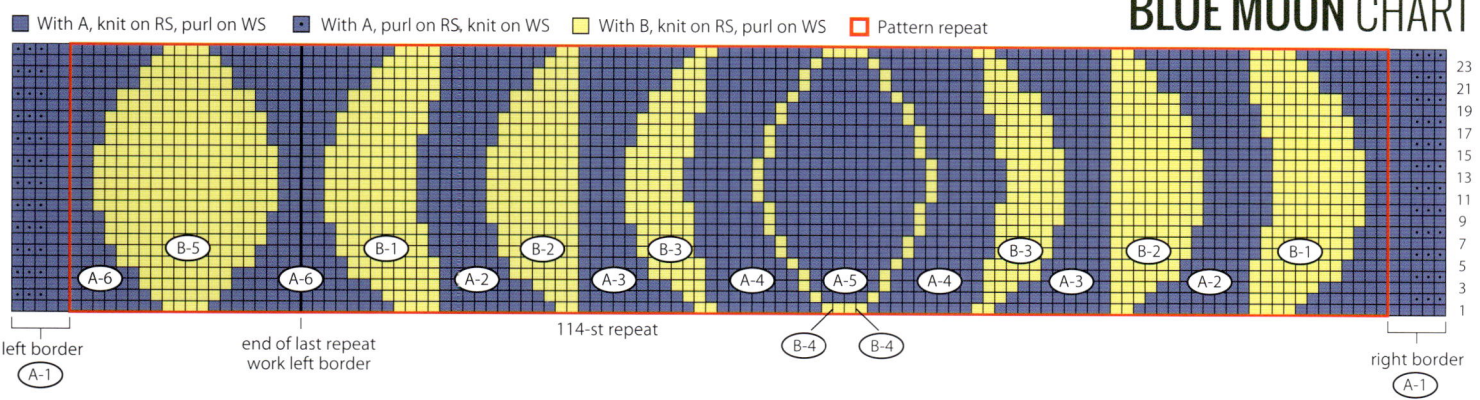

BLUE MOON CHART

Next row: (RS) Knit.

Next row: K3, purl to last 3 sts, k3.

Knit 2 rows.

Edging

Work as for Namanu Shawl (page 132).

FINISHING

Use chenille needle to bury all loose ends into links.

Machine wash on hand-wash setting, machine-dry until just damp.

Pin onto a flat surface with WS facing up and lightly press with a steam iron, if using wool. Allow to air-dry completely before removing pins. If yarn is not machine washable, hand-wash, roll into towels to remove excess moisture, and then proceed with pinning, ironing, and air-drying.

Sandy Hook Variation

The tragic events at Sandy Hook Elementary in December 2012 affected me deeply. Searching for comfort knitting, I decided to knit a Namanu Shawl in memory. I was startled to see that the pattern called for almost the same number of dolls (27) as there had been victims (26). Sarah Dimond of Plucky Knitter chose colors for the girls, boys, and teachers, plus an additional color for the 27th doll to represent "those who remember." Knitting the shawl helped me feel better, and I thought about every one of the people lost as I added the dolls to the border.

At the same time I was knitting Sandy Hook, Bobbie was working on the Tawanka Variation (page 150) and mentioned that she'd like a "pointy" edging for her shawl. I went to my trusty Barbara Walker library, and modified the Queen's edging. I test-knit the edging on Sandy Hook, using color for "those who remember," and loved the way it enveloped the dolls. The result is a garment that's very special to me and a testament to the way knitting can help us honor and love others.

Skill Level
Advanced beginner.

Finished Measurements
About 48" (122 cm) long and 12" (30.5 cm) tall.

Yarn
Plucky Knitter Primo Sport (75% merino, 20% cashmere, 5% nylon; 275 yd [251 m]/100 g): Flannel (gray; MC), 2 skeins; Abbey, 1 skein; up to 27 additional colors for dolls (8 used for sample), 4½ yd (4.1 m) each.

Needles
U.S. size 3 (3.25 mm): straight or 16" (40.5 cm) circular (circ) for body, 32" to 47" (81.5 to 120 cm) circ for border.

Adjust needle size if necessary to obtain correct gauge.

Notions
Chenille needle.

Stitch and Row Gauge
28 sts and 48 rows = 4" (10 cm) in garter st, after blocking; 32 sts and 40 rows = 4" (10 cm) in St st, after blocking.

Yarn Gauge
0.42.

Take time to check stitch, row, and yarn gauges.

Note
» When working the edging, odd-numbered rows are worked toward the shawl and the last stitch of the edging is worked together with the first stitch of the shawl, thereby decreasing (or "binding off") one shawl stitch.

YARN COLORS FOR DOLLS

Icey Audrey: girls Charlotte, Madeline, Grace, and Jessica.

Princess Phone: girls Olivia, Catherine, Emilie, and Avielle.

Bashful: girls Josephine, Ana, Caroline, and Alison.

Grady's Grouse: boys Jesse, Noah, and Daniel.

Doodlebug: boys Dylan, James, and Benjamin.

Skies of November: boys Chase and Jack.

Jazz Age: teachers Rachel, Anne Marie, and Victoria.

Edwardian: teachers Dawn, Lauren, and Mary.

Abbey: Those Who Remember.

YARN PREPARATION

The yarn amounts given here are based on the yarn and gauge specified and a yarn gauge of 0.42, and include 10" (25.5 cm) added for tails to be woven in. If your gauge or yarn gauge is different, knit a swatch and work your individual calculations (page 26) to determine the amount of yarn you'll need.

The yarn supplies needed for MC-1 and MC-3 are quite large; you could split these into two butterflies if desired. Yarn supplies of less than 2 yd (1.83 m) can be worked as single strands.

Yardages Needed for Sandy Hook Doll Chart

Color Block	Number Needed	S+R	Yards (Meters)
MC-1	1	199	3 (2.75)
CC-1	27	132	2¼ (2.00)
MC-2	26	144	2 (1.80)
MC-3	1	199	3 (2.70)
MC-4	54	35	¾ (0.68)
CC-2	27	90	2 (1.80)
CC-3	27	16	½ (0.46)
MC-5	27	37	1 (0.91)
CC-4	27	26	¾ (0.68)

SHAWL BODY

With MC, CO 1 st.

Work as for Namanu Shawl (page 132)—1 st rem.

Prepare yarn supplies as described above.

BORDER

Pick up sts, and work Rows 1–7 as for Blue Moon Shawl border (page 138).

Prepare yarn supplies as described above. Dolls are worked in the foll order: Charlotte, Daniel, Rachel, Olivia, Josephine, Dylan, Dawn, Madeline, Catherine, Chase, Jesse, Ana, Lauren, Those Who Remember, James, Anne Marie, Grace, Emilie, Jack, Mary, Noah, Caroline, Jessica, Avielle, Victoria, Benjamin, and Alison.

Work Rows 1–27 of Sandy Hook Doll chart (page 145), keeping first and last 3 sts in garter st for border, ending with a RS row.

Cont with MC only.

Next row: (WS) K3, purl to last 3 sts, k3.

Knit 2 rows even.

Cut yarn.

Edging

With edging yarn (the sample used Abbey), RS facing, and e-wrap (backward loop) method, CO 8 sts at the end of the needle—8 edging sts. See Edging chart on page 145.

Row 1: (RS) Sl 1 purlwise with yarn in back (purlwise wyb), k6, ssk, (last st of edging tog with next shawl st; see Notes)—8 edging sts.

Row 2: (WS) Sl 1 purlwise wyb, k7.

Row 3: Sl 1 purlwise wyb, k6, ssk,

Row 4: Sl 1 purlwise wyb, k7.

Row 5: Sl 1 purlwise wyb, k2, double yo, [k1, double yo] 3 times, k1, ssk—16 edging sts.

Row 6: Sl 1 purlwise wyb, [k2, p1] 4 times, k3.

Row 7: Sl 1 purlwise wyb, k14, ssk.

Row 8: Sl 1 purlwise wyb, k15.

Row 9: K12, wrapping yarn 3 times around the needle in each st, triple yo, k3, ssk—19 edging sts.

Row 10: Sl 1 purlwise wyb, k3, (k1, p1, k1 into triple yo), drop wraps in next 12 sts without working them to make 12 long loops, sl loops back onto needle and knit all tog as 1 st—8 edging sts rem.

Rep Rows 1–10 until all shawl sts have been BO, ending with Row 10 of edging.

With RS facing, BO all sts purlwise.

FINISHING

To make the dolls for Jesse, Noah, and Daniel stand out better against the MC background, use Doodlebug to duplicate stitch an outline around these figures.

Use chenille needle to bury all loose ends into links.

Machine wash on hand-wash setting, then machine-dry until just damp.

Pin onto a flat surface with WS facing up and lightly press with a steam iron, if using wool. Allow to air-dry completely before removing pins. If yarn is not machine washable, hand-wash, roll into towels to remove excess moisture, and then proceed with pinning, ironing, and air-drying.

EDGING CHART

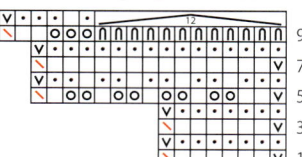

16-st repeat

- ☐ With A, knit on RS, purl on WS
- • With A, purl on RS, knit on WS
- ☐ ☐ With B, knit on RS, purl on WS
- ☐ Pattern repeat
- — Boundary between yarn sources
- ☐ knit on RS, purl on WS
- • purl on RS, knit on WS
- V Sl 1 purlwise wyb
- O yarn over
- ⧄ ssk last edging st tog with next shawl st
- ⩀ Wrapping yarn 3 times around needle, k1

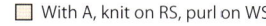

Sl next 12 sts to RHN, dropping extra wraps, sl the 12 long sts back to LHN and k them tog

SANDY HOOK DOLL CHART

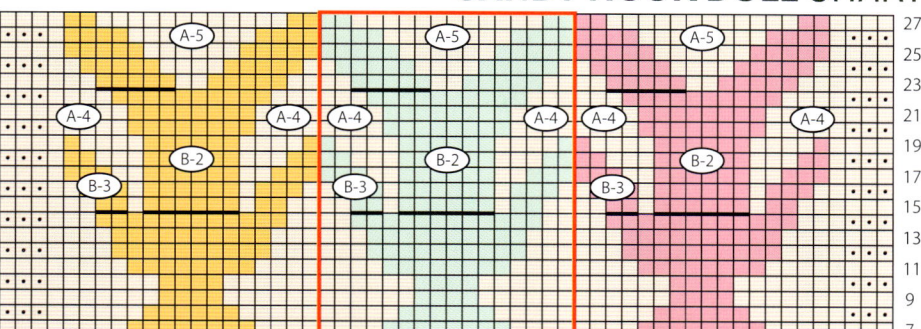

16-st repeat

Seneca Maples Variation

Designer: Valerie McPherson

Color motivates Valerie. Because of that, she says she is drawn to color before reason, which explains the variety of yarns used for the leaves in this shawl. Colors run from the first peek of chartreuse on bare, early spring branches to the autumn brown of fallen leaves turning to mulch. Using yarns that are the same weight as the shawl is certainly easier, but because the leaves simply had to be those colors, she used a variety of weights and brands (all in natural fibers). Hold the contrasting yarn more loosely and sometimes more tightly as necessary to achieve a consistent gauge.

Skill Level
Advanced beginner.

Finished Measurements
About 68" (172.5 cm) long and 16" (40.5 cm) tall.

Yarn
Berroco Ultra Alpaca Light (50% alpaca, 50% wool; 144 yd [131.5 m]/50 g): #4214 Steel Cut Oats (MC), 5 skeins.

Various yarns for leaves, including Kathryn Alexander's Hand-Dyed, Black Water Abbey, Rowan, Harrisville Shetland, Blue Sky Alpaca, Jamieson's Shetland: 119 yd (108.8 m) total; 8½ yd (7.77 m) per leaf.

Needles
U.S. size 5 (3.75 mm): straight or 16" (40.5 cm) circular for body and 40" (101.5 cm) circular for border.

U.S. size 4 (3.5 mm): 40" (101.5 cm) circular for picking up border sts and binding off (optional, for a tighter join and bound-off edge).

Adjust needle size if necessary to obtain correct gauge.

Notions
17 yarn bobbins; 18 markers (m); chenille needle.

Stitch and Row Gauge
22 sts and 32 rows = 4" (10 cm) in garter st, before blocking; 22 sts and 28 rows = 4" (10 cm) in St st, before blocking; 18 sts and 32 rows = 4" (10 cm) after blocking.

Yarn Gauge
0.86.

Note: Valerie knits loosely and achieved gauge with a size U.S. size 3 (3.25 mm) needle. Anne, a tighter knitter, achieved gauge with a size U.S. size 6 (4.00 mm) needle.

Take time to check stitch, row, and yarn gauges.

NOTES

» This version of the Namanu Shawl uses a combination of intarsia and stranded knitting. The leaves are worked with intarsia, but the main color is stranded across the work. If desired, the border can be worked entirely with intarsia, using separate yarn supplies for the MC between the leaves.

» The border rows are long. Instead of concentrating on completing rows, enjoy the color you're working with while anticipating the next color. If your color choices are beautiful, they will carry you through.

» Leaf stems may be added with duplicate stitch or worked with intarsia.

SHAWL BODY

With MC, CO 1 st.

Work as for Namanu Shawl (page 132), repeating 16 rows of increase shaping section 5 times total (60 sts total), 4 rows of center section 39 times total, and then rep Rows 1 and 2 of back section once more, (93 eyelets along outside edge plus 1 at tip), then work decrease shaping section 5 times total, and finish body as for Namanu Shawl—1 st rem; about 143 eyelets along inc edge (plus 1 at each tip).

TO STRAND OR NOT TO STRAND?

In traditional intarsia, stranding is "not done." Every section of color is worked with a separate source of yarn. For tiny sections of color, duplicate stitch may be added after knitting is complete.

In Annetarsia, stranding can be incorporated. I don't have any issues with combining the techniques. For example, in charts such as the bats for the Tawanka shawl (page 150), you have a choice whether to add strands of MC between the bats' feet or strand the MC behind them. Your choice will depend on how you want the private (wrong) side of the knitting to look, whether you have just the right lengths of leftover yarn, or what you feel like knitting at the time. If you want to strand some sections and work others in pure intarsia, it's completely up to you. As long as you maintain even tension, it won't make any difference on how the public (right) side of the knitting looks.

YARN PREPARATION

The yarn amounts given here are based on the yarn and gauge specified and a yarn gauge of 0.86, and include 10" (25.4 cm) added for tails to be woven in. If your gauge or yarn gauge is different, knit a swatch and work your individual calculations (page 26) to determine the amount of yarn you'll need.

For Stranded knitting: Each leaf is knitted with a single yarn supply that is stranded over MC at the edges as necessary for the leaf shaping.

For Intarsia knitting: Work Rows 1, 2, and 27–31 with the skein of MC, stranding it behind single stitches of other colors. In preparation for Row 3 of the chart, wind 19 yarn butterflies with MC in a size that's comfortable for you to work with. As yarn supplies of MC dwindle, join new yarn (page 33).

Yardages Needed for Seneca Maples Chart

Color Block	Number Needed	S+R	Yards (Meters)
Maple Leaf	17	338	8½ (7.77)

BORDER

For even distribution of pick-up sts, fold the work in half lengthwise. Then fold in half again two more times—8 sections. Place a removable marker at each fold, then pick up and knit alternately 66 sts and 67 sts in each section.

Pick-up row: With one size larger needle than used for body, pick up and knit (by inserting needle from front to back into the garter bump at the edge of each garter ridge) 5 sts for every 3 garter ridges along curved edge as foll: *[pick up and knit 1 st, yo] 2 times, pick up and knit 1 st; rep from * to end of curved edge—about 478 sts.

Row 1: (WS) With same size needle as used for body, knit all sts, while using the kfb method to inc 55 sts evenly spaced—about 533 sts.

Note: If you don't have 533 sts, inc (kfb) or dec (k2tog) evenly spaced as needed over the next 2 rows to reach 533 sts.

Rows 2 and 3: Knit.

Row 4: K3, purl to last 3 sts, k3.

Row 5: Knit.

Row 6: K3, [p31, pm] 16 times, p31, k3.

The maple leaves on this beautiful shawl remind me of my childhood…

Prepare yarn supplies as described on page 147.

Work Rows 1–35 of Seneca Maples chart, working the first 3 sts and last 3 sts in garter st.

Tip: When you get to the stems, lock in the contrasting color 1 or 2 stitches beyond the stem. This prevents distortion in the fabric.

Cont with MC only.

Next row: (WS) K3, purl to last 3 sts, k3.

Knit 2 rows.

Edging

Row 1: (RS) Knit.

Row 2: K3, *k5, [k3, yo] 2 times; rep from * to last 3 sts, k3—about 630 sts (the exact number is not crucial; this is simply to inc for a loose, lightly ruffled edge).

Row 3: Knit.

With WS facing and size 4 (3.5 mm) needle, BO all sts purlwise.

FINISHING

Use chenille needle to bury all loose ends into links.

Handwash gently in lukewarm water, squeeze out water, and then roll in towels to remove most moisture. Pin onto a flat surface with WS facing up and lightly press with a steam iron, if using wool. Allow to air-dry completely before removing pins.

SENECA MAPLES CHART

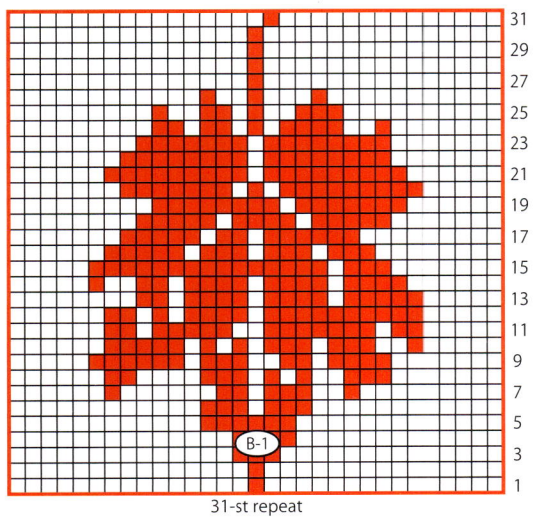

☐ With A, knit on RS, purl on WS
■ With B, knit on RS, purl on WS
▢ Pattern repeat

…maple syrup on fresh, hot, clover pancakes, mmmmm!

Tawanka Variation

Designer: Bobbie Hodges

Tawanka is a lodge at Camp Namanu used by counselors-in-training. It's the site of much learning, sharing, and hilarity. Bats have been known to shelter in the eaves, so this fun, beautiful shawl is named for the beloved site of many campfires and late-night talks.

Skill Level
Advanced beginner.

Finished Measurements
About 80" (203 cm) wide and 17" (43 cm) deep, after blocking.

Yarn
Dream in Color Starry (98% merino superwash, 2% lurex; 450 yd [411 m]/ 4 oz): Spanish Star (med. purple; A), Wisterious (purple/pink mix; B), Velvet Port (burgundy; C), and Purple Rain (dark purple; D), 1 skein each.

Note: Spanish Star (A) is no longer available; substitute Ruby River for a similar look.

Needles
U.S. size 4 (3.5 mm): straight for body and 40" (101.5 cm) circular (circ) for border.

Adjust needle size if necessary to obtain correct gauge.

Notions
Stitch markers (m); chenille needle.

Stitch and Row Gauge
28 sts and 48 rows = 4" (10 cm) in garter st; 28 sts and 36 rows = 4" (10 cm) in St st, before blocking.

Yarn Gauge
0.60.

Take time to check stitch, row, and yarn gauges.

NOTES

» To help keep track of where you are, place stitch markers between each chart area.

» Trust your instincts when it comes to the routes of your yarn sources. It's okay to change your mind about a certain pathway when you're knitting the motifs. Like life, there's more than one way to get where you're going.

SHAWL BODY

With A, and a needle to meet yarn gauge of 0.60, work as for Namanu Shawl (page 132), but rep the 4 rows of the center section a total of 37 times, then rep Rows 1 and 2 once more—87 eyelets along outside edge, plus 1 at tip.

Finish body as for Namanu Shawl— 1 st rem; about 138 eyelets along inc edge (plus 1 at each tip).

BORDER

Pick-up row: With A, pick up and knit (by inserting needle from front to back into the garter bump at the edge of each garter ridge) 5 sts for every 3 garter ridges along curved edge as foll: *[Pick up and knit 1 st, yo] 2 times, pick up and knit 1 st; rep from * to end of curved edge— about 469 sts.

I love bats! I used to hang around the old cathedral with a bunch of bat friends.

YARN PREPARATION

The yarn amounts given here are based on the yarn and gauge specified and a yarn gauge of 0.60, and include 10" (25.5 cm) added for tails to be woven in. If your gauge or yarn gauge is different, knit a swatch and work your individual calculations (page 26) to determine the amount of yarn you'll need.

Some of the yarn supplies are quite large; you could split these into two butterflies if desired. Yarn supplies of less than 2 yd (1.83 m) can be worked as single strands.

B is background color for chart. C is used for straight bat motifs (upside down and right side up), D is used for flying bats and center bat.

Yardages Needed for Border

Color Block	Number Needed	S+R	Yards (Meters)
B	10	810	14 (12.80)
B	2	329	6 (5.50)
B	2	396	7 (6.40)
B	1	163	3 (2.70)
C	5	14–42	1 (0.91)
C	4	61–92	2 (1.80)
C	1	253	5 (4.60)
C	3	371	7 (6.40)
C	3	467	9 (8.20)
D	24	18–25	1 (0.91)
D	6	92	2 (1.80)
D	6	385	7 (6.40)

Yardages for Specific Sections of Each Bat Chart

Note: Where yardage is not specified, use 1 yd or smaller strand.

Straight Bat (D):

Section	S+R	Yards (Meters)
D-3	385	7 (6.40)
D-1	25	
D-2	18	
D-4	92	2 (1.80)
D-5	24	

Right-Leaning Bat (C):

Section	S+R	Yards (Meters)
C-1	90	2 (1.80)
C-2	371	7 (6.40)

Left-Leaning Bat (C):

Section	S+R	Yards (Meters)
C-4	14	
C-3	467	9 (8.20)

Center Bat (C):

Section	S+R	Yards (Meters)
C-6	253	5 (4.60)
C-5	42	
C-7	61	
C-9	30	
C-8	2	

Note: If you don't have 469 sts, inc (kfb) or dec (k2tog) evenly spaced as needed over the next 3 rows to reach 469 sts.

Row 1: (RS) With A, knit.

Row 2: (WS) K3, purl to last 3 sts, k3.

Row 3: *K4 with A, k2 with B; rep from * to last st, k1 with A.

Row 4: K3 with B, p1 with B, *p2 with A, p4 with B; rep from * to last 7 sts, p4 with B, k2 with A, k1 with B.

Rows 5 and 6: With B, rep Rows 1 and 2.

Prepare yarn supplies as described on page 152.

Bat charts: Work Rows 1–30 of Bat charts (pages 154 and 155), maintaining garter st edging by knitting the first and last 3 sts of every row (not shown on chart) as foll.

Row 1 (RS): K3 with B, work Chart 1 over 41 sts, work Chart 2 over 28 sts, work Chart 3 over 41 sts, work Chart 4 over 28 sts, work Chart 1 over 41 sts, work Chart 2 over 28 sts, work Chart 5 over 49 sts, work Chart 2 over 28 sts, work Chart 3 over 41 sts, work Chart 4 over 28 sts, work Chart 1 over 41 sts, work Chart 2 over 28 sts, work Chart 3 over 41 sts, k3 with B.

Row 2 : (WS) K3 with B, work charts as established to last 3 sts, k3 with B.

Continue working chart through Row 30.

Row 31: (RS) *K4 with B, k2 with A; rep from * to last st, k1 with B.

Row 32: (WS) K3 with A, p1 with B, *p2 with B, purl 4 with A; rep from * to last 7 sts, p4 with A, k2 with B, k1 with A.

Rows 33 and 34: Knit with A.

Row 35: With A, k3, *k2tog, yo; rep from * to last 3 sts, k3.

Rows 36–38: Knit with A.

Rows 39 and 40: Knit with D.

Rows 41 and 42: Knit with A.

Row 43: (RS) With C, use the e-wrap also called backward-loop) method to CO 10 sts.

Work Rows 1–10 of edging for Sandy Hook Shawl (pages 144–145).

FINISHING

Use chenille needle to bury all loose ends into links.

Hand wash in warm water, rinse, and roll into towels to remove excess moisture.

Pin onto a flat surface with WS facing up and lightly press with a steam iron, if using wool. Allow to air-dry completely before removing pins.

This beautiful bat shawl speaks to me, but the pillows are calling me—I need a nap!

ALTERNATIVE VARIATIONS

Variation 1: For this variation, I used one skein each of Dream in Color Starry in Ruby River (A), Wisterious (purple/pink mix; B), Velvet Port (burgundy; C), and Purple Rain (dark purple; D), yarn gauge was 0.49 on U.S. size 3 (3.25 mm) needles. The finished shawl measures 74" (188 cm) wide and 15½" (39.5 cm) tall.

Variations knitted by Anne Berk.

Variation 2: For this variation, I used one skein each of Dream in Color Starry in Emerald Darkness (Green; A), Blue Lagoon (blue/green; B), Peacock Shadow (Dark blue; C), and Cocoa Kiss (Dark Gray; D), yarn gauge was 0.54 on U.S. size 5 (3.75 mm) needles. Color A was sufficient for body, but not enough yarn was available for use in the edging, so color D was substituted. The finished shawl measures 83" (211 cm) wide and 17" (43 cm) tall.

RIGHT-LEANING BAT CHART (Chart 1)

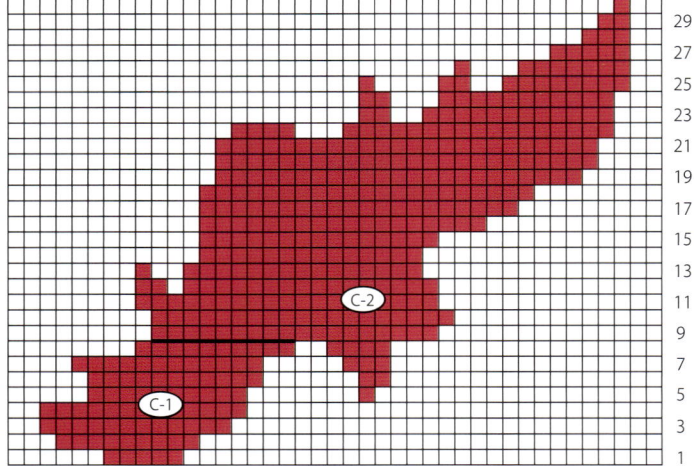

31-st repeat

STRAIGHT BAT CHART (Chart 2)

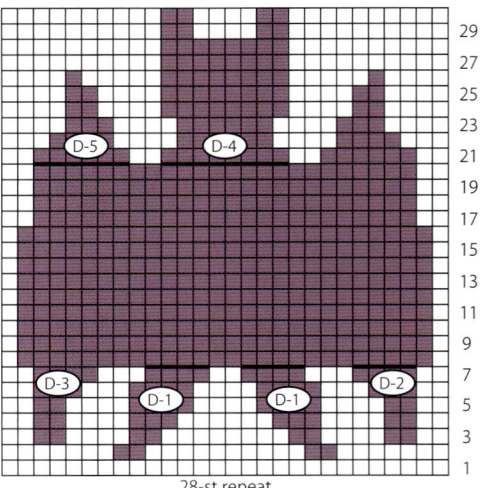

28-st repeat

LEFT-LEANING BAT CHART (Chart 3)

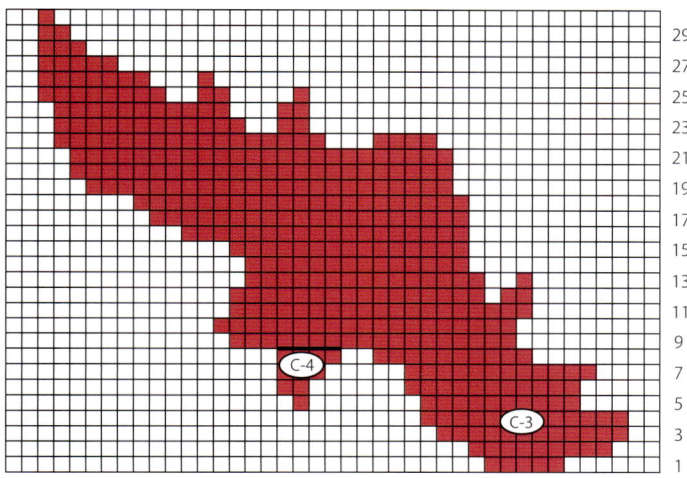

31-st repeat

- ☐ With B, knit on RS, purl on WS
- ■ With C, knit on RS, purl on WS
- ■ With D, knit on RS, purl on WS
- — Boundary between yarn sources

STRAIGHT BAT (UPSIDE-DOWN) CHART (Chart 4)

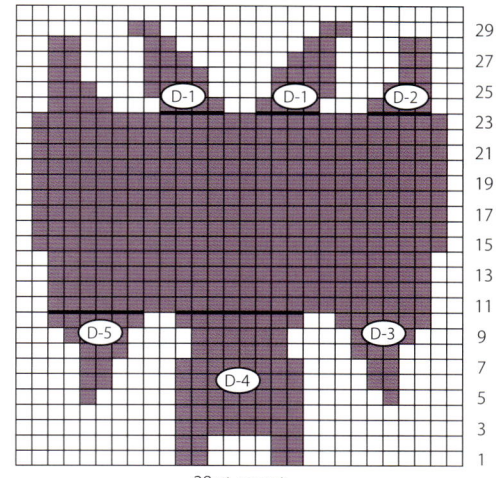

28-st repeat

CENTER BAT CHART (Chart 5)

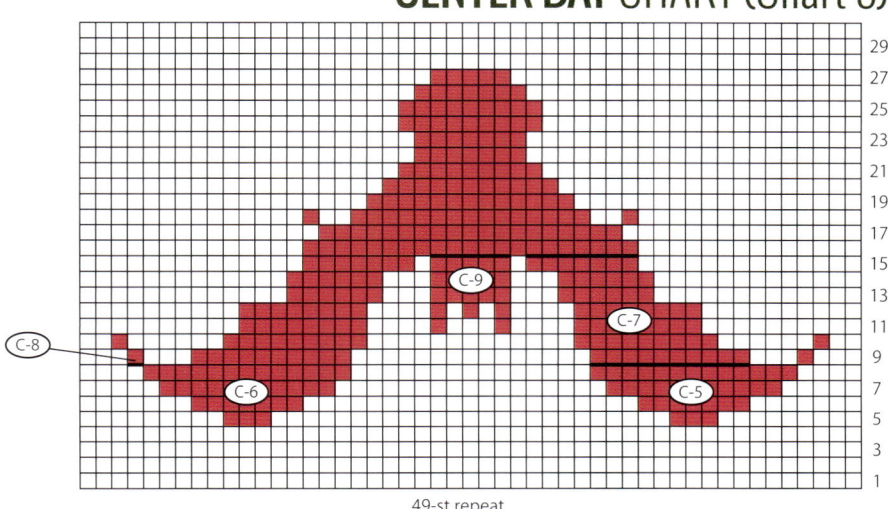

49-st repeat

155

Designing a Shawl
by Bobbie Hodges

It all started with a typing error. When one yarn was being discussed on Ravelry, I meant to say that I was knitting a hat with it. I typed "bat" instead of "hat." A couple of pages of hilarious posts ensued, including the posting of bat patterns and questions as to why I would knit a bat. I then thought it would be fun to knit Anne's Paper Doll Shawl with a bat motif. Because I'm much more comfortable knitting textured stitches than colorwork and had done only a smattering of intarsia, I knew this would be a challenge. Anne loved the idea and our journey was underway.

I emailed Anne a few images with an assortment of bat motifs. In no time at all, she emailed me a couple of color-coded charts based on my images…it was magic! She also calculated the S+R numbers, so that I could swatch.

What? I have to swatch? And calculate yarn gauge and measure yarn supplies? Could I really do all this? But now I was intrigued…I was an active member of a design team, with a real-live expert to help me translate my vision into a workable design!

My swatch was of the upside-down bat motif, which was a bit wonky, just as Anne had warned me it might be. This technique definitely takes a bit of practice. I made adjustments and knitted it again, this time with more success. Next, I knitted a swatch of the right-leaning bat motif. I was catching on faster than I had expected.

I planned to alternate upside down and right-side up "at rest" bats, as well as left- and right- leaning "flying bats." I gave Anne a vague description of "something pointy" for the edging. She not only found something quickly in one of Barbara Walker's stitch dictionaries, she modified it, tried it out, and then sent me photos and the pattern.

Determining the yarn amounts was by far the most challenging part of the project. Math doesn't especially scare me, but combined with a knitting technique that I'm not very familiar with, well, that's a different story. The body of the shawl was easy to knit. The only challenge was calculating how many rows of the body were needed to accommodate the pattern repeat in the edging. In order to do this, I had to finalize my plans for the intarsia border.

Faced with thirteen charts that had to go together, I began to doubt my ability to figure it all out. I'm a perfectionist so, of course, I wanted to get it "right." During the "virtual knitting," stress and doubt caused my brain to freeze. I decided to step away from the project for a few days, and work on another project. Anne supported me in this decision, while repeating over and over that I should relax with the process and not stress about doing it one "right" way.

When I got back to Tawanka, I reviewed my virtual knitting of the background. Not only would I follow the charts from right to left on right-side rows and from left to right on wrong-side rows, but I'd have to work the charts upside down. But, everything came together and I found knitting the border to be much easier than planning it. I simply had to follow the instructions and the route I'd planned. A few times I accidentally took a slightly different path. But, hey, it worked.

Designing this shawl was a rewarding, exciting, and valuable learning process. I now have the confidence as well as a good foundation to take on new knitting designs. What's next…cats?

The shawl is beautiful, but I think I see a future relative in the rocks.

Camp Namanu counselors modeling the Namanu Shawl and Variations.

Columbia Suit

The Columbia River borders the state of Oregon and has served as a source of food, transportation, energy, and inspiration for generations.

Inspired by Sally Melville's "Not Mrs. Doubtfire's suit" from *The Knitting Experience: Color*, this suit is a good first intarsia garment, as the intarsia involved is easily worked. For the skirt, the "in the round" (ITR) method is only needed for the rows that contain diamond motifs; where there are only two colors, the yarns are stranded. The top features intarsia bands on just the sleeves that are positioned where they don't interfere with the sleeve shaping.

Both fast and easy to knit, this versatile project is a good mix of creativity and rhythmic knitting.

WHAT YOU'LL NEED TO KNOW

Annetarsia "in the round" (ITR), page 12.

Stranded knitting.

Calculating yarn gauge, page 26.

Managing multiple yarn supplies, page 25.

Reading charts, page 39.

Burying ends, page 36.

Skill Level
Intermediate.

Finished Measurements
Skirt: About 31¼" (79.5 cm) waist circumference, relaxed, and 20½" (52 cm) long. Elastic waist can be adjusted to fit up to 46" (117 cm).

Top: About 36 (40, 44, 48, 52)" (91.5 [101.5, 112, 122, 132] cm) bust circumference and 23 (23, 23, 24, 24)" (58.5 [58.5, 58.5, 61, 61] cm) long.

Top shown measures 40" (101.5 cm) and includes about 2" (5 cm) positive ease.

Yarn
Toots LeBlanc Jacob/Alpaca Sport Weight (50% alpaca, 50% wool; 250 yd [229 m]/5oz):

Skirt: Dark Gray (A), 4 skeins; Light Gray (B) and White (C), 1 skein each.

Top: Dark Gray (A), 4 (4, 4, 5, 5) skeins; Light Gray (B) and White (C), 1 skein each.

Needles
U.S. sizes 4 and 5 (3.5 and 3.75 mm).

Adjust needle size if necessary to obtain correct gauge.

Notions
Markers (m); stitch holders for top; 1" (2.5 cm) elastic in length to fit waist plus 1" (2.5 cm) for skirt; tapestry needle; sharp-point sewing needle and matching thread for skirt; chenille needle.

Stitch and Row Gauge
Skirt: 24 sts and 34 rnds = 4" (10 cm) in St st on smaller needles, after blocking.

Top: 22 sts and 32 rnds = 4" (10 cm) in St st on larger needles, after blocking.

Yarn Gauge
0.61.

Take time to check stitch, row, and yarn gauges.

SKIRT

Prepare yarn supplies as described on page 161.

With A and smaller needles, CO 188 sts. Do not join for working in rnds.

Waistband

Work St st back and forth in rows until piece measures 1" (2.5 cm) from CO.

Place marker (pm) and join for working in rnds, being careful not to twist sts.

Set-up rnd: *K47, pm; rep from * to end—4 sections of 47 sts each.

Knit 1 rnd, then purl 1 rnd for turning ridge, then knit 3 rnds.

Body

Inc Rnd 1: *K2, M1 (see Special Abbreviations), knit to 2 sts before m, M1, k2, sl m; rep from * to end—8 sts increased.

Inc 8 sts in this manner every 4th rnd 4 more times, then every 8th rnd 3 times—252 sts total; 63 sts each section.

Inc Rnd 2: *K2, M1, k29, M1, knit to 2 sts before m, M1, k2, sl m; rep from * to end—264 sts total; 66 sts each section.

Knit 3 rnds even.

Inc Rnd 3: *K2, M1, k20, M1, k20, M1, knit to 2 sts before m, M1, k2; rep from * to end—280 sts total; 70 sts each section.

Knit 3 rnds even.

Inc Rnd 4: *K2, M1, k33, M1, knit to 2 sts before m, M1, k2; rep from * to end—292 sts total; 73 sts each section.

Knit 3 rnds even.

Inc Rnd 5: *K2, M1, k23, M1, k23, M1, knit to 2 sts before m, M1, k2; rep from * to end—308 sts total; 77 sts each section.

Knit 3 rnds even.

Work even in St st until piece measures 8" (20.5 cm) from turning ridge.

Border

[Purl 1 rnd, then knit 1 rnd] 2 times—2 garter ridges.

Change to larger needles.

Working Annetarsia ITR, work Rows 1–99 of Columbia Skirt chart (page 163) on each section—340 sts total; 85 sts each section.

NOTES

» Where a single contrast color travels diagonally on the main color of the Columbia Skirt chart, work by loosely stranding the unused color. Rows that can be worked in Annetarsia ITR are numbered on the left side of the chart.

» The top is worked in the round to the armholes, at which point it is worked back and forth in rows.

» The stretchiness of the fiber makes this a "one size fits most" pattern, as you can adjust the elastic of the waistband to accommodate most figures. If you choose to add or subtract stitches at the waist, be sure to increase gradually to the correct number of stitches needed for the motif.

SPECIAL ABBREVIATIONS

M1 (make 1): Use the left needle tip to lift the horizontal strand between the two needles from front to back, placing it on the left needle. Knit this lifted strand through the back loop to increase 1 stitch.

k1tbl: Knit 1 stitch through the back loop to twist it.

p1tbl: Purl 1 stitch through the back loop to twist it.

YARN PREPARATION

Prepare butterflies or loose strands for each block as follows. The yarn amounts given here are based on the yarn and gauge specified and a yarn gauge of 0.61, and include 10" (25.5 cm) added for tails to be woven in. If your gauge or yarn gauge is different, knit a swatch and work your individual calculations (page 26) to determine the amount of yarn you'll need.

Yarn supplies of less than 2 yd (1.83 m) can be worked as single strands.

Yardages Needed for Top

Color Block	Number Needed	S+R	Yards (Meters)
B-1	16 (16, 16, 18, 18)	30	¾ (0.69)
A-1	14 (14, 14, 16, 16)	12	½ (0.46)
C-1	14 (14, 14, 16, 16)	90	1¾ (1.60)
A-2	14 (14, 14, 16, 16)	247	4½ (4.11)
A-3	28 (28, 28, 32, 32)	33	¾ (0.69)
C-2	28 (28, 28, 32, 32)	12	½ (0.46)
B-2	7 (7, 7, 8, 8)	50	1¼ (1.14)

Yardages Needed for Skirt

Color Block	Number Needed	S+R	Yards (Meters)
A-1	4	27	¾ (0.69)
B-1	40	30	¾ (0.69)
A-2	36	12	½ (0.46)
A-3	36	24	¾ (0.69)
C-1	18	90	1¾ (1.60)
A-4	4	18	½ (0.46)
C-2	2	75	1½ (1.37)
C-3	2	12	½ (0.46)
A-5	4	54	1¼ (1.14)
A-6	4	36	1 (0.91)
B-2	16	50	1¼ (1.14)
B-3	4	7	½ (0.46)
A-7	2	27	¾ (0.69)
C-4	20	196	3½ (3.20)
B-4	30	46	1 (0.91)
B-5	4	41	1 (0.91)

Knit 2 rnds, removing all but the beg-of-rnd m.

[Purl 1 rnd, then knit 1 rnd] 3 times— 3 garter ridges.

BO all sts purlwise.

Finishing

Cut elastic to waist length adding 1" (2.5 cm) for seaming. With sharp-point sewing needle or chenille needle and matching thread, sew ends of elastic together. Fold waistband around elastic to the WS along turning ridge. With A threaded on a tapestry needle, sew CO edge to base of waistband to enclose elastic.

Use chenille needle to bury all loose ends into links.

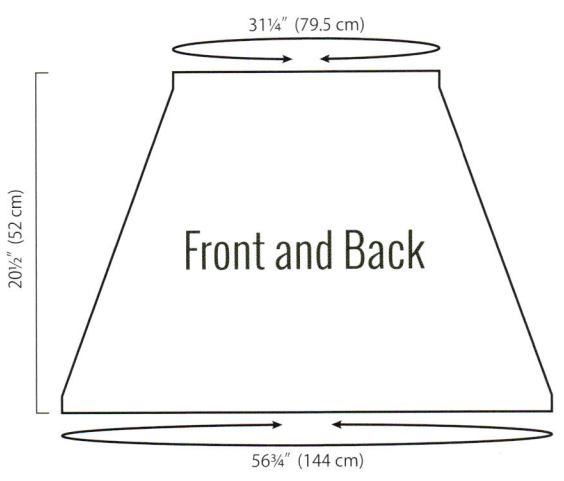

31¼" (79.5 cm)

20½" (52 cm)

Front and Back

56¾" (144 cm)

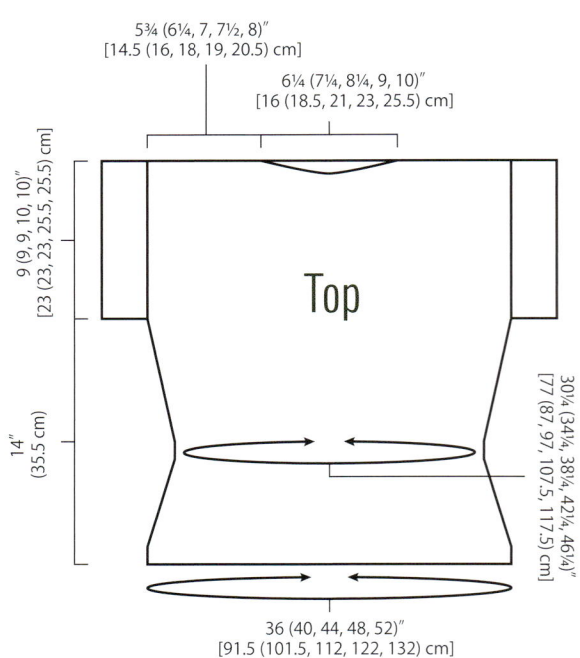

5¾ (6¼, 7, 7½, 8)"
[14.5 (16, 18, 19, 20.5) cm]

6¼ (7¼, 8¼, 9, 10)"
[16 (18.5, 21, 23, 25.5) cm]

9 (9, 9, 10, 10)"
[23 (23, 23, 25.5, 25.5) cm]

Top

14"
(35.5 cm)

30¼ (34¼, 38¼, 42¼, 46¼)"
[77 (87, 97, 107.5, 117.5) cm]

36 (40, 44, 48, 52)"
[91.5 (101.5, 112, 122, 132) cm]

COLUMBIA SLEEVE CHART

COLUMBIA SKIRT CHART

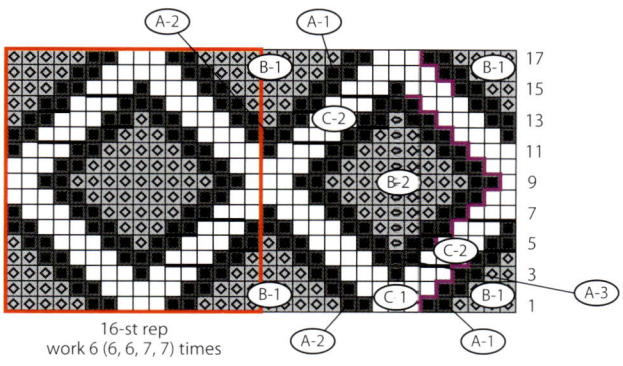

16-st rep
work 6 (6, 6, 7, 7) times

- ■ With A, knit on RS, purl on WS
- ◨ With B, knit on RS, purl on WS
- □ With C, knit on RS, purl on WS
- Ⓜ With A, M1
- Ⓜ With C, M1
- ▭ Pattern repeat
- Ⅰ Turning point
- ━ Boundary between yarn sources

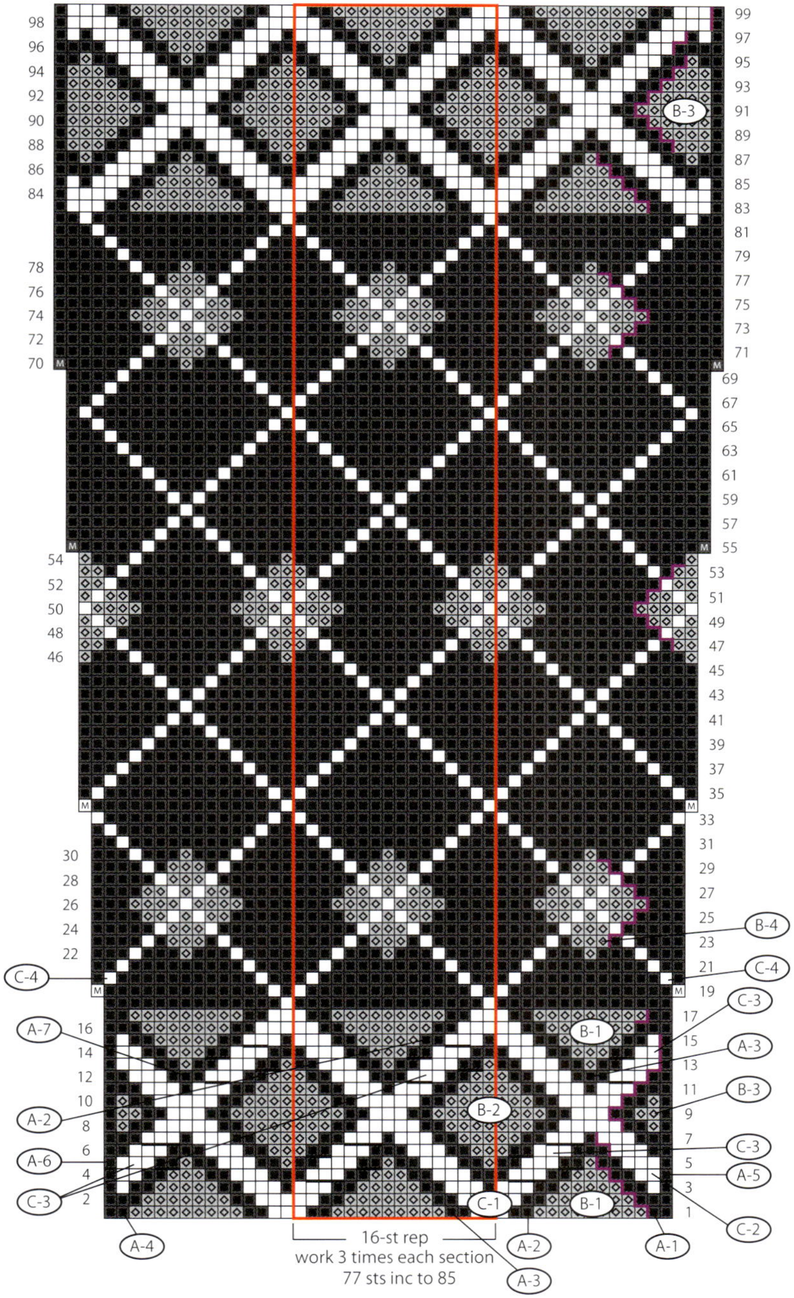

16-st rep
work 3 times each section
77 sts inc to 85

163

TOP

Prepare yarn supplies as described on page 161.

With A and smaller needles, CO 198 (220, 242, 264, 286) sts. Do not join for working in rnds.

Body

Knit 2 rows.

Change to larger needles.

Knit 1 row, then place marker (pm) and join for working in rnds, being careful not to twist sts.

Next rnd: K99 (110, 121, 132, 143), pm for side "seam," knit to end—99 (110, 121, 132, 143) sts each for front and back.

Knit 4 rnds.

Shape Waist

Note: Neck shaping is introduced while waist shaping is in progress; read to the end of this section before proceeding.

Dec rnd: K2, ssk, knit to 4 sts before side m, k2tog, k2, sl m, k2, ssk, knit to last 4 sts, k2tog, k2—4 sts decreased.

Knit 5 rnds even.

Rep the last 6 rnds 7 more times—166 (188, 210, 232, 254) total rem; 83 (94, 105, 116, 127) sts each for front and back.

Knit even until piece measures 7" (18 cm) from CO edge.

Inc rnd: K2, M1 (see Special Abbreviations), knit to 2 sts before side m, M1, k2, sl m, k2, M1, knit to last 2 sts, M1, k2—4 sts increased.

Knit 5 rnds even.

Rep the last 6 rnds 7 more times and at the same time, when front and back each have 95 (106, 117, 128, 139) sts and piece measures about 11½" (29 cm) from CO edge, shape neck as foll.

Shape Neck

Cont working side shaping as established, shape neck as foll:

Set up rnd: Mark neck sts on front as foll: k46 (51, 57, 62, 68), pm for neck, k3 (4, 3, 4, 3), pm for neck, knit to end.

Rnd 1: Knit to neck m, sl m, yo, k3 (4, 3, 4, 3), yo, sl m, knit to end—2 sts increased for neck.

Rnd 2: Knit to neck m, sl m, k1tbl (see Special Abbreviations), k3 (4, 3, 4, 3), k1tbl, sl m, knit to end.

Rnds 3 and 4: Knit.

Rep Rnds 1–4, working a yo inside each front neck marker every rep of Rnd 1 and working the yo through the back loop (tbl) every rep of Rnd 2.

When side incs are complete, continue neck incs as established until piece measures 14" (35.5 cm) from CO edge, ending with Rnd 2 of neck shaping.

Divide for Front and Back

Place 99 (110, 121, 132, 143) back sts on holder, removing side m.

Front

Work 109 (120, 131, 142, 153) front sts back and forth in rows as foll:

Row 1: Knit to m, sl m, yo, knit to m, yo, sl m, knit to end—2 sts increased for neck.

Row 2: Purl to m, sl m, p1tbl (see Special Abbreviations), purl to m, p1tbl, sl m, purl to end.

Row 3: Knit.

Row 4: Purl.

Rep Rows 1–4 until there are 47 (48, 47, 48, 47) sts between neck markers—143 (154, 165, 176, 187) sts total.

Work even in St st until armholes measure 9 (9, 9, 10, 10)" (23 [23, 23, 25.5, 25.5] cm), ending with a WS row.

BO 32 (35, 38, 41, 44) sts at beg of next 2 rows—79 (84, 89, 94, 99) sts rem.

Place rem sts onto holder.

Back

Return 99 (110, 121, 132, 143) held back sts onto larger needles.

Work even in St st until armholes measure 9 (9, 9, 10, 10)" (23 [23, 23, 25.5, 25.5] cm), ending with a WS row.

BO 32 (35, 38, 41, 44) sts at beg of next 2 rows—35 (40, 45, 50, 55) sts rem.

Place rem sts onto holder.

Sleeves

With A threaded on a tapestry needle, sew shoulder seams.

With A, smaller needles, RS facing, and beg at center of underarm, pick up and knit 112 (112, 112, 128, 128) sts evenly spaced around armhole. Pm and join for working in rnds.

Rnd 1: Purl.

Rnd 2: Knit.

Rep Rnds 1 and 2 once more.

Working Annetarsia ITR, work Rows 1–17 of Columbia Sleeve chart (page 163).

Cont with A as foll:

Rnd 1: Knit.

Rnd 2: Purl.

Rep these 2 rnds once, then rep Rnd 1 once again.

BO all sts purlwise.

Finishing

Place 114 (124, 134, 144, 154) held neck sts onto smaller needles. Join A at right shoulder seam and use the e-wrap (also called backward-loop) method to CO 2 sts with A.

Work I-cord BO as foll: *K1, k2tog, sl both sts to left needle tip; rep from * until all neck sts have been worked—2 I-cord sts rem.

Cut yarn, leaving a 10" (25.5 cm) tail and pull tail through rem sts to fasten off.

Thread tail on a tapestry needle and sew ends of neckband tog.

Use chenille needle to bury all loose ends into links.

Soak piece in tepid water with rinse-free wool soap for 30 min. Blot carefully with towel, lay flat, pin to measurements, and allow to air-dry completely before removing pins.

Sunriver Scarf

Sunriver, Oregon, a community in the high desert, is one of my favorite places on earth, as well as the location for the photography in this book. Like Sunriver, this scarf has universal appeal and can be worn by any age or gender. If you love the Dizzy Scarf (page 86), try this as your next step for working Annetarsia garter stitch. The chart was inspired by the tessellated #100 Puzzle chart in *Kaffe Fassett's Pattern Library*. I adjusted the section sizes in Kaffe's chart so that purl bumps would show up on both sides of the fabric to create a reversible appearance.

This is a wonderful stash-buster project. For impact, mix similar colors with contrasting ones to maintain a bold color statement.

WHAT YOU'LL NEED TO KNOW

Annetarsia garter stitch, page 54.

Calculating yarn gauge, page 26.

Managing multiple yarn supplies, page 25.

Reading charts, page 39.

Burying ends, page 36.

Skill Level
Intermediate.

Finished Measurements
About 8¼" (21 cm) wide and 70" (178 cm) long.

Yarn
Frog Tree Yarns Ewetopia, (50% superwash merino, 50% merino; 109 yd [100 m]/50 g): #1245 Kermit Green (A), #1226 Fuschia (B), #1246 Yellow Green (C), #1209 Medium Gray (D), #1205 Light Gray (E), and #1212 Dark Gray (F), 1 skein each.

Needles
U.S. size 6 (4 mm): straight.

Adjust needle size if necessary to obtain correct gauge.

Notions
Chenille needle.

Stitch and Row Gauge
20 sts and 28 rows = 4" (10 cm) in garter st Annetarsia patt, after blocking.

Yarn Gauge
0.60.

Take time to check stitch, row, and yarn gauges.

Notes
» The chart is worked in Annetarsia garter stitch—knit all stitches on all rows.

» Knit until you run out of yarn, or desired length. Sample ran out of dark gray first, after six full motifs had been worked. It was bound off on Row 65 of the seventh chart repeat.

YARN PREPARATION

The yarn amounts given here are based on the yarn and gauge specified and a yarn gauge of 0.60, and include 10" (25.5 cm) added for tails to be woven in. If your gauge or yarn gauge is different, knit a swatch and work your individual calculations (page 26) to determine the amount of yarn you'll need.

Yardage requirements vary for each section. Measure yarn supplies for Rows 1–35 separately from Rows 36–70 and store the supplies for each batch in a separate zip-top bag (or measure lengths as you go).

One length of yarn is needed for each section of each repeat of the pattern. Yarn supplies of less than 2 yd (1.83 m) can be worked as single strands.

Yardages Needed for Sunriver Scarf

Color Block	S+R	Yards (Meters)
A-1	61	1¼ (1.14)
B-1	117	2¼ (2.06)
A-2	251	4½ (4.11)
B-2	145	2¾ (2.51)
C-1	236	4¼ (3.89)
D-1	207	3¾ (3.43)
E-1	84	1¾ (1.60)
E-2	116	2¼ (2.06)
B-3	30	¾ (0.68)
F-1	264	4¾ (4.34)
E-3	69	1½ (1.37)
F-2	88	1¾ (1.60)
A-3	85	1¾ (1.60)
B-4	114	2¼ (2.06)
A-4	207	3¾ (3.43)
C-2	220	4 (3.66)
D-2	213	3¾ (3.43)
E-4	155	2¾ (2.51)
D-3	89	1¾ (1.60)
C-3	88	1¾ (1.60)
B-5	91	1¾ (1.60)
F-3	255	4½ (4.11)
E-5	30	¾ (0.68)
F-4	92	1¾ (1.60)

SCARF

Prepare yarn supplies as described on page 168.

With A, CO 41 sts.

Working Annetarsia garter st (page 54), rep Rows 1–70 of Sunriver Scarf chart (page 170) until piece measures desired length or you run out of yarn.

With the color of your choice, BO all sts.

FINISHING

Use chenille needle to bury all loose ends into links.

Sunriver, Oregon

SUNRIVER SCARF CHART

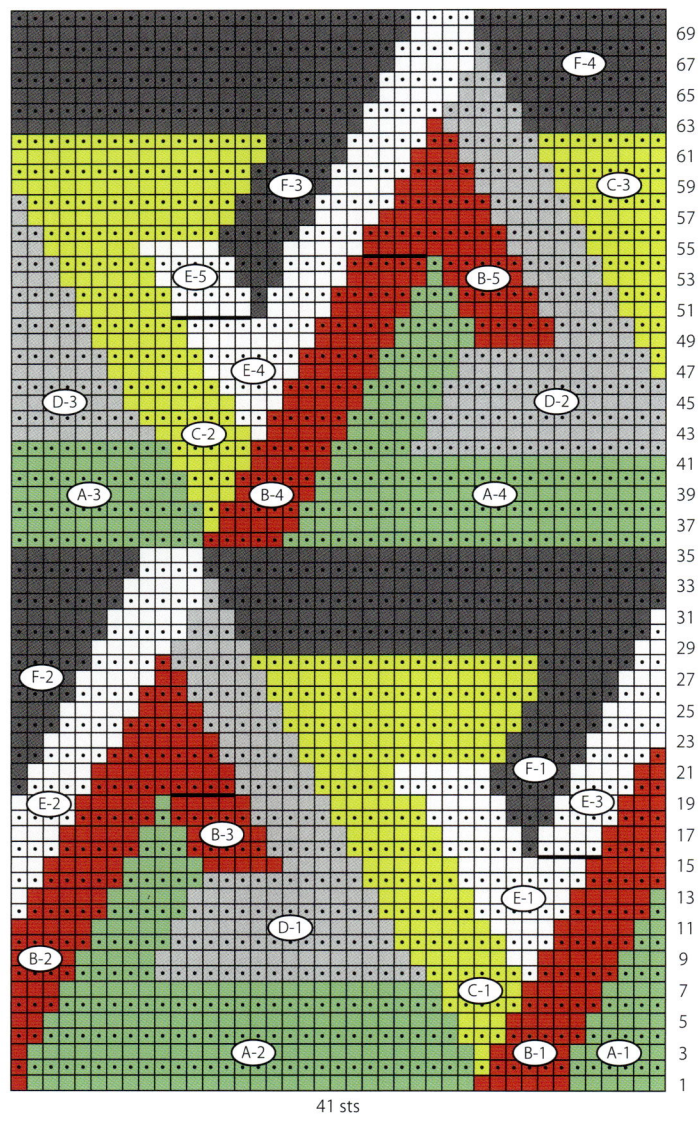

41 sts

- ▧ With A, knit on RS
- ▨ With A, knit on WS
- ▧ With B, knit on RS
- ▨ With B, knit on WS
- ▧ With C, knit on RS
- ▨ With C, knit on WS
- ▧ With D, knit on RS
- ▨ With D, knit on WS
- ☐ With E, knit on RS
- ⊡ With E, knit on WS
- ▧ With F, knit on RS
- ▨ With F, knit on WS
- — Boundary between yarn sources

ALTERNATIVE VARIATION

Knitted by Bobbie Hodges using:

A: Berroco Ultra Alpaca #6273 (Irwyn Green Mix)

B: Berroco Ultra Alpaca Tonal #6359 (Frambuesa)

C: Berroco Ultra Alpaca #6292 (Tiger's Eye Mix)

D: Berroco Ultra Alpaca #6283 (Lavender Mix)

E: Berroco Ultra Alpaca #6224 (Steel Blue)

F: Berroco Ultra Alpaca #6285 (Oceanic Mix)

Willamette Valley Socks

Designer: Marcia Weinert

Oregon's Willamette River valley is the site of thousands of lightning strikes every year. These socks feature a lightning-bolt motif and simple rolled cuffs (your links will peek out and reveal your magic powers!). With the exception of the toes, all sections of the socks are charted. Note that three of the lightning bolts end at the heel, but one crackles all the way down the instep. Pay careful attention while working the Ankle and Instep charts, in which there are irregular changes in the turning point, and some increases are worked on wrong-side rows. Or, just knit, letting your lightning bolts zig and zag at will. Enjoy your unique creation!

WHAT YOU'LL NEED TO KNOW

Annetarsia "in the round" (ITR), page 12.

Calculating yarn gauge, page 26.

Managing multiple yarn supplies, page 25.

Reading charts, page 39.

Burying ends, page 36.

Skill Level
Intermediate.

Finished Measurements
About 7½ (8½, 9½)" (19 [20.5, 24] cm) foot circumference and 8½" (21.5 cm) from back of heel to tip of toe. Socks shown in medium size.

Yarn
Dream in Color Everlasting 8-ply Sock (100% superwash merino; 420 yd [384 m]/100 g): Crisp (A) and Blue Fish (B), 1 skein each.

Needles
U.S. size 2 (2.75 mm): one circular (circ) at least 27" (68.5 cm) long.

Adjust needle size if necessary to obtain correct gauge.

Notions
Four markers; chenille needle.

Stitch and Row Gauge
16 sts and 20 rows = 2" (5 cm) in Annetarsia patt, after blocking.

Yarn Gauge
0.36.

Take time to check stitch, row, and yarn gauges.

YARN PREPARATION

The yarn amounts given here are based on the yarn and gauge specified and a yarn gauge of 0.36 and include 10" (25.5 cm) added for tails to be woven in. If your gauge or yarn gauge is different, knit a swatch and work your individual calculations (see page 26) to determine the amount of yarn you'll need.

You'll need between 8 and 11 yd (7.3 and 10 m) of yarn for each lightning-bolt motif, which can be contained in about 30 wraps around the hand.

SPECIAL ABBREVIATIONS

Loop 'n' lock: Pull yarn from the last section worked on the previous row, then lock it into place with the first stitch of the next row to form a loop.

w&t (wrap and turn): Slip 1 stitch purlwise from left to right needle tip, bring yarn between needle tips to opposite side of work, wrapping the slipped stitch, then return the slipped stitch to the left needle tip. Turn work.

M1 (make 1): Use the left needle tip to lift the horizontal strand between the two needles from front to back, placing it on the left needle. Knit this lifted strand through the back loop to increase 1 stitch.

Yardages Needed for Size Small

Color Block	Number Needed	S+R	Yards (Meters)
Short B Bolts	3	749	8 (7.30)
Long B Bolts	1	1,067	11 (10.00)
A sections	4	862	9 (8.20)

Yardages Needed for Size Medium

Color Block	Number Needed	S+R	Yards (Meters)
Short B Bolts	3	756	8 (7.30)
Long B Bolts	1	1074	11 (10.00)
A Sections	4	964	10 (9.10)

Yardages Needed for Size Large

Color Block	Number Needed	S+R	Yards (Meters)
Short B Bolts	3	763	8 (7.30)
Long B Bolts	1	1081	11¼ (10.30)
A Sections	4	1108	11½ (10.50)

LEG

Prepare yarn supplies as described above.

With A and using the long-tail method, CO 64 (72, 80) sts. Join for working in rnds, being careful to not twist sts.

Row 1: (WS) *With B, p8 (9, 10), with A, p8 (9, 10); rep from * 3 more times, linking each section.

Row 2: (RS) Loop 'n' lock (see Special Abbreviations). *K8 (9, 10) with A, k8 (9, 10) with B; rep from * 3 more times, linking each section.

Rows 3–7: Working a loop 'n' lock at the beg of each row, rep Rows 1 and 2 two more times, then work Row 1 once more.

Row 8: (RS; dec row) Loop 'n' lock. *With A, k1 (4, 10), [k2tog] 1 (1, 0) time, k2 (3, 0), [k2tog] 1 (0, 0) time; with B, k8 (4, 2), [k2tog] 0 (1, 1) time, k0 (3, 2), [k2tog] 0 (0, 1) time, k0 (0, 2); rep from * 3 more times—56 (64, 72) sts rem.

Following the chart for your size and working a loop 'n' lock at the beg of every row, work Rows 1–22 of Leg chart (page 176) 3 times, ending with a RS row.

ANKLE

Following the chart for your size, work Rows 1–24 of Ankle chart (page 177)— 84 (96, 108) sts.

Next row: (Row 25 of Ankle chart; WS) Loop 'n' lock. With B, p8; with A, p8 (10, 12), place marker for left instep, p8 (9, 10); link this yarn butterfly with both B and the next A butterflies; cont with the next A butterfly, p6 (7, 8), place marker for left sole, p15 (17, 19); link this yarn butterfly with both B and the next A butterflies; cont with the next A butterfly, p13 (15, 17), place marker for right sole, p8 (9, 10), drop this butterfly and the B butterfly through rem A loop; use A loop to p6 (7, 8), place marker for right instep, p12 (14, 16) to end of row.

Leaving the A and B butterflies next to the instep motif intact, carefully cut all other butterflies, leaving 6" (15 cm) tails.

Use chenille needle to bury all loose ends into links.

HEEL

(Row 26 of Ankle chart) Working with yarn attached to the ball of A (rather than a butterfly) work short-rows as foll:

Heel Turn

Row 1: (RS) Loop 'n' lock, knit to 2 sts before left sole m, w&t (see Special Abbreviations).

Row 2: (WS) Purl to 2 sts before right sole m, w&t.

Row 3: (RS) Knit to 1 st before wrapped st, w&t.

Row 4: (WS) Purl to 1 st before wrapped st, w&t.

Rep the last 2 rows 6 (7, 9) more times—10 (12, 12) sts rem between wrapped sts.

Next row: (RS) Knit to first wrapped st; *insert right needle under the wrap to lift it up, over, and to the left of the wrapped st, then knit the st tog with its wrap through their back loops (tbl); rep from * to 2 sts before left sole m, end by inserting the right needle under the next wrap to lift it up, over, and to the left of the wrapped st, then knit the st tog with its wrap and the last st before the marker as k3tog tbl, remove m, turn.

Next row: (WS) Sl 1, replace left sole m, purl to first wrapped st, *insert the right needle beneath the wrap from the knit (RS) side to lift it up, over, and to the left of the wrapped st, then purl the st tog with its wrap; rep from * to 2 sts before right sole m, end by inserting right needle under the last wrap from the knit (RS) side to lift it up, over, and to the left of the wrapped st, then purl the st tog with its wrap and the last st before the marker as p3tog, remove m, turn work.

Bottom of Heel

Row 1: (RS) Sl 1, replace right sole m (24 [28, 32] sts rem between sole markers), knit to left sole marker, slip marker (sl m), ssk, turn work.

SIZE SMALL LEG CHART

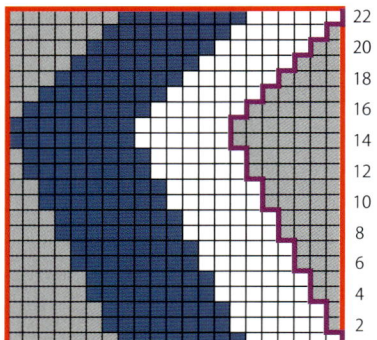

14-st repeat

SIZE MEDIUM LEG CHART

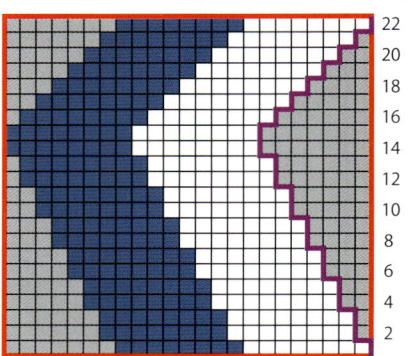

16-st repeat

SIZE LARGE LEG CHART

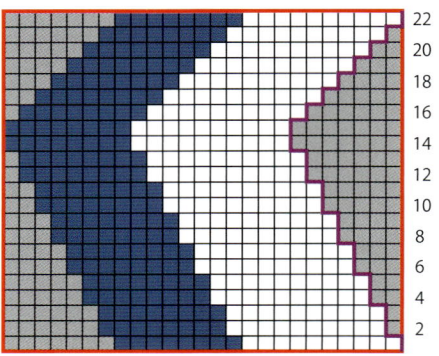

18-st repeat

INSTEP CHART

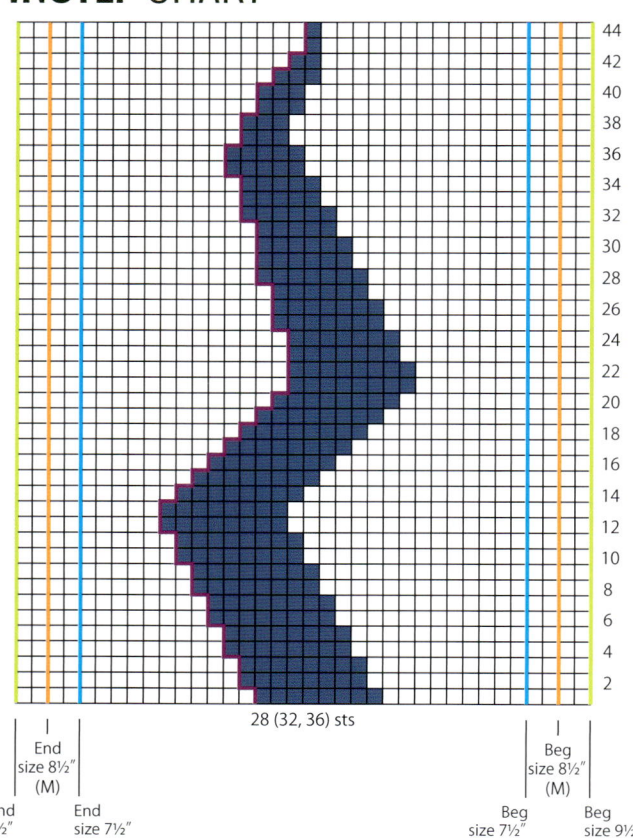

28 (32, 36) sts

- ☐ With A, knit on RS, purl on WS
- ■ With B, knit on RS, purl on WS
- ■ Heel sts; see instructions
- ■ No stitch
- M M1
- ☐ Pattern repeat
- | Turning point
- | Marker placement
- | Size 7½" (Small)
- | Size 8½" (Medium)
- | Size 9½" (Large)

SIZE SMALL ANKLE CHART

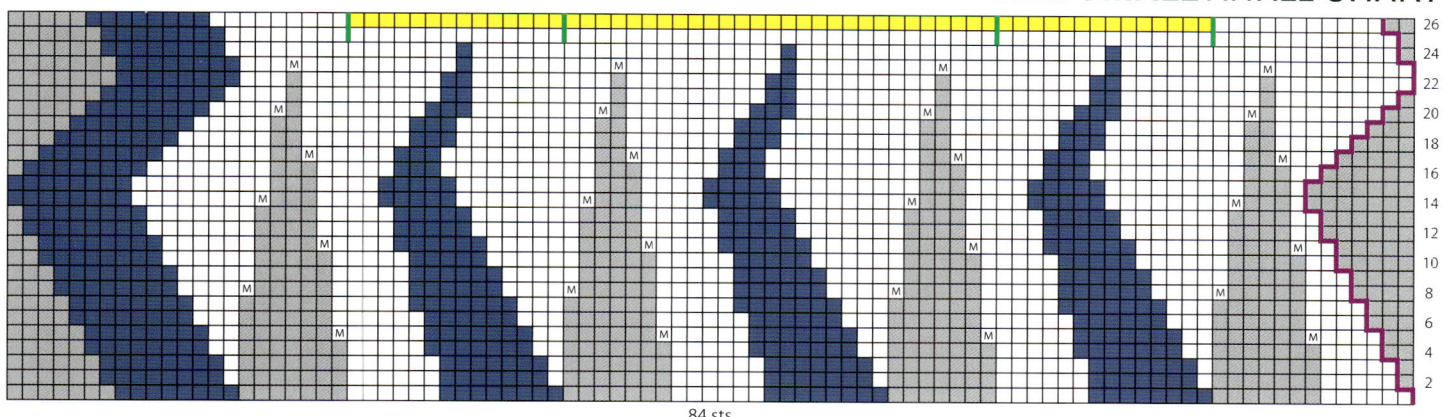

84 sts

SIZE MEDIUM ANKLE CHART

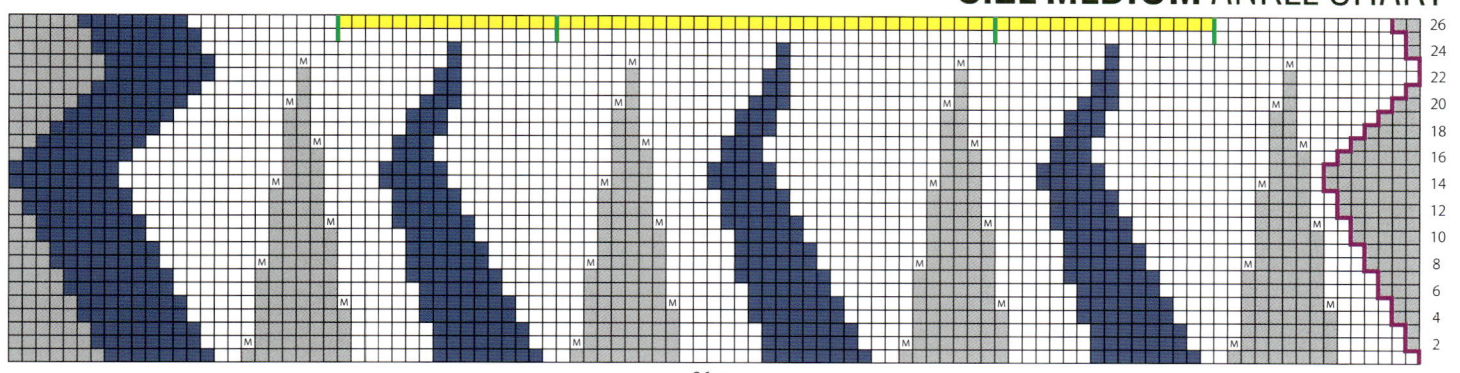

96 sts

SIZE LARGE ANKLE CHART

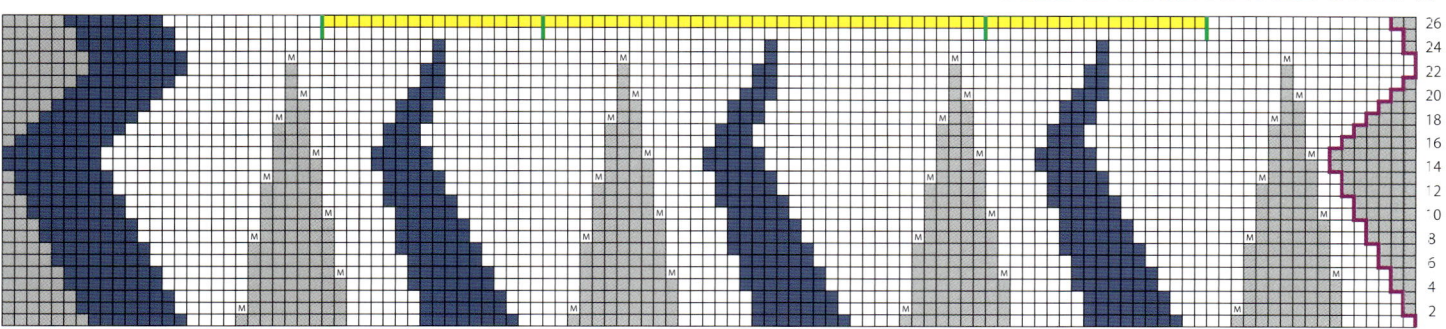

108 sts

Row 2: (WS) Sl 1, sl m, purl to right sole marker, sl m, p2tog, turn work.

Row 3: (RS) Sl 1, sl m, knit to left sole marker, sl m, ssk, turn work.

Row 4: (WS) Sl 1, sl m, purl to right sole marker, sl m, p2tog, turn work.

Rep the last 2 rows 8 (10, 12) more times—3 sts rem between sole and instep markers on each side.

Next row: (RS) Sl 1, sl right sole m, knit to left sole m, remove m, ssk, k1, sl left instep m, knit to start of B motif, drop A butterfly through B loop, use B loop to k8, turn work.

FOOT

Work Row 1 of Instep chart (page 176) as foll:

Row 1: (WS) Loop 'n' lock; with B, p8; with A, purl to left instep m, sl m, purl to right sole m, remove m, p2tog, p1, sl right instep m, purl to end—56 (64, 72) sts total; 28 (32, 36) sts each for sole and instep.

Keeping all sole sts in A and working a loop 'n' lock at the beg of every row, work through Row 44 of Instep chart. Cut B, leaving a 6" (15 cm) tail for burying.

With A, knit to right instep marker, which marks beg of rnd for the completion of the sock.

Work 4 (6, 8) rnds even, or until foot measures to the top of the little toe.

TOE

Rnd 1: *K1, ssk, knit to 3 sts before marker, k2tog, k1, sl m; rep from * once—4 sts decreased.

Rnd 2: Knit.

Rep these two rnds 7 (9, 11) more times—24 sts rem; 12 sts rem between markers.

Cut yarn, leaving a 12" (30.5 cm) tail.

FINISHING

Thread tail on a tapestry needle and use the Kitchener st to graft sts tog.

Use chenille needle to bury all loose ends into links.

ALTERNATIVE VARIATION

Perfect! Being a sheep, I need four of a kind!

Knit with Blue Moon Fiber Arts Socks that Rock Mediumweight (100% superwash merino; 405 yd [370 m]/170 g): Dark Shadows (A) and Festival of Lights (B), 1 skein each. Woman's sock shown in small size; man's sock shown in medium size, and is knitted with only one repeat of the leg chart. The heavier yarn used for this variation resulted in larger socks, although U.S. size 2 (2.75 mm) needles were used for all versions.

Variation sample knitted by Anne Berk.

These remind me of a blue sky over my favorite clover field. Suddenly, I want a clover smoothie!

Oaks Park Socks

Oaks Park may be the oldest continuously operating amusement park in America, serving as a community gathering place since 1905. It's a modest operation that caters to all ages and pocketbooks, with carnival rides and games that operate seasonally, an indoor skating rink that's open all year, and extensive picnic grounds along the Willamette River.

This is the sock mentioned in the introduction, the one that I was knitting that caught Cat Bordhi's attention and changed my life. I was inspired by her book *Personal Footprints for Insouciant Sock Knitters*, which lends itself very well to my ITR technique. If you'd like the socks to fit you perfectly, I highly recommend that you acquire Cat's book and follow her wonderful instructions.

Knitting this pattern with your personal numbers may result in a sock that looks different from mine, but will be beautiful with your individual patterning.

WHAT YOU'LL NEED TO KNOW

Annetarsia "in the round" (ITR), page 12.

Calculating yarn gauge, page 26.

Managing multiple yarn supplies, page 25.

Reading charts, page 39.

Burying ends, page 36.

Personal footprint technique from *Personal Footprints for Insouciant Sock Knitters* by Cat Bordhi (Passing Paws Press, 2009).

Skill Level
Intermediate.

Finished Measurements
About 8" (20.5 cm) foot circumference and 8½" (21.5 cm) foot length from back of heel to tip of toe.

Yarn
Holiday Yarns FlockSock (75% superwash merino, 25% nylon, 400 yd [366 m]/100 g); Burnt Orange (A) and Dirty Bird (B), 1 skein each.

Needles
U.S. size 1 (2.25 mm): 24" (60 cm) circular (circ) for "magic-loop" method. Double-pointed (dpn) or two circular needles may be substituted (dpn are preferred for binding off the heel).

Adjust needle size if necessary to obtain correct gauge.

Notions
Waste yarn; locking stitch marker (m); smooth waste yarn in a contrasting color for lifeline; chenille needle.

Stitch and Row Gauge
30 sts and 36 rows/rnds = 4" (10 cm) in patt.

Yarn Gauge
0.36.

Take time to check stitch, row, and yarn gauges.

NOTES

» These socks are worked in Annetarsia ITR. Remember to turn the work and make a new loop, every row—there are no exceptions! Continue the spiral as charted, working ITR through the entire pattern.

» Move the spirals of color one stitch every row. Count the stitches in each section every few rows to ensure that you're on track.

» The cast-on is fully described in *Personal Footprints for Insouciant Sock Knitters* by Cat Bordhi.

» To reverse the stripes for the second sock, work all spirals in the opposite direction.

SPECIAL ABBREVIATIONS

kfb: Knit into the front and back of the same stitch to increase 1 stitch.

M1 (make 1): Use the left needle tip to lift the horizontal strand between the two needles from front to back, placing it on the left needle. Knit this lifted strand through the back loop to increase 1 stitch.

Loop 'n' lock: Pull yarn from the last section worked on the previous row, then lock it into place with the first stitch of the next row to form a loop.

PF: The personal footprint as defined in Cat Bordhi's *Personal Footprints for Insouciant Sock Knitters*.

YARN PREPARATION

The toe will be knitted from the ball; the rest of the sock will be worked from butterflies.

Winding the yarn around your hand 40 times for each butterfly, make 10 butterflies of each color. If you prefer smaller butterflies, make 20–22 butterflies of 20 wraps each of each color.

TOE

Prepare yarn supplies as described on page 182.

Use Cat Bordhi's Personal Footprint Cast–On (or substitute Judy's Magic Cast-On) to cast on 12 stitches as foll:

Personal Footprint Cast-On: With A and leaving a 10" (25.5 cm) tail, make slipknot and place on one circ needle tip. Place the other tip above the first, then pull the ball yarn under the needles and up and away from you. Wrap the ball yarn toward you around the needles 3 times, ending behind and above the needle tips—3 wraps around both the lower and upper needle tips.

Pull the lower needle tip until the sts rest on the cable and the tip is in position to knit.

Rnd 1: K3 from upper needle.

Rotate the needles so that the slipknot is on the top needle tip. Pull lower needle tip until the sts are on the cable, slide the un-worked sts to the top needle, pull off the slipknot and tug it free, then hold the tail and the ball yarn together and k3 from lower needle.

Rotate the work clockwise so that the upper needle is now at the bottom and k3 from this needle—12 sts total; 6 sts worked with double yarn. Drop tail yarn.

Rnd 2: With ball yarn only, knit to end, working each loop of each double st separately—12 sts.

Rnd 3: [K1, kfb (see Special Abbreviations)] 6 times—18 sts.

Rnds 4, 6, and 8: Knit.

Rnd 5: [K2, kfb] 6 times—24 sts.

Rnd 7: [K3, kfb] 6 times—30 sts.

Rnd 9: [K4, kfb] 6 times—36 sts.

Rnds 10 and 11: Knit.

Rnd 12: [K5, kfb] 6 times—6 sts increased.

Rep Rnds 10–12, knitting 2 plain rnds followed by an inc rnd that adds 1 st before the kfb, until the toe just covers your toenails—60 sts in this example.

Note: Keep in mind that this Personal Footprint (PF; see Special Abbreviations) construction favors a tight fit for comfort and long wear.

FOOT

Row 1: (RS; Row 1 of Oaks Park chart; page 185) Add butterflies as foll: K6 with A, *k1 with B, cross A over B (Photo 1), then k5 with B (yarns linked), k1 with A, cross B over A, then k5 with A; rep from *—10 sections and 10 yarn butterflies. Turn work.

Row 2: (WS) Loop 'n' lock (see Special Abbreviations), then purl to end, following Row 2 of the chart.

Work ITR, shifting the colors 1 st every row and trying on the sock for fit as you go. When you approach the ankle, you may need to increase sts for best fit. Distribute these increases evenly around the foot circumference; they will be decreased later.

Inc rnd for left-leaning stripe: Work 30 sts in patt (the top of the foot), [k1, M1 (see Special Abbreviations), k5] 5 times—65 sts.

Inc rnd for right-leaning stripe: Work 30 sts in patt (the top of the foot), [k5, M1, k1] 5 times—65 sts.

Continue in patt as established until foot measures about 4" (10 cm) from last toe inc, or until the edge of the sock stretches to the center of your leg (near your ankle bone) or to the "leg line" of your PF, ending with a WS row (Photo 2).

Lifeline for the Leg Opening

Note: If there are more than 4 sts in a half-stripe on a lifeline, add a long loop to this section for burying ends. More than

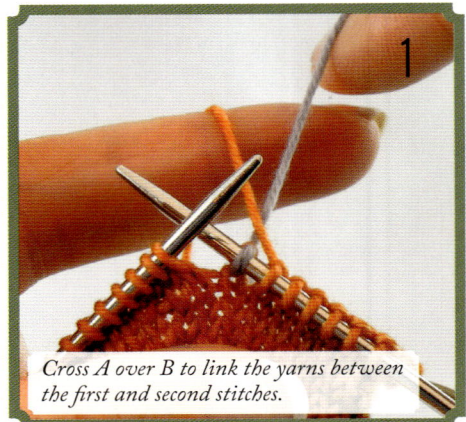
Cross A over B to link the yarns between the first and second stitches.

Leg Line.

Thread a lifeline.

Pull third stitch into long loop.

4 uncut sts at each end of the lifeline will not lie flat (see Lifelines box on page 186). Arrange sts so that half of the sts are on each needle tip.

For ease of adding a lifeline, slide sts onto the cable portion of the needle. With a narrow yarn needle, run smooth waste yarn through all sts on one needle, according to chart. These will be the front-of-leg sts (Photo 3).

Next row: (RS) K6 (first stripe), [k2, k1 with 10" (25.5 cm) loop (pull the long loops against the needle when knitting the next st, so that the loops don't shorten; Photo 4), k3] in each of the next 4 stripes

(or until all leg sts have been worked, leaving one section without a loop on each end of the needle), work to end.

Secure all of the long loops with a loose overhand knot close to the needle (Photo 5).

Bring the loops to the front of work so that they won't tangle with the yarn butterflies on the WS.

Next row: (WS) Work all sts in patt, then thread a second waste-yarn lifeline through all leg sts to match the first lifeline, according to chart. These will be the back-of-leg sts (Photo 6).

The single row between the two lifelines contains the middle sections that will be cut for the leg opening. The extra yarn that has been tied into half-hitch knots will allow you to bury the ends later.

Continue to work ITR, spiraling as established, until piece measures ½" (1.3 cm) from lifeline, or the work stretches over the PF to the "heel line."

HEEL

Set-up Row 1: (RS; dec row) [K1, k2tog, k4] 5 times—60 sts rem; 30 sts for instep, 30 sts for sole; 6 sts in each stripe.

Set-up Row 2: (WS) Work even in patt.

Row 1: (RS) [K3, k3tog, k1 with A, k6 with B] 5 times—55 sts rem.

Row 2 and all WS rows: Work even in patt.

Row 3: [K5 with A, k3, k2tog, k1 with B] 5 times—50 sts rem.

Row 5: Work even in patt (there are no decs this row).

Row 7: [K2, k2tog, k1 with A, k5 with B] 5 times—45 sts rem.

Row 9: [K4 with A, k2, k2tog, k1 with B] 5 times—40 sts rem.

Row 11: [K1, k2tog, k1 with A, k4 with B] 5 times—35 sts rem.

Row 13: [K3 with A, k1, k2tog, k1 with B] 5 times—30 sts rem.

Row 15: [K2tog, k1 with A, k2tog, k1 with B] 5 times—20 sts rem.

Row 17: [K2tog with A, k2tog with B] 5 times—10 sts rem.

Choose 1 strand to use for BO; cut rem strands and tuck ends inside the sock (Photo 7).

OAKS PARK CHART

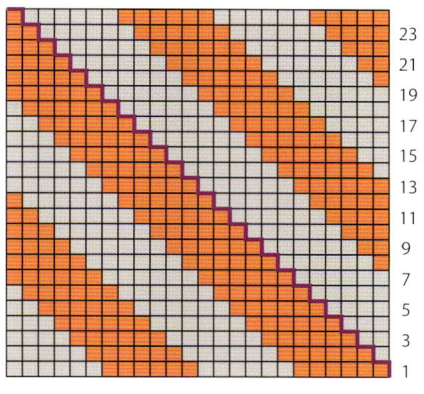

■ With A, knit on RS, purl on WS
☐ With B, knit on RS, purl on WS
❘ Turning point

When threading the second lifeline, don't forget the stitches on the end remain uncut.

Finished heel, ready to bind off.

LIFELINES

Lifelines will help immeasurably if you have to rip out the knitting to correct a mistake. They also will be used to mark the leg opening.

The following rules will help ensure success.

» The last two or three stitches on each end of the lifeline are worked for the leg, but not cut open.

» Placement of the lifeline will determine how the spirals connect at the ankle.

» The turning point and loop are not affected by the lifeline. The loop is easier to manage if it is outside the lifeline, but the turning point will not be affected by lifeline placement.

» When the leg opening is cut, the stitches on the top lifeline and the bottom lifeline will be knitted as a tube with the colors meeting at the sides, which will determine the width of the sections going up the leg.

» The stitches held on both lifelines should match in color and number. The second lifeline is shifted over two stitches to accommodate the spiral movement over the two rows knit to the second lifeline.

» The total number of stitches on the lifelines should equal the number of stitches desired for the leg circumference.

» Divide the end sections for the spirals that will grow out of the ankle spiral (for example, if there are six stitches in the middle stripes on the lifelines, there will be three stitches in each end section, so that there will be six total stitches in every stripe around the leg).

» Start and end the lifeline at the edge of complete sections for spirals that merge together and flow over the ankle.

» Only two or three stitches should be left uncut on each end of the lifeline. If more than five total stitches are left uncut, the stitches will not lie flat. If the sections on the edge of the lifeline need to be cut, simply add long knotted loops on these sections, as well as on the middle sections, for weaving in ends after cutting the yarn.

» For Version 2, reverse the order of colors on the lifelines for the second sock to create a mirrored effect on the leg, placing the wide stripes in the different color. The colors on each end of the lifeline will be wide stripes.

» For ease of knitting, work increases and decreases about ½" (1.3 cm) away from the lifelines.

» If you wish the width of the leg stripes to match the width of the foot stripes, work increases and decreases for the foot only on the 50% of the stitches that are not included in the lifelines. The lifeline stitches will become the leg

Divide the sections in half for spirals that grow out of the ankle. Here, there are 6 stitches in each stripe but 3 stitches in each section next to the ankle.

Start and end the lifeline at the edge of complete sections for spirals that merge together and flow over the ankle.

stitches, so you will need them to have the same number of stitches all of the way up the sock.

» Work increases and decreases in the middle of a section.

» The number of stitches in the lifeline and the width of any sections are adjustable for size as long as the above rules are followed.

Place 5 sts on one needle tip and rem 5 sts on the other needle tip. With WS facing tog and RS facing out, use the three-needle method to BO these sts (Photo 8). The loose sts on the final row will make the BO look odd, but it will be corrected later.

LEG

Note: For more information on how to create the leg opening, see Cat's book, or see the bibliography (page 223) for a link to her excellent video tutorial.

Place the 30 sts held on one lifeline onto one needle tip, then place the 30 sts held on the second lifeline onto the other needle tip—60 sts total; 30 sts on each needle tip (Photo 9).

Move the sts to cable portion of the circ needle and remove the lifelines.

Use the three-needle method to bind off the heel stitches.

Following the lifelines, insert the needles into the stitches.

The completed foot.

Remove the 4 slipknots, cut each long loop in half (Photo 10), then ravel each side of these four sections (Photo 11).

Bury the ends in links on the WS. Do not cut or ravel the partial sections on the ends (3 sts of A on one end and 3 sts of B on the other end). Those sections will be continued up the leg, preserving the ankle/leg/foot continuity and making the join look invisible.

The heel is complete. Try on the foot and admire your work!

Note: Because the pattern moved along the diagonal when lifelines were placed, you'll need to restore the stripe patt so that there are 6 sts in each stripe when you begin the leg.

Leg: With RS facing and the toe in front, skip the sts in the uncut section, leaving them to the end of the row. Using a new yarn supply for each section (leaving 5" [12.5 cm] tails) and maintaining the diagonal shift, k24 sts from the side of leg facing the toe, k6 sts in the uncut section to maintain the proper color sequence, k24 sts from the side of the leg facing the heel, and k6 sts from the second uncut section—60 sts total.

Cont as charted until leg measures 5½" (14 cm) or desired length from ankle.

RIBBING

Leaving one strand of A for the ribbing, cut the other strands, leaving 5" (12.5 cm) tails.

With A, work in k1, p1 rib for 2" (5.1 cm) or desired length.

BO all sts in patt.

FINISHING

Tighten ends inside the heel. Use chenille needle to bury all loose ends into links.

Remove the lifelines and cut each loop in half.

Unravel the stitches on each side of the four sections.

The inside of the heel.

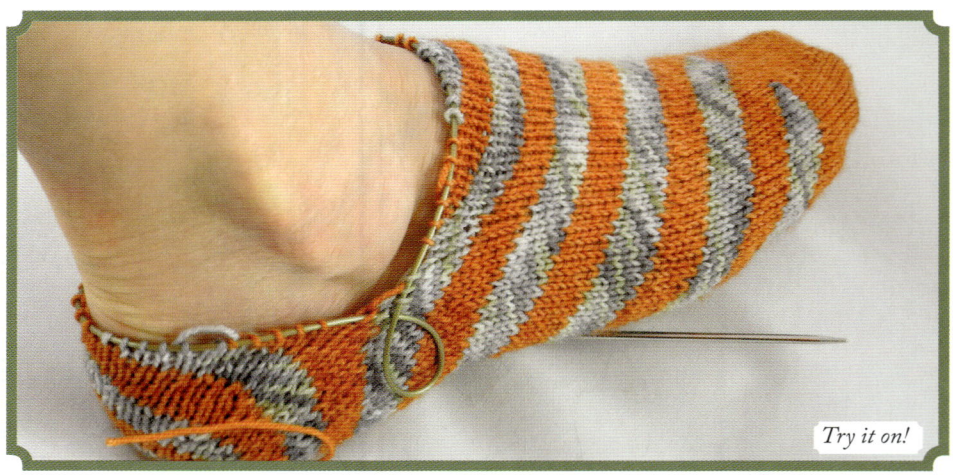
Try it on!

ALTERNATIVE VARIATIONS

Pink and Green Variation: Blue Moon Socks that Rock Lightweight, 100% Superwash Merino in Sophie and Mr. Greenjeans. Variation sample knitted by Anne Berk.

Beth Popp's "Luna Park" Variation (pictured below): Beth used Mountain Colors Crazy Foot (90% merino, 10% nylon; 425 yd [388 m]/100 g) in Harmony Iris (Purple) and North Wind (Blue) for this variation. She used about 36 g (1.25 ounces) of each color.

Beth followed the instructions given with the following modifications:

» The completed toe had six sections of 9 sts each; 54 sts total.

» Three sections of each color were added, alternating Color A (Purple) and Color B (Blue).

» When piece measured 2½" (6.5 cm) from beg of colorwork, 1 st was increased in the middle of every section—six stripes of 10 sts each; 60 sts total.

» When piece measured 3¾" (9.5 cm) from beg of colorwork, 1 st was increased in the middle of every section—six stripes of 11 sts each; 66 sts total.

» When piece measured 6" (15 cm) from beg of colorwork, lifelines were added so that the following color sequence was on both Needle 1 and Needle 2: 11 sts A, 11 sts B, 11 sts A.

» The leg opening was cut over the center 27 sts on the lifeline; 33 sts from each lifeline were placed on needles—four sections of color on each needle: 22 A, 11 B, 22 A, 11 B; 66 sts total.

» Working ITR, new yarn sources were added for each color and the spirals continued in the same direction as previously established.

» When piece measured 5" (12.5 cm) from leg opening, all yarns were cut, leaving 5" (12.5 cm) tails to be buried later.

» With B, k1, p1 ribbing was worked for 1" (2.5 cm).

» All sts were BO in ribbing.

OK ballet class, feet in the First Position. Not so easy for a dizzy sheep!

Kelly Sweater

During workshops at Wynona Studios in Oregon City, Oregon, I asked knitters which types of projects they'd like to knit to use their newfound skills. Many of them wanted to knit personalized sweaters for children and grandchildren. The Kelly Sweater is a basic raglan construction that can be customized for appropriate motifs and sizing. It's designed for a loose, casual fit, and the sleeve and body can be lengthened as the child grows. The body and sleeves are knitted in the round from the lower edges to the armholes, then joined together and the yoke is knitted in one piece to the shoulders, with the neck shaped along the way. The motifs are worked in the Annetarsia ITR technique.

The sweater is shown in two versions, named for Noah and Drew Kelly, whose grandma, Tammie, participated in the Wynona workshop and test-knit some of the motif swatches included in Chapter 4.

WHAT YOU'LL NEED TO KNOW

Annetarsia "in the round" (ITR), page 12.

Calculating yarn gauge, page 26.

Managing multiple yarn supplies, page 25.

Reading charts, page 39.

Burying ends, page 36.

Kitchener stitch or three-needle bind-off.

Duplicate stitch.

Skill Level
Advanced beginner to advanced, depending on the complexity of the motifs added.

Finished Measurements
About 22¾ (27, 29½, 32, 34½, 36¼)" (58 [68.5, 75, 81.5, 87.5, 92] cm) chest circumference.

Drew's sweater (left) measures 27" (68.5 cm) and Noah's sweater (right) measures 32" (81.5 cm).

Yarn
Brown Sheep Lamb's Pride Superwash Worsted (100% wool; 200 yd [182 m]/100 g): 2 (3, 4, 4, 6, 7) skeins for MC; additional colors as needed for motifs.

Needles
U.S. sizes 6 (optional; see Notes) and 7 (4 and 4.5 mm): 24" (60 cm) circular (circ) and set of 4 or 5 double-pointed (dpn).

Adjust needle size if necessary to obtain correct gauge.

Notions
Markers (m); stitch holders; waste yarn or spare circular needle; tapestry needle; chenille needle.

Stitch and Row Gauge
19 sts and 29 rnds/rows = 4" (10 cm) in St st on larger needles, after blocking.

Yarn Gauge
0.80.

Take time to check stitch, row, and yarn gauges.

NOTES

» Smaller needles may be used for hem facings. When hems are let down to extend length for growth, this will cause the additional fabric to slightly hug the body. Size U.S. 6 (4 mm) needles are recommended for a slightly tighter fabric, but smaller sizes can be used to further tighten the gauge. Swatching is recommended for best results.

» Choose motifs from Chapter 5 (or another source), placing them as desired on the front, back, and sleeves, and following the ITR method.

SPECIAL ABBREVIATIONS

M1 (make 1): Use the left needle tip to lift the horizontal strand between the two needles from front to back, placing it on the left needle. Knit this lifted strand through the back loop to increase 1 stitch.

kfb: Knit into the front and back of the same stitch to increase 1 stitch.

BODY

With CC and smaller circ needle (if snug hem is desired) CO 104 (124, 136, 148, 160, 168) sts.

Place marker (pm) and join for working in rnds, being careful not to twist sts.

Knit all rnds until piece measures 2½" (6.5 cm), or desired length for hem facing.

Change to larger circ needle.

Turning ridge: Join MC, [kfb (see Special Abbreviations), p35 (30, 33, 36, 39, 41)] 2 times, pm for side "seam," [kfb, p25 (30, 33, 36, 39, 41)] 2 times—108 (128, 140, 152, 164, 172) sts.

With MC, knit 1 rnd.

Replace markers with locking markers at the turning ridge to mark side "seam." The "loop" will mark the last section of every row.

Cont even in St st until piece measures 7 (7½, 9, 10½, 13, 14½)" (18 [19, 23, 26.5, 33, 37] cm) or desired length from turning ridge to underarm.

Cut yarn, leaving a 5" (12.5 cm) tail. Place sts on waste yarn or spare circ needle.

KELLY SWEATER SCHEMATIC

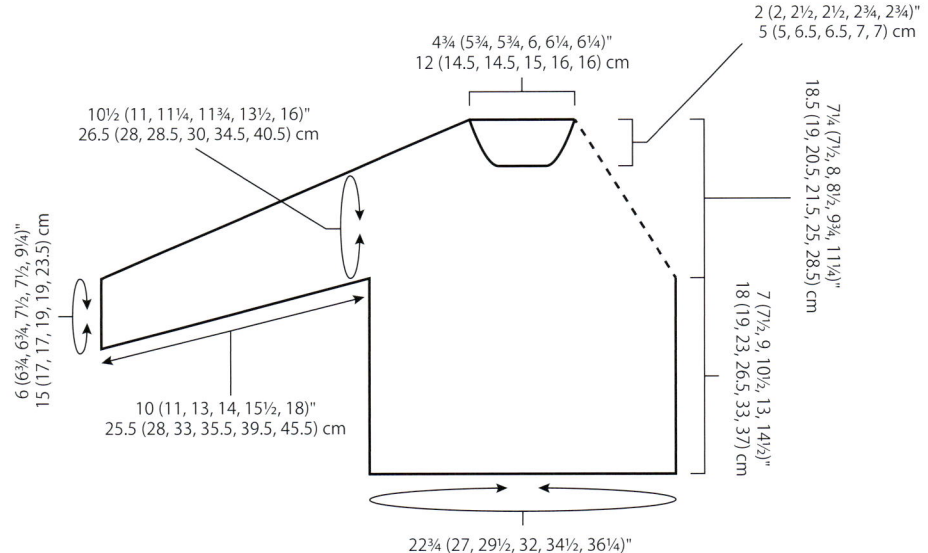

SLEEVES (MAKE 2)

With MC and dpn (in smaller size, if snug hem is desired), CO 32 (36, 36, 40, 40, 48) sts.

Pm and join for working in rnds, being careful not to twist sts.

Hem

Note: Stitches are decreased in the facing to provide a good fit when the hem is turned to the inside. If the hem is later let out to allow for growth, there will be a slight bell shape to the cuff. See the photos below to see both the tucked and untucked versions.

Knit 5 rnds.

Dec rnd: *K6 (7, 7, 8, 8, 10), k2tog; rep from * to end—28 (32, 32, 36, 36, 44) sts rem.

Knit 5 rnds.

Turning rnd: With MC, purl all sts.

Knit 5 rnds.

Inc rnd: *K7 (7, 7, 8, 8, 10), M1 (see Special Abbreviations); rep from * to end—32 (36, 36, 40, 40, 48) sts.

Shape Sleeve

Knit 5 rnds.

Inc rnd: K1, M1, knit to last st, M1, K1—2 sts increased.

Rep inc rnd every 6th rnd 6 (4, 2, 1, 2, 2) more times, then every 8th rnd 2 (3, 6, 6, 9, 11) times—50 (52, 54, 56, 64, 76) sts.

Cont even in St st until piece measures 10 (11, 13, 14, 15½, 18)" (25.5 [28, 33, 35.5, 39.5, 45.5] cm) from turning ridge or desired length to underarm.

Next rnd: Knit to 5 (5, 5, 5, 7, 7) sts before m, place next 10 (10, 10, 10, 14, 14) sts onto holder (removing m when you come to it)—40 (42, 44, 46, 50, 62) sts rem.

Cut yarn, leaving a 5" (12.5 cm) tail. Place sts on waste yarn or spare circular needle.

YOKE

Joining rnd: K44 (54, 60, 64, 68, 72) body sts, pm, place next 10 (10, 10, 10, 14, 14) body sts onto holder (remove m when you come to it), k40 (42, 44, 46, 50, 62) sleeve sts, pm, k44 (54, 60, 66, 68, 72) body sts, pm, place next 10 (10, 10, 10, 14, 14) body sts onto holder (remove m when you come to it), pm, k40 (42, 44, 46, 50, 62) sleeve sts, pm—168 (192, 208, 220, 236, 268) sts total.

Work even until piece measures 1" (2.5 cm) from joining rnd.

Shape Raglan

Notes: Neck shaping is introduced while raglan shaping is in progress; read all the way through the next sections before

RAGLAN DECREASE OPTIONS

There are several ways to work the raglan decreases, depending on the look you want. In each option, one stitch is decreased each side of each raglan marker.

Option 1: Work (ssk, k2) before each marker and work (k2, k2tog) after each marker.

Option 2: Work (k2tog, k2) before each marker and work (k2, ssk) after each marker.

Option 3: Work (k2tog, yo, ssk, k1) before each marker and work (k1, k2tog, yo, ssk) after each marker.

From left to right: Option 1 (used in Drew's sweater), Option 2 (used in Noah's sweater), Option 3.

proceeding. See box on page 194 for alternative ways to work raglan decreases.

Dec rnd: K2, ssk, work to 4 sts before next m, k2tog, k2, slip marker (sl m); rep from * 3 more times—8 sts decreased.

Rep dec rnd every other rnd 10 (11, 12, 12, 12, 13) more times, then every 4th rnd 2 (3, 4, 5, 6, 9) times.

At the same time, when piece measures 12 (13, 14, 15½, 19½, 23)" (30.5 [33.0, 35.5, 39.5, 49.5, 58.5] cm) from joining rnd or desired length to base of neck opening, shape neck as foll.

Shape Neck

Cont working raglan shaping as established, shape neck as foll:

Dividing row: Work to the center 9 (9, 9, 11, 12, 12) front sts (between the first and second markers), place these 9 (9, 9, 11, 12, 12) sts onto a holder, turn work.

Working back and forth in rows and working raglan shaping as established, dec 1 st at each neck edge every RS row 5 (5, 5, 5, 6, 6) times.

Cont even until all raglan decreases have been completed—45 (53, 53, 55, 62, 62) sts rem when all shaping is complete.

Work 1 WS row even.

Neck Edging

Change to smaller needle if desired.

Pick-up rnd: (RS) K45 (53, 53, 55, 62, 62), pick up and knit about 10 sts along neck shaping, k9 (9, 9, 11, 12, 12) held center front sts, pick up and knit about 10 sts along neck shaping—about 74 (82, 82, 86, 94, 94) sts total.

Pm and join for working in rnds.

Work in k1, p1 ribbing (inc 1 st at end of rnd if necessary to end with p1) until piece measures 1" (2.5 cm) from pick-up rnd or desired length.

Loosely BO all sts in patt.

FINISHING

Place each set of 10 (10, 10, 10, 14, 14) held underarm sts on an empty needle. With MC threaded on a tapestry needle, use the Kitchener st to graft the sts tog, or use the three-needle method to BO the sts tog.

Use chenille needle to bury all loose ends into links.

If using superwash wool, machine wash and dry. If using other fiber, wash and block according to the ball-band directions. Turn up hems, if desired: thread MC on a tapestry needle to sew in place.

NOAH'S VERSION

This version (below), designed for 7-year-old Noah, includes motifs of his favorite sports—soccer and football—and follows the general instructions for a 32" (81.5 cm) circumference. With different motifs on the front and back, this version shows how several motifs can be used to customize a sweater. For simplicity, the name is added to the center of the upper back with duplicate stitch.

The main color (SW03 Gray Heather) is worked from the skein, except for small amounts used in the jersey number charts. All other yarn supplies can be wound into butterflies or bobbins or kept as loose strands for easy management: SW125 Lemon Ice, SW01 Red Wing, SW11 White Frost, SW05 Onyx, SW117 Sable.

The large jersey number (6" Numbers chart on pages 218–221) is centered when the back measures 7½" (19 cm) from the turning ridge; the small jersey number (4" Numbers chart on pages 216–217) is centered when the front measures 8½" (21.5 cm) from the turning ridge; the Soccer Ball chart (page 212) is centered when the right sleeve measures 4" (10 cm) from the turning ridge (it is worked in color stranding, which creates a dense fabric); the Football chart (page 208) is centered when the left sleeve measures 5" (12.5 cm) from the turning ridge.

The yoke is shaped with Raglan Decrease Option 2, as described on page 194.

DREW'S VERSION

Designed for 4-year-old Drew, this 27" (68.5 cm) version (above) features a train motif that occupies just 20 rows around the body. Add or subtract cars to accommodate narrower or wider circumferences.

The main color (SW115 Oats N' Cream) is worked from the skein and can be stranded behind the other colors if desired. The motif requires a few yards (used as loose strands) of each of the following colors: SW01 Red Wing, SW11 White Frost, SW176 Bon Vivant Blue, SW125 Lemon Ice, SW117 Sable, SW05 Onyx, SW165 Frosted Fuschia, and SW90 Northern Lights.

The train motif (page 215) begins on the first row after the turning ridge on the body; the knitting begins with the caboose and ends with the engine as you work from right to left. Note that the turning point shifts slightly at the right edge of the motif (the end of the caboose).

The yoke is shaped with Raglan Decrease Option 1, as described on page 194.

OTHER DIZZY PROJECTS

It is my pleasure to introduce the following photo collection of beautiful projects: a whole gallery of Annetarsia projects knitted by the very talented Dizzyites! I can't decide which is my favorite—I'll have to knit them all!

Knitted by Paula Lane using Malabrigo Finito #856 (Azules) and #40 (Estragon).

Knitted by Beth Popp using Berroco Ultra Alpaca Light #4279 (Potting Mix) and #4217 (Tupelo).

Knitted by Barbara Mauger, using Malabrigo Silky Merino #30 (Purple Mystery) and #204 (Velvet Grapes).

Knitted by Susan Zuris using Plymouth Select Merino Superwash DK #1110 (Mystic Purple) and #1117 (Lt Gray).

Knitted by Erin Brown using Malabrigo Silky Merino #30 (Purple Mystery) and #403 (Coral), and adding beads.

Knitted by Caralyn Miller Ross using Berroco Vintage DK # #2102 (Buttercream) and #2179 (Chocolate).

Knitted by Lynn Charles using Malabrigo Finito #40 (Estragon) and #862 (Piedras).

Knitted by Andi Simmonsen using Plymouth Select Merino Superwash DK #1019 (Cornflower) and #1111 (Navy).

Knitted by Karen Petito using the official Dizzy Scarf colors.

Knitted by Sarah Reilly using the official Dizzy Scarf colors.

Knitted by Esther Waldman using Cascade 220 #9419 (Vermeer Blue) and #7802 (Cerise).

Knitted by Bobbie Hodges using Cascade 220 #2422 (Lavender) and #8904 (Prune), and Plymouth Gina #0008.

Such knitting talent is so inspiring! Good job everybody!

If only I could ride a bike…Ah, a beautiful scarf flowing in the wind and everyone admiring the outstanding colors. Wait—that's my namesake scarf!

Chapter 4:
Motif Library

The wonderful thing about intarsia is that you can knit any isolated motif into your back-and-forth knitting; the wonderful thing about Annetarsia is that you can knit those motifs in the round as well. I asked participants in the Wynona workshops for additional motifs they'd like to use and charted them for this chapter. Thanks to two of the Wynona knitters, Shan Davis and Tammie Stafford, you can examine swatches along with the charts. All were all knitted with Brown Sheep Lamb's Pride Superwash Worsted yarn on size 7 (4.5 mm) needles.

It's important to note that although any motif can be knitted, not all are easily done so. The ones I've included here have been tested for ease of knitting—the boundaries between colors shift only a few stitches at a time and the images evolve as intuitively as possible. Keep in mind that the image is created one stitch and one row at a time, and some images don't take recognizable shape until the knitting is complete and viewed from a distance.

Before knitting any motif, critique the chart stitch by stitch. Examine the odd-numbered rows from right to left, even-numbered rows from left to right, and make notes of when new sections of color begin. If a color jumps several stitches from one row to the next, consider whether it would be more efficient to strand the color across the gap or add a new source of yarn. In general, if the color won't be used in its previous position again, it's easiest to strand it to the new position; if, however, the color will be needed again in its previous position, it's usually best to add a new source of yarn.

If you'd like to change the size of a motif, simply scan or photocopy it onto a fresh piece of paper, then enlarge or shrink it to the desired size on the computer or photocopier. Trace the revised motif onto graph paper and you're ready to swatch. Knitter's graph paper represents the size and shape of knitted stitches fairly closely, but you'll still need to swatch.

Swatching will determine if it will work as well in knitting as it looks on paper. There's no substitute for knitting a swatch, which can be just as much fun and just as important as any other aspect of knitting.

To chart a motif that has an excellent chance of swatching perfectly the first time, follow these simple steps (see photos on page 43):

Step 1. Knit a plain stockinette swatch with the yarn and needles you plan to use for the background. Make the swatch large enough to have a ½" (1.3 cm) border around the motif area.

Step 2. Trace the motif onto the center of a piece of stiff paper that's a bit larger than the size of the final knitted motif.

Step 3. Use scissors to cut the motif out of the center and place it aside. You'll use the piece with the motif cut out of it as a frame.

Step 4. Place the frame on your swatch, aligning the base of the cut-out window with a row of stitches.

Step 5. Count the number of stitches in each row that appear in the window, including partial stitches in which at least half of the stitch appears, and chart them on a piece of graph paper. Don't count partial stitches in which less than half of the stitch appears.

Step 6. When all rows have been charted, look at the charted motif critically and adjust the edge stitches for the best overall effect.

Step 7. Now knit another swatch, including your charted motif! Examine the swatch, make additional adjustments to the chart, if needed, then knit another swatch.

Repeat Step 7 until you're satisfied with the results.

Keep in mind that you can embellish simple motifs to turn them into something completely different. For example, a simple circle can become a balloon, a ball of yarn, or a peace sign.

This library is meant to be a springboard for your own ideas; feel free to change and adapt the charts for your particular needs. Once you make changes, whether they're to the motif, yarn, needle size, or color, you've taken the first step in knitwear designing. Congratulations!

Motif Library Contents

203 *Bell*

204 *Butterflies*

205 *Cats*

207 *Circles*

207 *Cupcake*

208 *Football*

208 *Hearts*

209 *Kites*

210 *Leaf*

211 *Geometric Shapes*

211 *Soccer Ball*

212 *Stars*

213 *Sun and Clouds*

214 *Trains*

215 *4" Numbers*

217 *6" Numbers*

221 *Large Alphabet*

222 *Small Alphabet*

222 *Symbols*

BELL

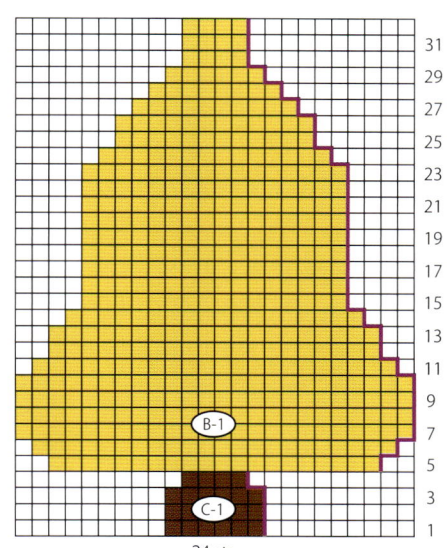

☐ With A, knit on RS, purl on WS
🟨 With B, knit on RS, purl on WS
⬛ With C, knit on RS, purl on WS
▌ Turning point

24 sts

BUTTERFLIES

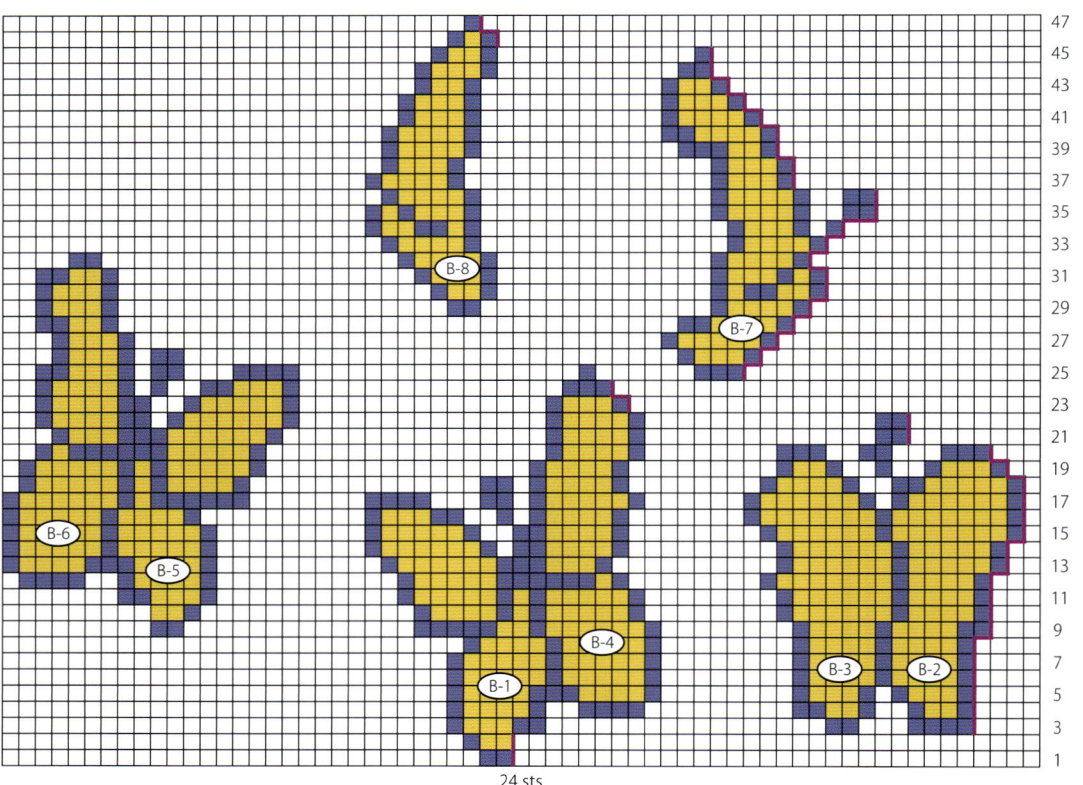

- ☐ With A, knit on RS, purl on WS
- ☐ With B, knit on RS, purl on WS
- ☐ With C, knit on RS, purl on WS
- ☐ With E, knit on RS, purl on WS
- | Turning point
- — Boundary between yarn sources

CAT 1

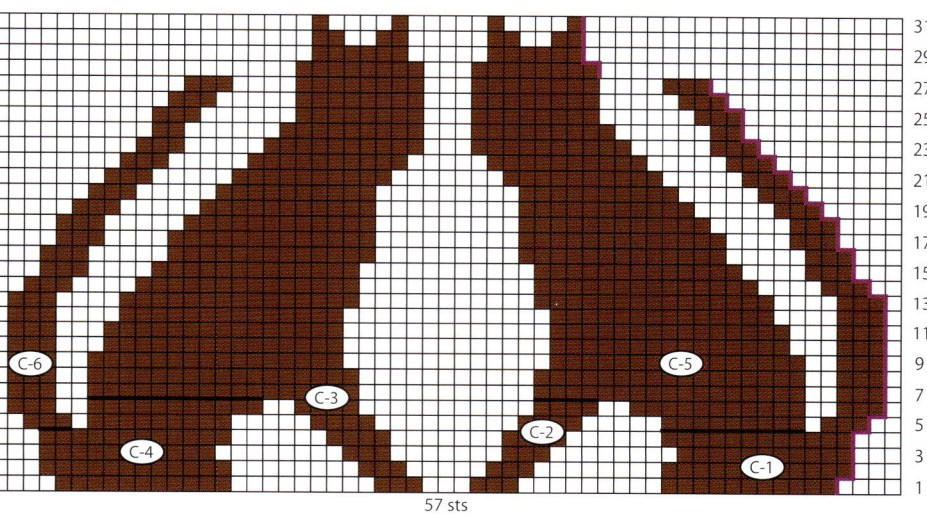

57 sts

CAT 2

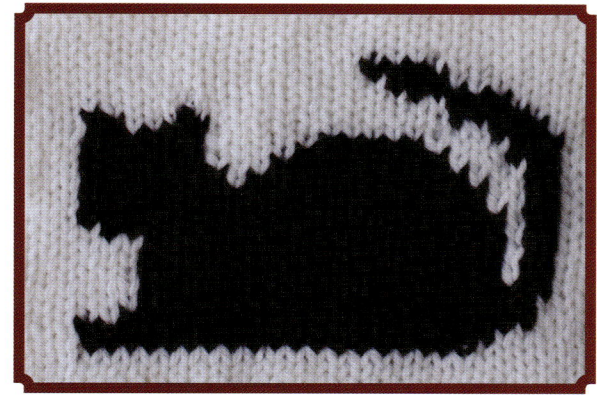
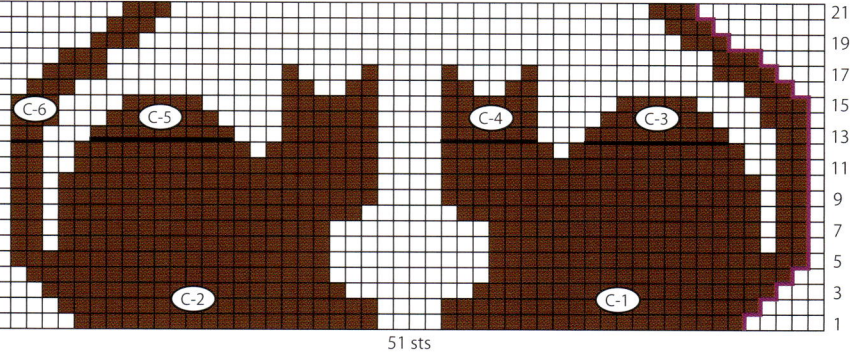

51 sts

CAT 3

☐ With A, knit on RS, purl on WS
☐ With B, knit on RS, purl on WS
☐ With C, knit on RS, purl on WS
☐ With D, knit on RS, purl on WS
☐ With F, knit on RS, purl on WS
☐ With G, knit on RS, purl on WS
▌ Turning point
▬ Boundary between yarn sources

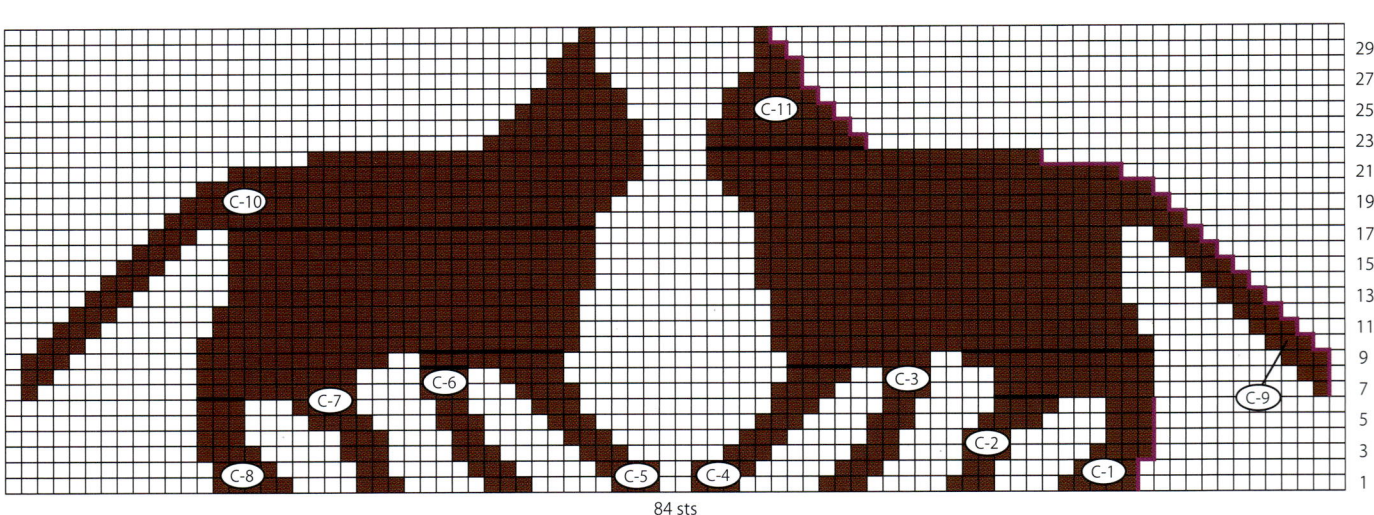

84 sts

CIRCLES

33 sts

CUPCAKE

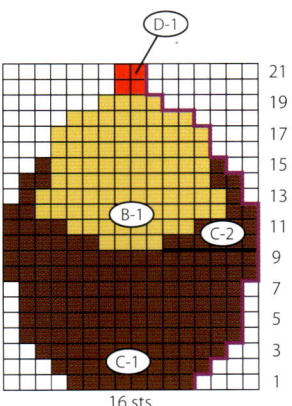

16 sts

FOOTBALL

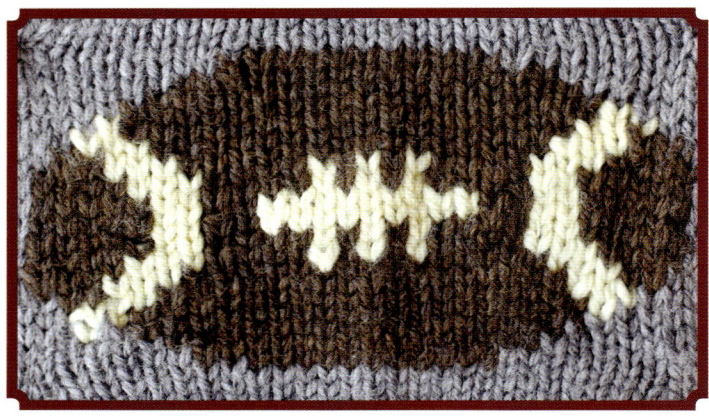

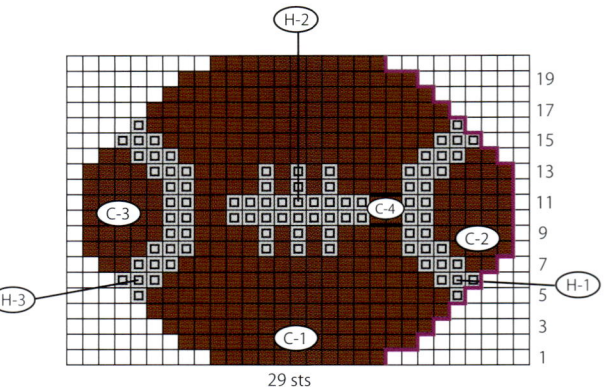

29 sts

HEART 1

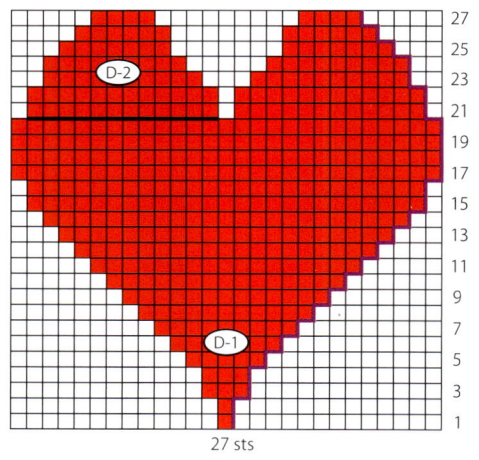

27 sts

- ☐ With A, knit on RS, purl on WS
- ☐ With B, knit on RS, purl on WS
- ☐ With C, knit on RS, purl on WS
- ☐ With D, knit on RS, purl on WS
- ☐ With E, knit on RS, purl on WS
- ☐ With F, knit on RS, purl on WS
- ☐ With G, knit on RS, purl on WS
- ☐ With H, knit on RS, purl on WS
- ❘ Turning point
- ─ Boundary between yarn sources

HEART 2

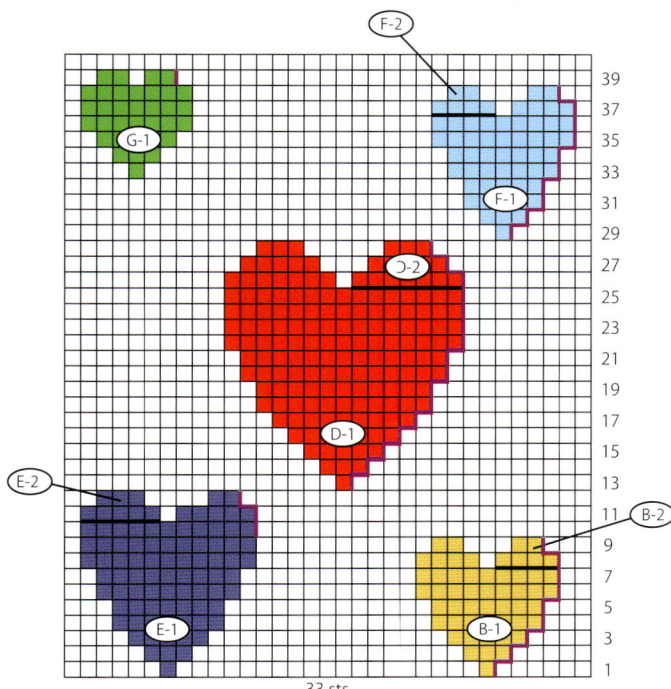

33 sts

KITES

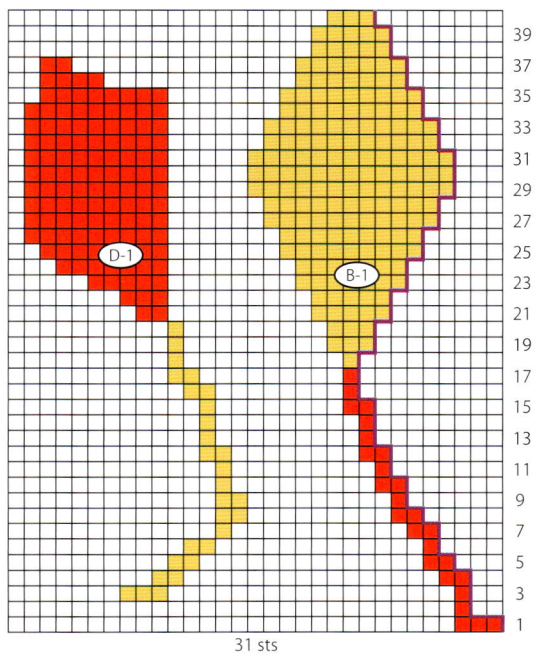

31 sts

LEAF

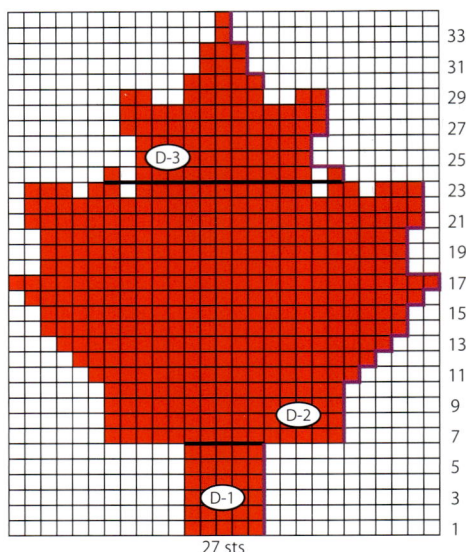

27 sts

☐ With A, knit on RS, purl on WS
☐ With B, knit on RS, purl on WS
☐ With D, knit on RS, purl on WS
☐ With E, knit on RS, purl on WS
☐ With F, knit on RS, purl on WS
☐ With G, knit on RS, purl on WS
☐ With H, knit on RS, purl on WS
☐ With I, knit on RS, purl on WS
| Turning point
— Boundary between yarn sources

GEOMETRIC SHAPES

SOCCER BALL

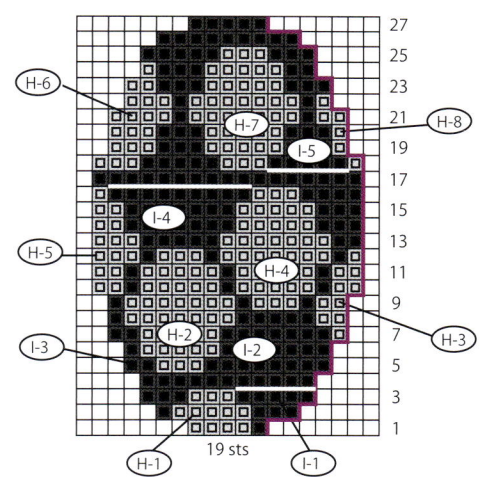

*The white lines on this chart signify the boundary between yarn sources, which is normally a black line.

STAR 1

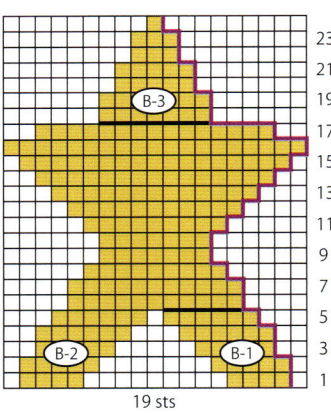

19 sts

STAR 2

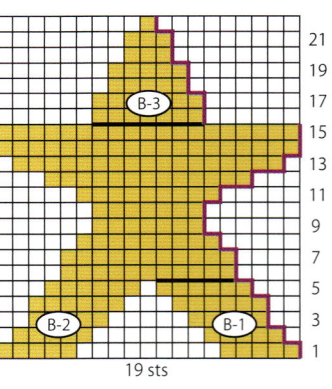

19 sts

☐ With A, knit on RS, purl on WS
▨ With B, knit on RS, purl on WS
▨ With E, knit on RS, purl on WS
▣ With H, knit on RS, purl on WS
▏ Turning point
▬ Boundary between yarn sources

SUN AND CLOUDS

70 sts

TRAINS

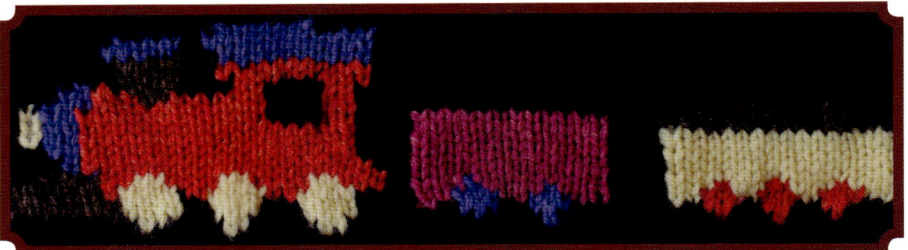

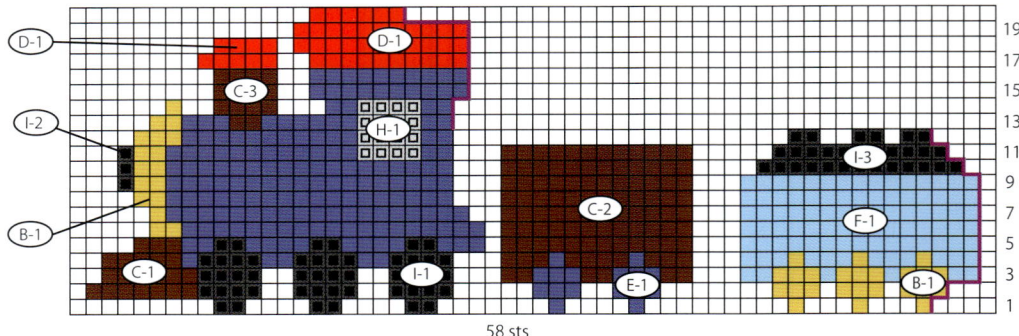

58 sts

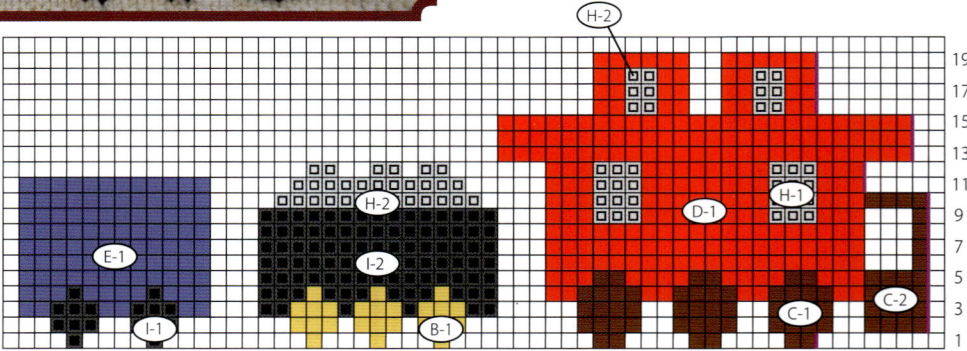

59 sts

4" NUMBERS

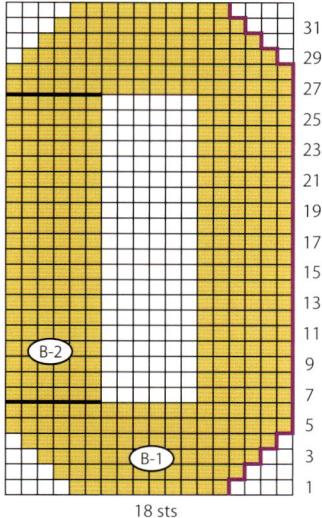
18 sts

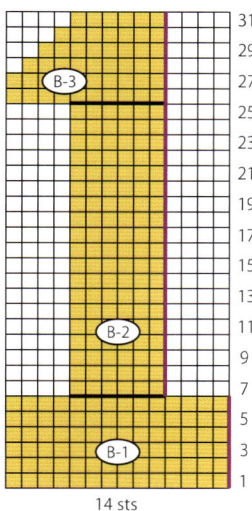
14 sts

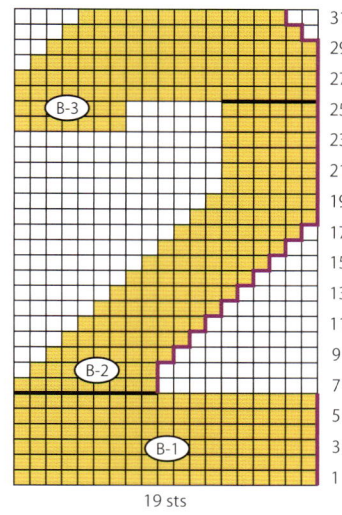
19 sts

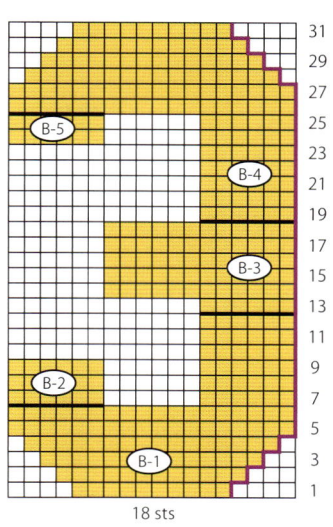
18 sts

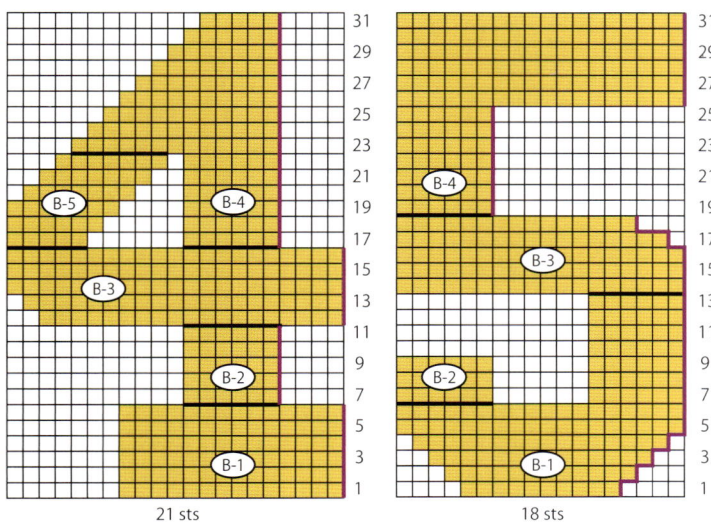
21 sts   18 sts

☐ With A, knit on RS, purl on WS
🟨 With B, knit on RS, purl on WS
■ With C, knit on RS, purl on WS
■ With D, knit on RS, purl on WS
■ With E, knit on RS, purl on WS
■ With F, knit on RS, purl on WS
▣ With H, knit on RS, purl on WS
■ With I, knit on RS, purl on WS
❘ Turning point
━ Boundary between yarn sources

4" NUMBERS

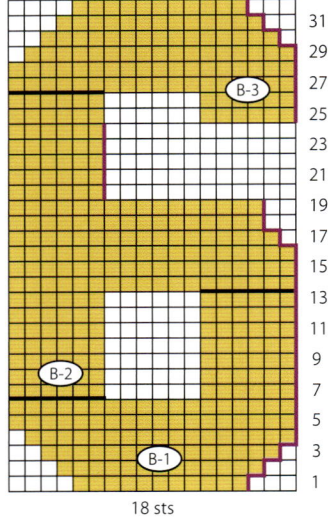
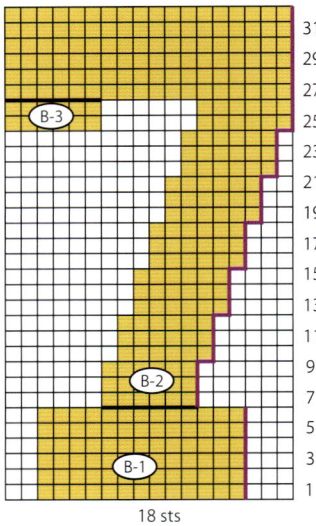
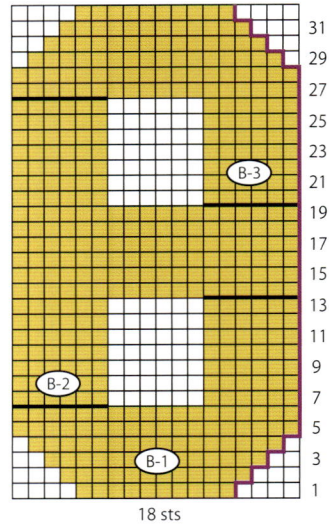
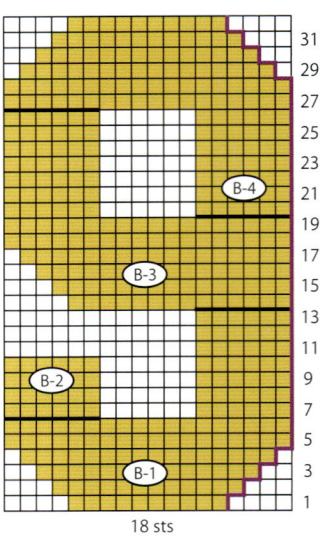

☐ With A, knit on RS, purl on WS
▨ With B, knit on RS, purl on WS
| Turning point
— Boundary between yarn sources

6" NUMBERS

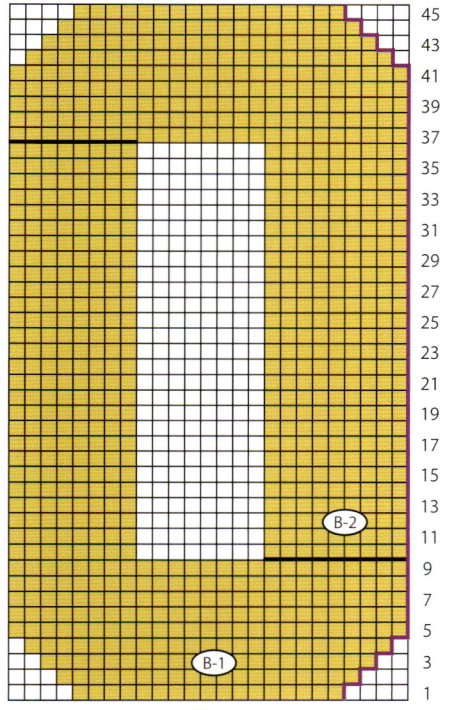

25 sts

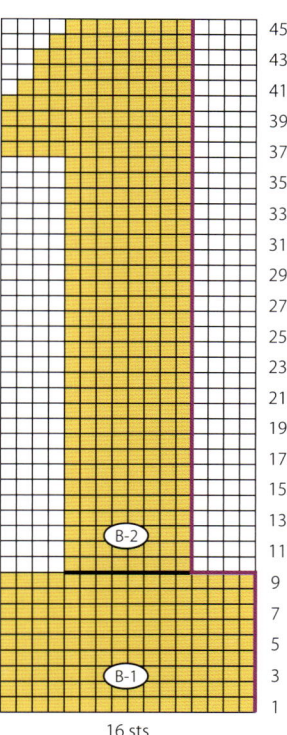

16 sts

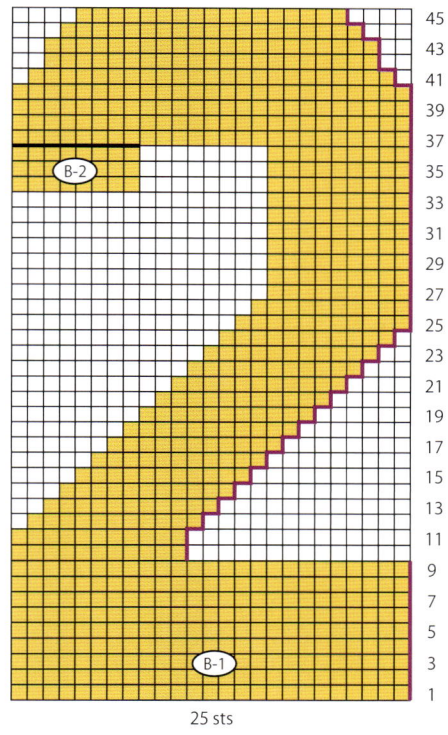

25 sts

6" NUMBERS

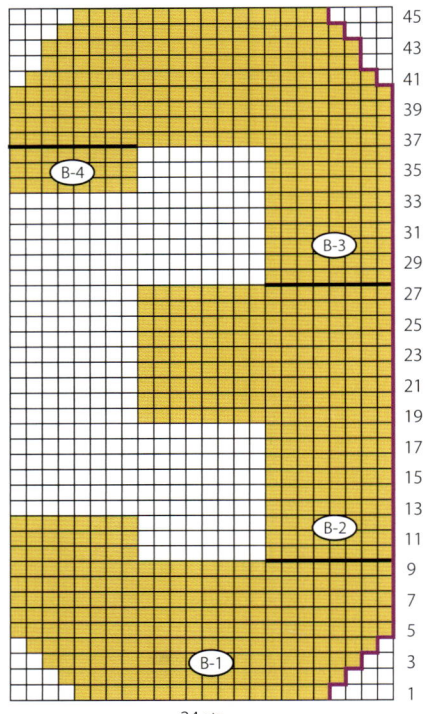

24 sts

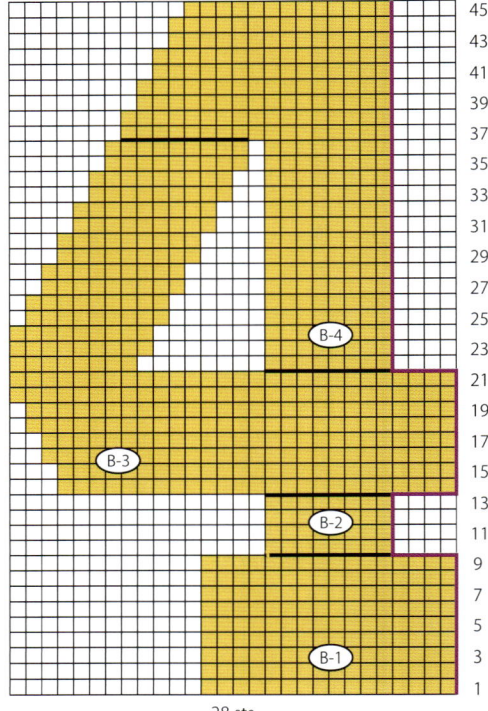

28 sts

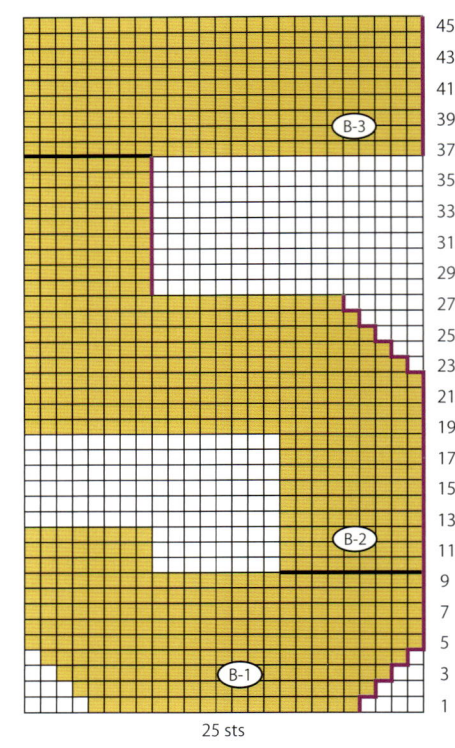

25 sts

☐ With A, knit on RS, purl on WS
▨ With B, knit on RS, purl on WS
▮ Turning point
▬ Boundary between yarn sources

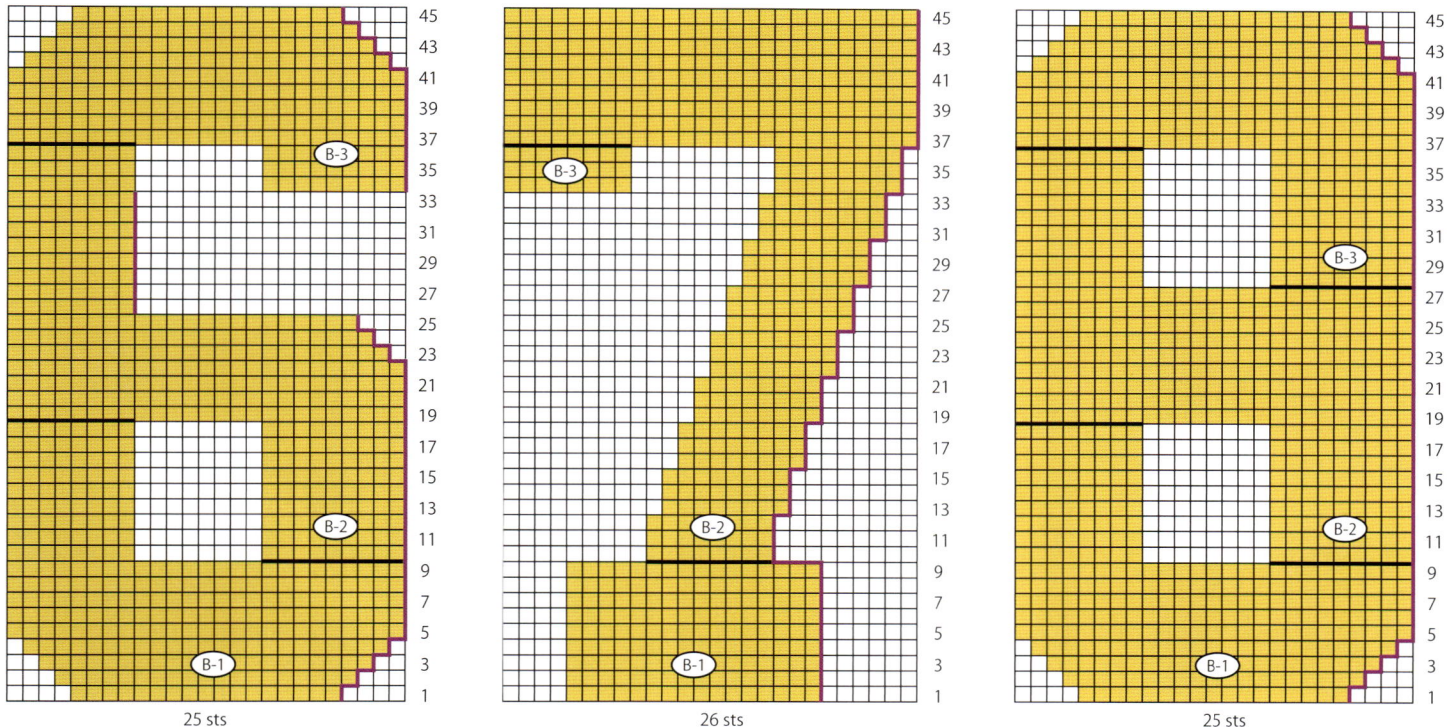

6" NUMBERS

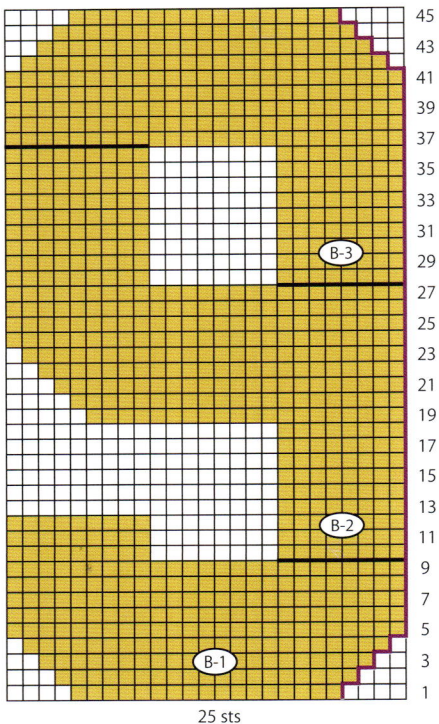

25 sts

- ☐ With A, knit on RS, purl on WS
- ☐ With B, knit on RS, purl on WS
- ▌ Turning point
- ▬ Boundary between yarn sources

LARGE ALPHABET

SMALL ALPHABET

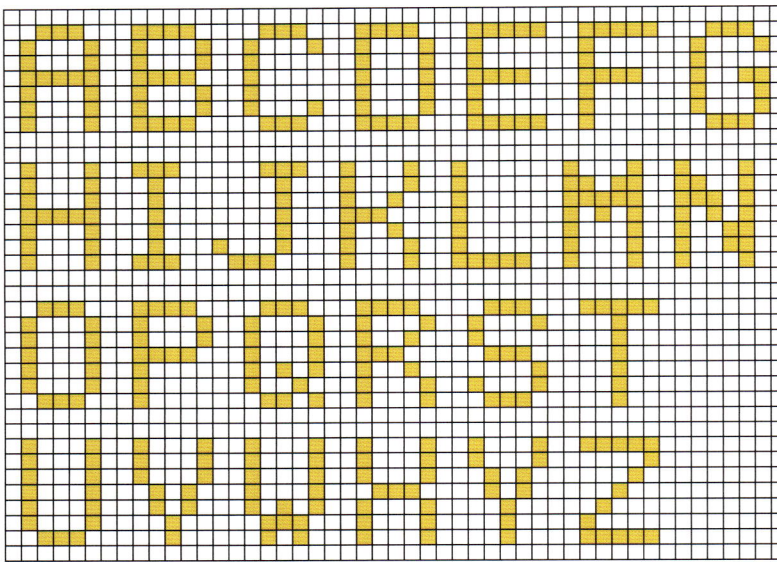

SYMBOLS

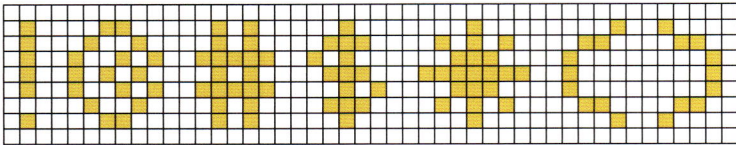

☐ With A, knit on RS, purl on WS
■ With B, knit on RS, purl on WS

NOTE
Because these alphabet and symbol charts are best worked with duplicate stitch or with the main color stranded behind, no turning points are given.

Abbreviations

beg(s)	begin(s); beginning
BO	bind off
CC	contrast color
circ	circular
cm	centimeter(s)
CO	cast on
cont	continue(s); continuing
dec(s)('d)	decrease(s); decreasing; decreased
dpn	double-pointed needles
foll	follow(s); following
inc(s)('d)	increase(s); increasing; increase(d)
k	knit
kf&b	knit into the front and back of same stitch
k2tog	knit 2 stitches together
kwise	knitwise, as if to knit
m	marker(s)
mm	millimeter(s)
M1	make one (increase)
MC	main color
p	purl
patt(s)	pattern(s)
pm	place marker
psso	pass slipped stitch over
pwise	purlwise, as if to purl
rem	remain(s); remaining
rep	repeat(s); repeating
rnd(s)	round(s)
RS	right side
sl	slip
ssk	slip, slip, knit (decrease)
st(s)	stitch(es)
St st	stockinette stitch
tbl	through back loop
tog	together
WS	wrong side
wyb	with yarn in back
yd	yard(s)
yo	yarnover
*	repeat starting point

BIBLIOGRAPHY

Books

Bordhi, Cat. *New Pathways for Sock Knitters Book One*. Passing Paws Press, 2007.

———. *Personal Footprints for Insouciant Sock Knitters*. Passing Paws Press, 2009.

Falick, Melanie. *Knitting in America*. Artisan, 1997.

Fassett, Kaffe. *Kaffe Fassett's Pattern Library*. Taunton Press, 2003.

Melville, Sally. *The Knitting Experience Book 3: Color*. XRX Publishing, 2005.

Menz, Deb. *Color Works*. Interweave Press, 2004.

Thomas, Mary. *Mary Thomas's Knitting Book*. Dover Publications, 1973.

Walker, Barbara G. *A Second Treasury of Knitting Patterns*. Schoolhouse Press ed. 1998

Resources, DVDs, and Videos

Berk, Anne. *Knitting Daily Workshop: Inside Intarsia*. www.interweavestore.com.

———. *Knitting Daily Workshop: Intarsia InDepth*. www.interweavestore.com.

Bordhi, Cat. Personal Footprints: Opening up the Leg. YouTube video (http://www.youtube.com/watch?v=ztbI4T373PU).

Callahan, Gail. *ColorGrid*, www.kangaroodyer.com.

Neatby, Lucy. *Intarsia Untangled 1*. www.lucyneatby.com.

———. *Intarsia Untangled 2*. www.lucyneatby.com

YARN SUPPLIERS

Berocco: www.berocco.com

Blue Moon Fiber Arts: www.bluemoonfiberarts.com

Brown Sheep Yarns: www.brownsheep.com

Dream in Color: www.dreamincoloryarn.com

Frog Tree Yarns: www.frogtreeyarns.com

Holiday Yarns: www.holidayyarns.com

KnitPicks: www.knitpicks.com

Miss Babs Hand-Dyed Yarns and Fibers, Inc: www.missbabs.com

Plucky Knitter: www.thepluckyknitter.com

Simply Socks Yarn Company: www.simplysockyarn.com

Toots LeBlanc: www.tootsleblanc.com

INDEX

Adding New Yarn, 32–35
    Adding a New Color, 32–33
    Joining a New Source of the Same Color, 33–35

Annetarsia "In the Round" (ITR), 12–16, 38
    Helpful Hints, 16
    Knit "Round" (Right-Side Row), 14–15
    Purl "Round" (Wrong-Side Row), 12–14
    Shortcut Directions, 15

Bobbins, 27

Butterflies, 28–29
    How to Wind, 29

Calculating Yarn Supplies, 25–27
    Add Extra for Tails, 26
    Calculate the Yarn Gauge, 26
    Determine S+R, 26
    Knit a Swatch, 25
    Multiply Yarn Gauge by S+R, 26

Charts
    Anatomy of a, 40
    Keeping Track of Your Place, 41
    What to Look for, 40–41
    When to Strand a Yarn, 42

Chenille Sewing Needles, 38

Color
    Forgot to Shift a Color, 79
    In Charts, 41
    Wrong Color Used, 78–80

Copyright Issues, 45

End Allowance, 26–27, 38

Ends
    Burying, 36
    Fringe, 37
    Knots, 36–37
    Managing Ends, 37–38
    Weaving, 36

ITR, (see Annetarsia "In the Round")

Knitting Needles, 38

Linking Yarn, 31–32
    Omitted Links, 76
    Right-Side Rows, 31
    Wrong-Side Rows, 31–32

Loops, 38
    There are Two Loops, 80

Loop 'n' Lock, 38

Loose Strands, 27

Managing Tangles, 30

"Missing" Stitches at Motif Edges, 79–80

Motifs
    Charting, 42–44
    Library, 200

Pull-Skeins and Balls, 27

Raglan Decrease Options, 194

Russian Join, 35

Simple Join, 33

Spit-Splice, 34–35

Stitches Plus Rows (S+R), 26, 39

Stitch Markers, 38

Turning Point, 39
    At an Awkward Position, 80–81

Yarn Choice, 20–21
    Color, 21
    Fiber Content, 20
    Texture, 20

Color Play, 22–24

Yarn Gauge, 26, 39

Yarn Supply, 39
    Choices, 27